Other Books and Series by Jeff Bowen

Applications for Enrollment of Chickasaw Newborn Act of 1905
Volumes I thru VII

Cherokee Intermarried White 1906 Volume I thru X

Applications for Enrollment of Creek Newborn Act of 1905
Volumes I thru XIV

Applications for Enrollment of Choctaw Newborn Act of 1905
Volume I, II, III, IV, V, VI, VII, VIII, IX, X, XI, XII, XIII, XIV, XV & XVI

Visit our website at **www.nativestudy.com** to learn more about these and other books and series by Jeff Bowen

APPLICATIONS FOR ENROLLMENT OF CHOCTAW NEWBORN ACT OF 1905

VOLUME XVII

TRANSCRIBED BY
JEFF BOWEN

NATIVE STUDY
Gallipolis, Ohio
USA

Other Books and Series by Jeff Bowen

1901-1907 Native American Census Seneca, Eastern Shawnee, Miami, Modoc, Ottawa, Peoria, Quapaw, and Wyandotte Indians (Under Seneca School, Indian Territory)

1932 Census of The Standing Rock Sioux Reservation with Births And Deaths 1924-1932

Census of The Blackfeet, Montana, 1897- 1901 Expanded Edition

Eastern Cherokee by Blood, 1906-1910, Volumes I thru XIII

Choctaw of Mississippi Indian Census 1929-1932 with Births and Deaths 1924-1931   Volume I
Choctaw of Mississippi Indian Census 1933, 1934 & 1937, Supplemental Rolls to 1934 & 1935 with Births and Deaths 1932-1938, and Marriages 1936-1938 Volume II

Eastern Cherokee Census Cherokee, North Carolina 1930-1939
Census 1930-1931 with Births And Deaths 1924-1931 Taken By Agent L. W. Page Volume I
Eastern Cherokee Census Cherokee, North Carolina 1930-1939
Census 1932-1933 with Births And Deaths 1930-1932 Taken By Agent R. L. Spalsbury   Volume II
Eastern Cherokee Census Cherokee, North Carolina 1930-1939
Census 1934-1937 with Births and Deaths 1925-1938 and Marriages 1936 & 1938 Taken by Agents R. L. Spalsbury And Harold W. Foght Volume III

Seminole of Florida Indian Census, 1930-1940 with Birth and Death Records, 1930-1938

Texas Cherokees 1820-1839 A Document For Litigation 1921

Choctaw By Blood Enrollment Cards 1898-1914 Volumes I thru XVII

Starr Roll 1894 (Cherokee Payment Rolls) Districts: Canadian, Cooweescoowee, and Delaware Volume One
Starr Roll 1894 (Cherokee Payment Rolls) Districts: Flint, Going Snake, and Illinois   Volume Two
Starr Roll 1894 (Cherokee Payment Rolls) Districts: Saline, Sequoyah, and Tahlequah; Including Orphan Roll   Volume Three

Cherokee Intruder Cases Dockets of Hearings 1901-1909 Volumes I & II

Indian Wills, 1911-1921 Records of the Bureau of Indian Affairs
Books One thru Seven;
Native American Wills & Probate Records 1911-1921

Other Books and Series by Jeff Bowen

Turtle Mountain Reservation Chippewa Indians 1932 Census with Births & Deaths, 1924-1932

Chickasaw By Blood Enrollment Cards 1898-1914 Volume I thru V

Cherokee Descendants East An Index to the Guion Miller Applications Volume I
Cherokee Descendants West An Index to the Guion Miller Applications Volume II (A-M)
Cherokee Descendants West An Index to the Guion Miller Applications Volume III (N-Z)

Applications for Enrollment of Seminole Newborn Freedmen, Act of 1905

Eastern Cherokee Census, Cherokee, North Carolina, 1915-1922, Taken by Agent James E. Henderson
    Volume I (1915-1916)
    Volume II (1917-1918)
    Volume III (1919-1920)
    Volume IV (1921-1922)

Complete Delaware Roll of 1898

Eastern Cherokee Census, Cherokee, North Carolina, 1923-1929, Taken by Agent James E. Henderson
    Volume I (1923-1924)
    Volume II (1925-1926)
    Volume III (1927-1929)

Applications for Enrollment of Seminole Newborn Act of 1905 Volumes I & II

North Carolina Eastern Cherokee Indian Census 1898-1899, 1904, 1906, 1909-1912, 1914 Revised and Expanded Edition

1932 Hopi and Navajo Native American Census with Birth & Death Rolls (1925-1931) Volume 1 - Hopi
1932 Hopi and Navajo Native American Census with Birth & Death Rolls (1930-1932) Volume 2 - Navajo

Western Navajo Reservation Navajo, Hopi and Paiute 1933 Census with Birth & Death Rolls 1925-1933

Cherokee Citizenship Commission Dockets 1880-1884 and 1887-1889 Volumes I thru V

Copyright © 2013
by Jeff Bowen

ALL RIGHTS RESERVED
No part of this publication may be reproduced
or used in any form or manner whatsoever
without previous written permission from the
copyright holder or publisher.

Originally published:
Baltimore, Maryland
2013

Reprinted by:

Native Study LLC
Gallipolis, OH
www.nativestudy.com
2020

Library of Congress Control Number: 2020918113

ISBN: 978-1-64968-110-2

Made in the United States of America.

This series is dedicated to the descendants of the Choctaw newborn listed in these applications.

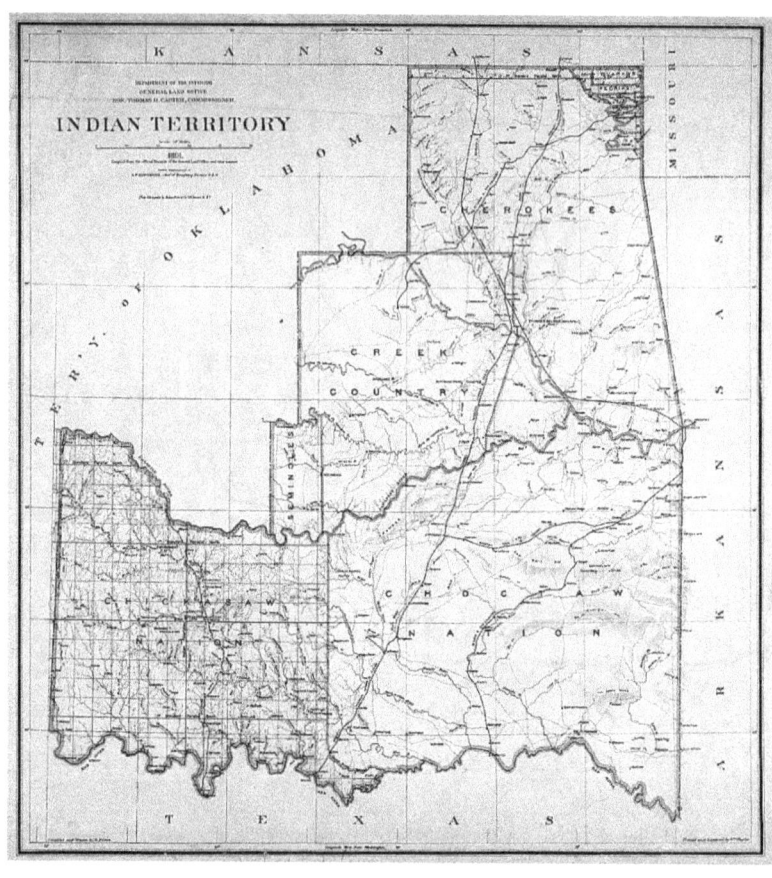

This map of Indian Territory shows how large the Choctaw and Chickasaw Nations' land base was that contained huge deposits of asphalt and coal. Just the size and territory involved was flooded with the "Grafters".

DEPARTMENT OF THE INTERIOR.
Commissioner to the Five Civilized Tribes.

NOTICE.

Opening of Land Office at Wewoka,
IN THE SEMINOLE NATION, INDIAN TERRITORY.

Notice is hereby given that on Monday, September 4, 1905, the Commissioner to the Five Civilized Tribes will establish a land office at Wewoka, in the Seminole Nation, Indian Territory, for the purpose of allowing citizens and freedmen of the Seminole Nation to select allotments of land for their minor children enrolled under the Act of Congress approved March 3, 1905 (33 Stat. L 1060), and for the further purpose of allowing citizens and freedmen of the Seminole Nation, whose allotments are incomplete, to select additional land in order to bring the value of their allotments up to the standard of $309.09, as nearly as may be practicable.

Each child whose enrollment in accordance with the Act of March 3, 1905, has been duly approved by the Secretary of the Interior, is entitled to receive an alllotment of forty acres without regard to the character or value of the land selected.

Selection of allotments for minor children must be made by their citizen or freedmen parents or by a duly appointed guardian, or curator, or by a duly appointed administrator.

TAMS BIXBY,
Commissioner.

Muskogee, Indian Territory,
July 29, 1905.

This particular notice for the Seminole and Creek Newborn makes mention of the Act of 1905. It is likely that a similar notice was posted in the Choctaw and Chickasaw Nations for the registration of newborn children.

DEPARTMENT OF THE INTERIOR,
Commission to the Five Civilized Tribes.

Rules and Regulations Governing the Selection of Allotments and the Designation of Homesteads in the Choctaw and Chickasaw Nations.

1. Selections of allotments and designations of homesteads for adult citizens and selections of allotments for adult freedmen must be made in person except as herein otherwise provided.

2. Applications to have land set apart and homesteads designated for duly identified Mississippi Choctaws must be made personally before the Commission to the Five Civilized Tribes. Fathers may apply for their minor children and if the father be dead the mother may apply. Husbands may apply for wives. Applications for orphans, insane persons and persons of unsound mind may be made by duly appointed guardian or curator, and for aged and infirm persons and prisoners by agents duly authorized thereunto by power of attorney, in the discretion of said Commission.

3. At the time of the selection of allotment each citizen and duly identified Mississippi Choctaw shall designate as a homestead out of said selection land equal in value to one hundred and sixty acres of the average allottable land of the Choctaw and Chickasaw Nations, as nearly as may be.

4. Each Choctaw and Chickasaw freedman, at the time of selection shall designate as his or her allotment of the lands of the Choctaw and Chickasaw Nations, land equal in value to forty acres of the average allottable land of the Choctaw and Chickasaw Nations.

5. Citizens, freedmen and identified Mississippi Choctaws who are married, whether they have attained their majority or not, will be regarded as of age for the purpose of making selections.

6. Selections may be made by citizen and freedman parents for unmarried male children under twenty-one years of age and for unmarried female children under eighteen years of age, and a male citizen or freedman may make selection for his wife, if she is entitled to make selection, unless she shall, at the time or previously thereto, protest in writing.

7. Where the father of an unmarried minor citizen, freedman or identified Mississippi Choctaw is a non-citizen, the citizen, freedman or identified Mississippi Choctaw mother of such children must make selection in person in behalf of said children.

8. Selections of allotments and designations of homesteads for minor citizens and selections of allotments for minor freedmen may be made by the citizen father or mother or freedman father or mother, as the case may be, or by a guardian, curator, or an administrator having charge of their estate, in the order named.

9. Selections of allotments and designations of homesteads for citizen, and selections of allotment for freedmen, prisoners, convicts, aged and infirm persons and soldiers and sailors of the United States on duty outside of Indian Territory, may be made by duly appointed agents under power of attorney, and for incompetents by guardians, curators, or other suitable person akin to them.

10. Selections may be made and homesteads designated by duly identified Mississippi Choctaws, who have, within one year after the date of their identification as such, made satisfactory proof of bona fide settlement within the Choctaw-Chickasaw country, at any time within six months after the date of their said identification.

11. Persons authorized to make selections by power of attorney, as provided in rules 2 and 9 hereof, must be the husband or wife, or a relative not further removed than a cousin of the first degree of the person for whom such selection is made.

12. It shall be the duty of the Commission to the Five Civilized Tribes to see that selections of allotments and designations of homesteads for the classes of persons mentioned in rules 2, 6, 7, 8 and 9 hereof, are made for the best interests of such persons.

13. Selections of allotments for citizens, freedmen and identified Mississippi Choctaws who have died subsequent to September 25, 1902, and before making a selection of allotment, shall be made by a duly appointed administrator or executor. If, however, such administrator or executor be not duly and expeditiously appointed, or fails to act promptly when appointed, or for any other cause such selections be not so made within a reasonable and practicable time, the Commission to the Five Civilized Tribes shall designate the lands thus to be allotted.

14. In determining the value of a selection the appraised value of the land selected shall be increased by the appraised value of such pine timber on such land as has heretofore been estimated by the Commission to the Five Civilized Tribes.

15. Selections of allotments may be made only by citizens and freedmen whose enrollment has been approved by the Secretary of the Interior, and by persons duly identified by the Commission to the Five Civilized Tribes as Mississippi Choctaws, and by none others.

16. When a selection of land has been made by a citizen, freedman or identified Mississippi Choctaw, and the land so selected is claimed by a person whose rights as a citizen or freedman have not been finally determined, contest for the land so selected may be instituted by the person claiming the land, formal application for the land being first made as is required by the Rules of Practice in Choctaw and Chickasaw allotment contest cases.

THE COMMISSION TO THE FIVE CIVILIZED TRIBES.

TAMS BIXBY, Chairman.

Muskogee, Indian Territory, March 24, 1903.

The above statement published prior to 1905, was established for what was supposed to be a set of guidelines when it came to allotments. But with supplemental agreements and Congressional legislation, time frames as well as rules and regulations often changed and were not the same for every tribe.

INTRODUCTION

The *Applications for Enrollment of Choctaw Newborn Act of 1905*, National Archive film M-1301, Rolls 50-57, are found under the heading of Applications for Enrollment of the Commission to the Five Civilized Tribes. For this series, I have transcribed the application forms filled out by individuals applying for enrollment in the Five Civilized Tribes under the Dawes Commission. These applications contain considerably more information than stated on the census cards found in series M-1186. M-1301 possesses its own numerical sequence, separate from M-1186. To find each party's roll number you would have to reference M-1186.

The Choctaw as well as the Chickasaw allotments were likely some of the most sought after properties in Indian Territory. There was supposed to be a 25-year restriction on the sale or lease of any Indian lands so as to insure that the owners wouldn't be swindled, but that isn't what happened. This fact is borne out in the Dawes Commission General Allotment Act, of February 8, 1887, Section 5, which "Provides that after an Indian person is allotted land, the United States will hold the land 'in trust [1] for the sole use and benefit of the Indian' (or his heirs if the Indian landowner dies) for a period of 25 years. (Land held in trust by the United States government cannot be sold or in anyway alienated by the Indian landowner, since the United States government considers the underlying ownership of the land held by itself and not the tribe. After the period of trust ends, the Indian landowner is free to sell the land and is free from any encumbrance from the United States.)"[1] Instead, Native Americans were exploited by the devious. The Choctaw and Chickasaw Districts both had huge asphalt and coal deposits, so there was pressure from outsiders to acquire them from the minute they were discovered. After repeated attacks throughout the years and many legislative changes, President "Roosevelt finally signed the Five Tribes Bill at noon on April 26, 1906, the forces seeking to end all restrictions were disappointed. Section 19 removed restrictions from the sale of all inherited land but directed that no full-bloods could sell their land for twenty-five years. The Act also prohibited leases for more than one year without the approval of the Secretary of the Interior."[2]

Angie Debo described the opportunists that wanted these Native American allotments as, "Grafters". The parents of the newborns enumerated within this series would no sooner receive the approval for their child's allotment than there would be someone there with cash in hand holding a new deed or lease for the parents to sign their child's birthright away. Angie Debo said it best, "As the business incapacity of the allottees became apparent, a horde of despoilers fastened themselves upon their property." According to Debo, "The term 'grafter' was applied as a matter of course to dealers in Indian land, and was frankly accepted by them. The speculative fever also affected Government employees so that it was almost impossible to prevent them from making personal investments."[3]

---

[1] General Allotment Act, Act of Feb. 8, 1887 (24 Stat. 388, ch. 119, 25 USCA 331)
[2] The Dawes Commission and the Allotment of the Five Civilized Tribes, 1893-1914 by Kent Carter, pg. 173
[3] And Still the Waters Run, Angie Debo, p. 92.

INTRODUCTION

According to the Department of Interior in 1905, "It is estimated that there will be added to the final rolls of the citizens and freedmen of the Choctaw and Chickasaw nations the names of 2,000 persons, including 1,500 new-born children to be enrolled under the provisions of the act of Congress approved March 3, 1905."[4]

The quote below explains, in detail, the requirements for qualifying as a newborn Choctaw, "By the act of Congress approved March 3, 1905 (H.R. 17474), entitled 'An act making appropriations for the current and contingent expenses of the Indian Department and for fulfilling treaty stipulations with various Indian tribes for the fiscal year ending June 30, 1906, and for other purposes,' it was provided as follows:

'That the Commission to the Five Civilized Tribes is hereby authorized for sixty days after the date of the approval of this act to receive and consider applications for enrollment of infant children born prior to September twenty-fifth, nineteen hundred and two, and who were living on said date, to citizens by blood of the Choctaw and Chickasaw tribes of Indians whose enrollment has been approved by the Secretary of the Interior prior to the date of the approval of this act; and to enroll and make allotments to such children.'

'That the Commission to the Five Civilized Tribes is authorized for sixty days after the date of the approval of this act to receive and consider applications for enrollment of children born subsequent to September twenty-fifth, nineteen hundred and two, and prior to March fourth, nineteen hundred and five, and who were living on said latter date, to citizens by blood of the Choctaw and Chickasaw tribes of Indians whose enrollment has been approved by the Secretary of the Interior prior to the date of the approval of this act; and to enroll and make allotments to such children.'

"Notice is hereby given that the Commission to the Five Civilized Tribes will, up to and inclusive of midnight, May 2, 1905, receive applications for the enrollment of infant children born prior to September 25, 1902, and who were living on said date, to citizens by blood of the Choctaw and Chickasaw tribes of Indians whose enrollment has been approved by the Secretary of the Interior prior to March 3, 1905."[5]

Following is the scope of these transcriptions: Besides the applications themselves, researchers will find the identities of other individuals within these applications -- doctors, lawyers, mid-wives, and other relatives -- that may help with you genealogical research.

Jeff Bowen
Gallipolis, Ohio
NativeStudy.com

---

[4] Annual Reports of the Department of the Interior For the Fiscal Year Ended June 30, 1905, p. 609.
[5] Annual Reports of the Department of the Interior For the Fiscal Year Ended June 30, 1905, p. 593.

Applications for Enrollment of Choctaw Newborn
Act of 1905   Volume XVII

Choctaw New Born 1242
   Sadie Aline Harris
   (Born April 8, 1903)

BIRTH AFFIDAVIT.

DEPARTMENT OF THE INTERIOR.
COMMISSION TO THE FIVE CIVILIZED TRIBES.

IN RE APPLICATION FOR ENROLLMENT, as a citizen of the Choctaw Nation, of Sadie Aline Harris, born on the 8th day of April, 1903

Name of Father: Walter C Harris   a citizen of the Choctaw Nation.
Name of Mother: Sarah E Harris   a citizen of the Choctaw Nation.

Postoffice   Norwood, Ind. Ter.

AFFIDAVIT OF MOTHER.

UNITED STATES OF AMERICA, Indian Territory,
   Central   DISTRICT.

I, Sarah E. Harris, on oath state that I am 20 years of age and a citizen by marriage, of the Choctaw Nation; that I am the lawful wife of Walter C. Harris, who is a citizen, by blood of the Choctaw Nation; that a female child was born to me on 8th day of April, 1903; that said child has been named Sadie Aline Harris, and was living March 4, 1905.

   Sarah E Harris

Witnesses To Mark:
   S.E. Morris
   Alice M Byrn

Subscribed and sworn to before me this 11th day of April, 1905

   Wirt Franklin
   Notary Public.

Applications for Enrollment of Choctaw Newborn
Act of 1905 Volume XVII

AFFIDAVIT OF ATTENDING PHYSICIAN OR MID-WIFE.

UNITED STATES OF AMERICA, Indian Territory,
Central   DISTRICT.

I, Laura Smith, a mid wife, on oath state that I attended on Mrs. Sarah E Harris, wife of Walter C Harris on the 8th day of April, 1903; that there was born to her on said date a Female child; that said child was living March 4, 1905, and is said to have been named Sadie Aline Harris

                                                  her
                                          Laura x Smith
Witnesses To Mark: mark
  { John E Harris
    John F Spagle

Subscribed and sworn to before me this 21 day of April, 1905

                              W.R. Kirby
                                    Notary Public.

NEW BORN AFFIDAVIT

No ....

CHOCTAW ENROLLING COMMISSION

IN THE MATTER OF THE APPLICATION FOR ENROLLMENT as a citizen of the Choctaw Nation, of Sadie Aline Harris born on the 8th day of April 190 3

Name of father Walter C Harris   a citizen of Choctaw   Nation,
final enrollment No. 2903
Name of mother Sarah E Harris   a citizen of Choctaw   Nation,
final enrollment No. 890

                                    Norwood, I.T.   Postoffice.

Applications for Enrollment of Choctaw Newborn
Act of 1905 Volume XVII

AFFIDAVIT OF MOTHER

UNITED STATES OF AMERICA
   INDIAN TERRITORY
DISTRICT   Central

I Sarah E Harris , on oath state that I am 20 years of age and a citizen by Intermarriage of the Choctaw Nation, and as such have been placed upon the final roll of the Choctaw Nation, by the Honorable Secretary of the Interior my final enrollment number being 890 ; that I am the lawful wife of Walter C Harris , who is a citizen of the Choctaw Nation, and as such has been placed upon the final roll of said Nation by the Honorable Secretary of the Interior, his final enrollment number being 2903 and that a female child was born to me on the 8th day of April 190 3; that said child has been named Sadie Aline Harris , and is now living.

Sarah E Harris

WITNESSETH:
  Must be two witnesses { WA Coleman
  who are citizens   Louis Dyer

Subscribed and sworn to before me this, the 13th day of March , 190 5

W.A. Shoney
Notary Public.

My Commission Expires: Jan 10, 1909

Affidavit of Attending Physician or Midwife

UNITED STATES OF AMERICA,
   INDIAN TERRITORY,
Central   DISTRICT

I, Laura Smith a midwife on oath state that I attended on Mrs. Sarah E Harris wife of Walter C Harris on the 8th day of April , 190 3, that there was born to her on said date a female child, that said child is now living, and is said to have been named Sadie Aline Harris

Laura Smith   ~~M.D~~.

Subscribed and sworn to before me this the 13th day of March 1905

W A Shoney
Notary Public.

WITNESSETH:
  Must be two witnesses { WA Coleman
  who are citizens and
  know the child.   Louis Dyer

Applications for Enrollment of Choctaw Newborn
Act of 1905 Volume XVII

We hereby certify that we are well acquainted with Laura Smith a midwife and know her to be reputable and of good standing in the community.

Must be two citizen witnesses. { WA Coleman
Louis Dyer

Choctaw New Born 1243
    Jesse Thompson
    (Born March 25, 1904)

NEW BORN

CHOCTAW
NEW BORN

1243

Jesse Thompson

(Born March 25, 1904)

ACT OF CONGRESS APPROVED MARCH 30, 1905.

CANCELLED

transferred to CHICKASAW
card no NEW BORN 546
JAN 3- 1906

Applications for Enrollment of Choctaw Newborn
Act of 1905 Volume XVII

Choctaw New Born 1244
    Jesse Thomas Witt
    (Born April 29, 1903)

BIRTH AFFIDAVIT.

DEPARTMENT OF THE INTERIOR.
COMMISSION TO THE FIVE CIVILIZED TRIBES.

IN RE APPLICATION FOR ENROLLMENT, as a citizen of the Choctaw Nation, of Jessie Thomas Witt, born on the 29 day of April, 1903

Name of Father: Marion Witt   a citizen of the Choctaw Nation. by entermarriage[sic]
Name of Mother: Peggy Witt   a citizen of the Choctaw Nation.

Postoffice   Nashoba Ind Ter

AFFIDAVIT OF MOTHER.

UNITED STATES OF AMERICA, Indian Territory, }
    Central   DISTRICT.

    I, Peggy Witt, on oath state that I am 40 years of age and a citizen by blood, of the Choctaw Nation; that I am the lawful wife of Marion Witt, who is a citizen, by entermarriage of the Choctaw Nation; that a male child was born to me on the 29 day of April, 1903; that said child has been named Jessie Thomas Witt, and was living March 4, 1905.

                                 her
                           Peggy x Witt
Witnesses To Mark: mark
  { John Williams
    (Name Illegible)

    Subscribed and sworn to before me this 22 day of April, 1905

                       F.M. Fuller
                           Notary Public.

Applications for Enrollment of Choctaw Newborn
Act of 1905   Volume XVII

AFFIDAVIT OF ATTENDING PHYSICIAN OR MID-WIFE.

UNITED STATES OF AMERICA, Indian Territory,
Central   DISTRICT.

    I, Minnie Williams, a mid wife, on oath state that I attended on Mrs. Peggy Witt, wife of Marion Witt on the 29 day of April, 1903; that there was born to her on said date a male child; that said child was living March 4, 1905, and is said to have been named Jessie Thomas Witt

                                      Minnie Williams

Witnesses To Mark:
    Mary Wheat
    J.W. Wheat

    Subscribed and sworn to before me this 22 day of April, 1905

                              F.M. Fuller
                                  Notary Public.

My commission expires April 18th 1908

                                                            7-5572.

                Muskogee, Indian Territory, April 28, 1905.

Marion Witt,
        Nashoba, Indian Territory.

Dear Sir:

    Receipt is hereby acknowledged of the affidavits of Peggy Witt and Minnie Williams to the birth of Jessie Thomas Witt, son of Marion and Peggy Witt, April 29, 1903, and the same have been filed with our records as an application for the enrollment of said child.

                      Respectfully,

                                      Chairman.

Applications for Enrollment of Choctaw Newborn
Act of 1905 Volume XVII

Choctaw New Born 1245
    Beulah Grace Woods
    (Born April 20, 1903)

BIRTH AFFIDAVIT.

DEPARTMENT OF THE INTERIOR.
COMMISSION TO THE FIVE CIVILIZED TRIBES.

IN RE APPLICATION FOR ENROLLMENT, as a citizen of the Choctaw Nation, of Bulah[sic] Grace Woods, born on the 20 day of April, 1903

Name of Father: Gilbert W Woods   a citizen of the Choctaw Nation.
Name of Mother: Lizzie (Anderson) Woods   a citizen of the Choctaw Nation.

    Postoffice   Talihina I.T.

AFFIDAVIT OF MOTHER.

UNITED STATES OF AMERICA, Indian Territory,
    Central   DISTRICT.

    I, Lizzie Woods, on oath state that I am 20 years of age and a citizen by blood, of the Choctaw Nation; that I am the lawful wife of Gilbert W Woods, who is a citizen, by Blood of the Choctaw Nation; that a female child was born to me on 20 day of April, 1903; that said child has been named Bulah Grace Woods, and was living March 4, 1905.

                                          Lizzie Woods

Witnesses To Mark:
{

    Subscribed and sworn to before me this 6th day of July, 1905

                                 T.B. Lunsford
My com. expires   Notary Public.
Feb. 4, 1908

Applications for Enrollment of Choctaw Newborn
Act of 1905 Volume XVII

AFFIDAVIT OF ATTENDING PHYSICIAN OR MID-WIFE.

UNITED STATES OF AMERICA, Indian Territory, }
Central   DISTRICT.

I, Kizzie F Woods, a mid wife, on oath state that I attended on Mrs. Lizzie Woods, wife of Gilbert W Woods on the 20 day of April, 1903; that there was born to her on said date a female child; that said child was living March 4, 1905, and is said to have been named Bulah Grace Woods

Kizzie F Woods

Witnesses To Mark:
{

Subscribed and sworn to before me this 6th day of July, 1905

T.B. Lunsford
My com. expires   Notary Public.
Feb. 4, 1908

BIRTH AFFIDAVIT.

DEPARTMENT OF THE INTERIOR.
COMMISSION TO THE FIVE CIVILIZED TRIBES.

IN RE APPLICATION FOR ENROLLMENT, as a citizen of the Choctaw Nation, of Beulah Grace Woods, born on the 20 day of April, 1903

Name of Father: Gilbert W Woods   a citizen of the Choctaw Nation.
Name of Mother: Lizzie (Anderson) Woods   a citizen of the Choctaw Nation.

Postoffice   Talihina I.T.

AFFIDAVIT OF MOTHER.

UNITED STATES OF AMERICA, Indian Territory, }
Central   DISTRICT.

I, Lizzie (Anderson) Woods, on oath state that I am about 20 years of age and a citizen by Blood, of the Choctaw Nation; that I am the lawful wife of Gilbert W Woods, who is a citizen, by Blood of the Choctaw Nation; that a female child was born to me on 20 day of April, 1903; that said child has been named Beulah Grace Woods, and was living March 4, 1905.

Lizzie E Woods

Applications for Enrollment of Choctaw Newborn
Act of 1905   Volume XVII

Witnesses To Mark:
{

    Subscribed and sworn to before me this 22 day of April , 1905

Sam T. Roberts Jr
Notary Public.

AFFIDAVIT OF ATTENDING PHYSICIAN OR MID-WIFE.

UNITED STATES OF AMERICA, Indian Territory, }
   Central   DISTRICT.

    I, Kizzie F Woods , a Midwife , on oath state that I attended on Mrs. Lizzie Anderson Woods , wife of Gilbert W Woods on the 20 day of April , 1903; that there was born to her on said date a female child; that said child was living March 4, 1905, and is said to have been named Beulah Grace Woods

Kizzie F Woods

Witnesses To Mark:
{

    Subscribed and sworn to before me this 22 day of April , 1905

Sam T. Roberts Jr
Notary Public.

7-4732.

Muskogee, Indian Territory, April 28, 1905.

Gilbert W. Woods,
    Talihina, Indian Territory.

Dear Sir:

    Receipt is hereby acknowledged of the affidavits of Lizzie E. Woods and Kizzie F. Woods to the birth of Beulah Grace Woods, daughter of Gilbert W. and Lizzie E. Woods, April 20, 1903, and the same have been filed with our records as an application for the enrollment of said child.

Respectfully,

Chairman.

Applications for Enrollment of Choctaw Newborn
Act of 1905 Volume XVII

7-NB-1245.

Muskogee, Indian Territory, June 19, 1905.

Gilbert W. Woods,
    Talihina, Indian Territory.

Dear Sir:

    There is enclosed herewith for execution application for the enrollment of your infant child, Beulah Grace Woods, born April 20, 1903.

    In the affidavits heretofore filed in this office your wife signed her name as Lizzie E. Woods.. Her name appears upon the records of the Commission as Lizzie Anderson. In the enclosed affidavits her name is inserted as Lizzie Woods as it would now be since her marriage to you. You will please have her sign her name as it appears in the affidavit, omitting the initial E.

    The attending physician or midwife should sign his or her name as the same appears in the body of the affidavits. In having these affidavits executed, if either of the persons are unable to write, signature by mark must be attested by two witnesses. Each affidavit must be executed before a Notary Public and the notarial seal and signature of the officer must be attached to each separate affidavit.

    You are requested to give this matter your immediate attention as no further action can be taken until these affidavits are filed with the Commission.

    Respectfully,

    Chairman.

DeB--3/19

Choctaw New Born 1246
    Sallie Ann Gibson
    (Born Feb. 20, 1904)

Applications for Enrollment of Choctaw Newborn
Act of 1905   Volume XVII

BIRTH AFFIDAVIT.

DEPARTMENT OF THE INTERIOR.
COMMISSION TO THE FIVE CIVILIZED TRIBES.

IN RE APPLICATION FOR ENROLLMENT, as a citizen of the Choctaw Nation, of Sallie Ann Gibson, born on the 20th day of February, 1904

Name of Father: Harrison Gibson   a citizen of the Choctaw Nation.
Name of Mother: Emma Gibson   a citizen of the Choctaw Nation.

Postoffice   Antlers, Ind. Ter.

AFFIDAVIT OF MOTHER.

UNITED STATES OF AMERICA, Indian Territory,
Central   DISTRICT.

I, Emma Gibson, on oath state that I am 26 years of age and a citizen by blood, of the Choctaw Nation; that I am the lawful wife of Harrison Gibson, who is a citizen, by blood of the Choctaw Nation; that a female child was born to me on 20th day of February, 1904; that said child has been named Sallie Ann Gibson, and was living March 4, 1905.

         her
Emma x Gibson
Witnesses To Mark: mark
   Robert Anderson
   Vester W Rose

Subscribed and sworn to before me this 25th day of April, 1905

Wirt Franklin
Notary Public.

AFFIDAVIT OF ATTENDING PHYSICIAN OR MID-WIFE.

UNITED STATES OF AMERICA, Indian Territory,
Central   DISTRICT.

I, Nancy Lewis, a mid-wife, on oath state that I attended on Mrs. Emma Gibson, wife of Harrison Gibson on the 20th day of February, 1904; that there was born to her on said date a female child; that said child was living March 4, 1905, and is said to have been named Sallie Ann Gibson

         her
Nancy x Lewis
         mark

Applications for Enrollment of Choctaw Newborn
Act of 1905   Volume XVII

Witnesses To Mark:
{ Robert Anderson
{ Vester W Rose

Subscribed and sworn to before me this 25 day of   April   , 1905

Wirt Franklin
Notary Public.

NEW BORN AFFIDAVIT

No ....

CHOCTAW ENROLLING COMMISSION

IN THE MATTER OF THE APPLICATION FOR ENROLLMENT as a citizen of the Choctaw Nation, of   Sallie Ann Gibson   born on the 20th day of February   190 4

Name of father   Harrison Gibson   a citizen of   Choctaw   Nation, final enrollment No. 4966
Name of mother   Emma Gibson   a citizen of   Choctaw   Nation, final enrollment No. 4967

Antlers I.T.   Postoffice.

AFFIDAVIT OF MOTHER

UNITED STATES OF AMERICA }
INDIAN TERRITORY }
DISTRICT   Central

I   Emma Gibson   , on oath state that I am 28 years of age and a citizen by blood of the   Choctaw   Nation, and as such have been placed upon the final roll of the Choctaw   Nation, by the Honorable Secretary of the Interior my final enrollment number being 4967 ; that I am the lawful wife of   Harrison Gibson   , who is a citizen of the   Choctaw   Nation, and as such has been placed upon the final roll of said Nation by the Honorable Secretary of the Interior, his final enrollment number being 4966   and that a Female child was born to me on the 20th day of February 190 4; that said child has been named   Sallie Ann Gibson   , and is now living.

Attest
S.P. Davenport

her
Emma x Gibson
mark

Applications for Enrollment of Choctaw Newborn
Act of 1905   Volume XVII

WITNESSETH:

Must be two witnesses { Gabriel Nelson
who are citizens   { Isaac Simpson

Subscribed and sworn to before me this, the   16   day of   Feby   , 190 5

A.J. Arnote
Notary Public.

My Commission Expires:
May 16th 1907

Affidavit of Attending Physician or Midwife

UNITED STATES OF AMERICA, }
INDIAN TERRITORY,   }
Central   DISTRICT   }

I,   Nancy Lewis   a   Mid wife on oath state that I attended on Mrs. Emma Gibson   wife of   Harrison Gibson on the   20th   day of   Feby , 190 4, that there was born to her on said date a   Female child, that said child is now living, and is said to have been named   Sallie Ann Gibson

Attest   her
S.P. Davenport   Nancy x Lewis   MiDwife
                                           mark

Subscribed and sworn to before me this the   16   day of   Feby   1905

A.J. Arnote
Notary Public.

WITNESSETH:

Must be two witnesses { Gabriel Nelson
who are citizens and   {
know the child.   { Isaac Simpson

We hereby certify that we are well acquainted with   Nancy Lewis   a   Mid wife   and know   her   to be reputable and of good standing in the community.

Must be two citizen { Gabriel Nelson
witnesses.   { Isaac Simpson

Applications for Enrollment of Choctaw Newborn
Act of 1905   Volume XVII

Choctaw New Born 1247
    Archie M. Gray
    (Born Aug. 24, 1904)

BIRTH AFFIDAVIT.

DEPARTMENT OF THE INTERIOR.
COMMISSION TO THE FIVE CIVILIZED TRIBES.

IN RE APPLICATION FOR ENROLLMENT, as a citizen of the Choctaw Nation, of Archie M. Gray, born on the 24 day of August, 1904

Name of Father: George W. Gray   a citizen of the United States ~~Nation~~.
Name of Mother: Malina Gray (nee Dick)   a citizen of the Choctaw Nation.

    Postoffice   Coalgate IT

AFFIDAVIT OF MOTHER.

UNITED STATES OF AMERICA, Indian Territory, }
    Central   DISTRICT.

    I, Malina Gray (nee Malina Dick), on oath state that I am 20 years of age and a citizen by blood, of the Choctaw Nation; that I am the lawful wife of George W Gray, who is a citizen, ~~by~~ of the United States ~~Nation~~; that a Male child was born to me on 24th day of August 1904, 1........; that said child has been named Archie M. Gray, and was living March 4, 1905.

                               Malina Gray
Witnesses To Mark: nee Malina Dick

    Subscribed and sworn to before me this 25th day of April, 1905

                              W.H. Angell
                                  Notary Public.

AFFIDAVIT OF ATTENDING PHYSICIAN OR MID-WIFE.

UNITED STATES OF AMERICA, Indian Territory, }
    Central   DISTRICT.

    I, W.M. Hume, a physician, on oath state that I attended on Mrs. Malina Gray (nee Dick), wife of George W Gray on the 24th day of

Applications for Enrollment of Choctaw Newborn
Act of 1905 Volume XVII

August , 1904; that there was born to her on said date a Male child; that said child was living March 4, 1905, and is said to have been named Archie M Gray

Witnesses To Mark:

Subscribed and sworn to before me this 25th day of April , 1905

W.H. Angell
Notary Public.

NEW BORN AFFIDAVIT

No

CHOCTAW ENROLLING COMMISSION

IN THE MATTER OF THE APPLICATION FOR ENROLLMENT as a citizen of the Choctaw Nation, of Archie M Gray born on the 24 day of Aug 190 4

Name of father Geo Gray a citizen of United States Nation, final enrollment No. ———

Name of mother Malina Gray a citizen of Choctaw Nation, final enrollment No. 3948

Coalgate IT Postoffice.

AFFIDAVIT OF MOTHER

UNITED STATES OF AMERICA
INDIAN TERRITORY
DISTRICT Central

(nee Malina Dick)

I Malina Gray , on oath state that I am 20 years of age and a citizen by blood of the Choctaw Nation, and as such have been placed upon the final roll of the Choctaw Nation, by the Honorable Secretary of the Interior my final enrollment number being 3948 ; that I am the lawful wife of Geo Gray, who is a citizen of the US ~~Nation, and as such has been placed upon the final roll of said Nation by the Honorable Secretary of the Interior, his final enrollment number~~ being .... and that a Male child was born to me on the 24 day of August 190 4; that said child has been named Archie M Gray , and is now living.

Malina Gray

Applications for Enrollment of Choctaw Newborn
Act of 1905 Volume XVII

WITNESSETH:
Must be two witnesses { D W Hodges
who are citizens { Chas La Flore

Subscribed and sworn to before me this, the 27 day of Feby , 190 5

PE Wilhelm
Notary Public.

My Commission Expires: Feby 1st 1905[sic]

Affidavit of Attending Physician or Midwife

UNITED STATES OF AMERICA, }
INDIAN TERRITORY, }
Central   DISTRICT }

I, W.M. Hume a physician on oath state that I attended on Mrs. Malina Gray wife of Geo Gray on the 24 day of August , 190 4, that there was born to her on said date a Male child, that said child is now living, and is said to have been named Archie M Gray

W.M. Hume   M. D.

Subscribed and sworn to before me this the 27 day of Feby 1905

PE Wilhelm
Notary Public.

WITNESSETH:
Must be two witnesses { D.W. Hodges
who are citizens and {
know the child.   { Chas La Flore

We hereby certify that we are well acquainted with W.M. Hume a physician and know him to be reputable and of good standing in the community.

Must be two citizen { D.W. Hodges
witnesses.   { Chas La Flore

Applications for Enrollment of Choctaw Newborn
Act of 1905 Volume XVII

Muskogee, Indian Territory, July 3, 1905.

George W. Gray,
Coalgate, Indian Territory.

Dear Sir:

Receipt is hereby acknowledged of your letter of June 29, asking if the application for the enrollment of your child, Archie M. Gray, has been received.

In reply you are advised that the application for the enrollment of your child, Archie M. Gray, has been received and filed, and the name of your child has been placed upon a schedule of citizens by blood of the Choctaw Nation prepared for forwarding to the Secretary of the Interior. You will be notified when his enrollment is approved by the Department.

Respectfully,

Commissioner.

Choctaw New Born 1248
Escar Nichols
(Born Jan. 10, 1904)

BIRTH AFFIDAVIT.

DEPARTMENT OF THE INTERIOR.
COMMISSION TO THE FIVE CIVILIZED TRIBES.

IN RE APPLICATION FOR ENROLLMENT, as a citizen of the   Choctaw   Nation, of Escar Nichols   , born on the 10th   day of   January , 1904

Name of Father: Levi Nichols   a citizen of the   Choctaw   Nation.
Name of Mother: Emma Nichols   a citizen of the   Choctaw   Nation.

Postoffice   Antlers, Ind. Ter.

Applications for Enrollment of Choctaw Newborn
Act of 1905   Volume XVII

AFFIDAVIT OF MOTHER.

UNITED STATES OF AMERICA, Indian Territory, }
Central   DISTRICT.

I, Emma Nichols, on oath state that I am 27 years of age and a citizen by blood, of the Choctaw Nation; that I am the lawful wife of Levi Nichols, who is a citizen, by marriage of the Choctaw Nation; that a male child was born to me on 10th day of January, 1904; that said child has been named Escar Nichols, and was living March 4, 1905.

Emma Nichols

Witnesses To Mark:
{

Subscribed and sworn to before me this 25th day of April, 1905

Wirt Franklin
Notary Public.

AFFIDAVIT OF ATTENDING PHYSICIAN OR MID-WIFE.

UNITED STATES OF AMERICA, Indian Territory, }
Central   DISTRICT.

I, M.J. Wise, a mid-wife, on oath state that I attended on Mrs. Emma Nichols, wife of Levi Nichols on the 10th day of January, 1904; that there was born to her on said date a male child; that said child was living March 4, 1905, and is said to have been named Escar Nichols

M.J. Wise

Witnesses To Mark:
{

Subscribed and sworn to before me this 25th day of April, 1905

Wirt Franklin
Notary Public.

Applications for Enrollment of Choctaw Newborn
Act of 1905 Volume XVII

Choctaw New Born 1249
    Sophia Graman
    (Born July 30, 1904)

BIRTH AFFIDAVIT.

DEPARTMENT OF THE INTERIOR.
COMMISSION TO THE FIVE CIVILIZED TRIBES.

IN RE APPLICATION FOR ENROLLMENT, as a citizen of the Choctaw Nation, of Sophia Graman, born on the 30th day of July, 1904

Name of Father: Jackson Graman   a citizen of the Choctaw Nation.
Name of Mother: Sallie Graman   a citizen of the Choctaw Nation.

        Postoffice   Antlers, Ind. Ter.

AFFIDAVIT OF MOTHER.

UNITED STATES OF AMERICA, Indian Territory, }
   Central   DISTRICT.   }

    I, Sallie Graman, on oath state that I am 41 years of age and a citizen by blood, of the Choctaw Nation; that I am the lawful wife of Jackson Graman, who is a citizen, by blood of the Choctaw Nation; that a female child was born to me on 30th day of July, 1904; that said child has been named Sophia Graman, and was living March 4, 1905.

                                  her
                            Sallie x Graman
Witnesses To Mark: mark
  { Robert Anderson
    Vester W Rose

    Subscribed and sworn to before me this 25th day of April, 1905

                            Wirt Franklin
                              Notary Public.

Applications for Enrollment of Choctaw Newborn
Act of 1905   Volume XVII

AFFIDAVIT OF ATTENDING PHYSICIAN OR MID-WIFE.

UNITED STATES OF AMERICA, Indian Territory, }
Central   DISTRICT.

I, Malissa Gibson, a mid-wife, on oath state that I attended on Mrs. Sallie Graman, wife of Jackson Graman on the 30th day of July, 1904; that there was born to her on said date a female child; that said child was living March 4, 1905, and is said to have been named Sophia Graman

Malissa x Gibson
her mark

Witnesses To Mark:
{ Robert Anderson
{ Vester W Rose

Subscribed and sworn to before me this 25th day of April, 1905

Wirt Franklin
Notary Public.

NEW-BORN AFFIDAVIT.

Number..............

...Choctaw Enrolling Commission...

IN THE MATTER OF THE APPLICATION FOR ENROLLMENT, as a citizen of the Choctaw Nation, of Sophia Graman

born on the 30th day of July 1904

Name of father   Jackson Graman   a citizen of   Choctaw Nation
Nation final enrollment No...............
Name of mother Sallie Graman   a citizen of   Choctaw
Nation final enrollment No. ....

Postoffice   Antlers

AFFIDAVIT OF MOTHER.

UNITED STATES OF AMERICA
INDIAN TERRITORY
Central   DISTRICT

I Sallie Graman, on oath state that I am 39 years of age and a citizen by blood of the Choctaw Nation, and as such have been placed upon the final roll of the Choctaw Nation, by the Honorable

Applications for Enrollment of Choctaw Newborn
Act of 1905   Volume XVII

Secretary of the Interior my final enrollment number being ....; that I am the lawful wife of   Jackson Graman , who is a citizen of the   Choctaw   Nation, and as such has been placed upon the final roll of said Nation by the Honorable Secretary of the Interior, his final enrollment number being .... and that a   Female   child was born to me on the 30th   day of July   190 4; that said child has been named   Sophia Graman , and is now living.

her
Sallie x Graman
mark

Witnesseth.

Must be two Witnesses who are Citizens. } Morris Gibson
Allen Greenwood

Subscribed and sworn to before me this 24   day of   March   190 5

John Cocke
Notary Public.

My commission expires:
Dec 6" 1908

AFFIDAVIT OF ATTENDING PHYSICIAN OR MIDWIFE

UNITED STATES OF AMERICA
INDIAN TERRITORY
  Central   DISTRICT

I,   Melessa Gibson   a   midwife on oath state that I attended on Mrs.   Sallie Graman   wife of   Jackson Graman   on the 30th   day of July , 190 4, that there was born to her on said date a   Female   child, that said child is now living, and is said to have been named   Sophia Graman

her
Melessa x Gibson   M.D.
mark   Midwife

WITNESSETH:

Must be two witnesses who are citizens and know the child. { Morris Gibson
Allen Greenwood

Subscribed and sworn to before me this, the   24th   day of   March   190 5

John Cocke   Notary Public.

We hereby certify that we are well acquainted with   Melessa Gibson   a   midwife   and know   her   to be reputable and of good standing in the community.

{ Morris Gibson
Allen Greenwood

Applications for Enrollment of Choctaw Newborn
Act of 1905   Volume XVII

7-1699.

Muskogee, Indian Territory,

May 4, 1905.

Jackson Graman,
    Antlers, Indian Territory.

Dear Sir:

Receipt is hereby acknowledged of the affidavits of Sallie Graman and Melessa Gibson to the birth of Sophia Graman, daughter of Sallie and Jackson Graman, July 30, 1904, and the same have been filed with our records as an application for the enrollment of said child.

Respectfully,

Chairman.

Choctaw New Born 1250
    Texanna Farr
    (Born Sept. 11, 1904)

BIRTH AFFIDAVIT.

DEPARTMENT OF THE INTERIOR.
COMMISSION TO THE FIVE CIVILIZED TRIBES.

IN RE APPLICATION FOR ENROLLMENT, as a citizen of the   Choctaw   Nation, of Texanna Farr   , born on the   11th   day of   September   , 1904

Name of Father: Arthur T Farr   a citizen of the   Choctaw   Nation.
Name of Mother: Lena Eliza Farr   a citizen of the   Choctaw   Nation.

Postoffice   Antlers, Ind. Ter.

AFFIDAVIT OF MOTHER.

UNITED STATES OF AMERICA, Indian Territory, }
    Central   DISTRICT.   }

I,   Lena Eliza Farr   , on oath state that I am   24   years of age and a citizen by   marriage   , of the   Choctaw   Nation; that I am the lawful wife of   Arthur

Applications for Enrollment of Choctaw Newborn
Act of 1905   Volume XVII

T Farr, who is a citizen, by blood of the Choctaw Nation; that a female child was born to me on 11th day of September, 1904; that said child has been named Texanna Farr, and was living March 4, *1905; and that said child died on April 5, 1905.*

                                          Lena Eliza Farr

Witnesses To Mark:
{

    Subscribed and sworn to before me this 25th day of April, 1905

                                           Wirt Franklin
                                           Notary Public.

AFFIDAVIT OF ATTENDING PHYSICIAN OR MID-WIFE.

UNITED STATES OF AMERICA, Indian Territory,}
Central   DISTRICT.}

    I, M. J. Wise, a mid-wife, on oath state that I attended on Mrs. Lena Eliza Farr, wife of Arthur T. Farr on the 11th day of September, 1904; that there was born to her on said date a female child; that said child was living March 4, 1905, and is said to have been named Texanna Farr

                                           M.J. Wise

Witnesses To Mark:
{

    Subscribed and sworn to before me this 25th day of April, 1905

                                           Wirt Franklin
                                           Notary Public.

<u>Choctaw New Born 1251</u>
    Marie Dillard[sic]
    (Born April 6, 1904)

Applications for Enrollment of Choctaw Newborn
Act of 1905   Volume XVII

BIRTH AFFIDAVIT.

DEPARTMENT OF THE INTERIOR.
COMMISSION TO THE FIVE CIVILIZED TRIBES.

IN RE APPLICATION FOR ENROLLMENT, as a citizen of the   Choctaw   Nation, of Marie Dilliard   , born on the   6th   day of   April   , 1904

Name of Father: Le Flore Dilliard   a citizen of the   Choctaw   Nation.
Name of Mother: Cora Dilliard   a citizen of the   Choctaw   Nation.

Postoffice   Antlers, Ind. Ter.

AFFIDAVIT OF MOTHER.

UNITED STATES OF AMERICA, Indian Territory, }
Central   DISTRICT.

I,   Cora Dilliard   , on oath state that I am   29   years of age and a citizen by marriage   , of the   Choctaw   Nation; that I am the lawful wife of   Le Flore Dilliard   , who is a citizen, by   blood   of the   Choctaw   Nation; that a   female   child was born to me on   6th   day of   April   , 1904; that said child has been named   Marie Dilliard   , and was living March 4, 1905.

Cora Dilliard

Witnesses To Mark:
{

Subscribed and sworn to before me this   25th   day of   April   , 1905

Wirt Franklin
Notary Public.

AFFIDAVIT OF ATTENDING PHYSICIAN OR MID-WIFE.

UNITED STATES OF AMERICA, Indian Territory, }
Central   DISTRICT.

I,   M. J. Wise   , a   mid-wife   , on oath state that I attended on Mrs.   Cora Dilliard   , wife of   LeFlore Dilliard   on the   6th   day of   April   , 1904; that there was born to her on said date a   female   child; that said child was living March 4, 1905, and is said to have been named   Marie Dilliard

M. J. Wise

Witnesses To Mark:
{

Applications for Enrollment of Choctaw Newborn
Act of 1905 Volume XVII

Subscribed and sworn to before me this 25th day of April, 1905

Wirt Franklin
Notary Public.

7-NB-1251

Muskogee, Indian Territory, August 10, 1905.

Leflore Dillard,
    Antlers, Indian Territory.

Dear Sir:

Replying to that portion of your letter of July 19, 1905, in which you ask if you can now file for Marie Dilard[sic], you are advised that on August 2, 1905, the Secretary of the Interior approved the enrollment of Marie Dillard as a citizen by blood of the Choctaw Nation and selection of allotment may now be made in her behalf in accordance with the rules and regulations governing the selection of allotments and the designation of homesteads in the Choctaw and Chickasaw Nations.

Respectfully,

Acting Commissioner.

Choctaw New Born 1252
    Virgie Lou Shillings
    (Born Nov. 26, 1903)

BIRTH AFFIDAVIT.

DEPARTMENT OF THE INTERIOR.
COMMISSION TO THE FIVE CIVILIZED TRIBES.

IN RE APPLICATION FOR ENROLLMENT, as a citizen of the Choctaw Nation, of Virgie Lou Shillings, born on the 26th day of November, 1903

Name of Father: William C. Shillings   a citizen of the United States ~~Nation~~.
Name of Mother: Mary Shillings   a citizen of the Choctaw Nation.

Postoffice   Finley, Ind. Ter.

Applications for Enrollment of Choctaw Newborn
Act of 1905 Volume XVII

AFFIDAVIT OF MOTHER.

UNITED STATES OF AMERICA, Indian Territory, }
Central DISTRICT.

I, Mary Shillings, on oath state that I am 21 years of age and a citizen by blood, of the Choctaw Nation; that I am the lawful wife of William C. Shillings, who is a citizen, ~~by~~ of the United States ~~Nation~~; that a female child was born to me on 26th day of November, 1903; that said child has been named Virgie Lou Shillings, and was living March 4, 1905.

Mary Shillings

Witnesses To Mark:
{

Subscribed and sworn to before me this 25th day of April, 1905

Wirt Franklin
Notary Public.

AFFIDAVIT OF ATTENDING PHYSICIAN OR MID-WIFE.

UNITED STATES OF AMERICA, Indian Territory, }
Central DISTRICT.

I, W. N. John, a physician, on oath state that I attended on Mrs. Mary Shillings, wife of William C. Shillings on the 26th day of November, 1903; that there was born to her on said date a female child; that said child was living March 4, 1905, and is said to have been named Virgie Lou Shillings

W.N. John

Witnesses To Mark:
{

Subscribed and sworn to before me this 25th day of April, 1905

Wirt Franklin
Notary Public.

Applications for Enrollment of Choctaw Newborn
Act of 1905 Volume XVII

Choctaw New Born 1253
    Jesse James Terrell
    (Born Oct. 9, 1904)

BIRTH AFFIDAVIT.

DEPARTMENT OF THE INTERIOR.
COMMISSION TO THE FIVE CIVILIZED TRIBES.

IN RE APPLICATION FOR ENROLLMENT, as a citizen of the Choctaw Nation, of Jesse James Terrell , born on the 9th day of October , 1904

Name of Father: Houston Terrell   a citizen of the Choctaw Nation.
Name of Mother: Louisa Terrell nee James   a citizen of the Choctaw Nation.

Postoffice   Kinta I.T.

AFFIDAVIT OF MOTHER.

UNITED STATES OF AMERICA, Indian Territory,
    Western   DISTRICT.

    I, Louisa Terrell , on oath state that I am 18 years of age and a citizen by blood , of the Choctaw Nation; that I am the lawful wife of Houston Terrell , who is a citizen, by blood of the Choctaw Nation; that a male child was born to me on 9th day of October , 1904; that said child has been named Jesse James Terrell , and was living March 4, 1905.

                                      Louisa Terrell
Witnesses To Mark:

    Subscribed and sworn to before me this 20 day of April , 1905

                             (Name Illegible)
                               Notary Public.
My commission expires March 4th 1907

Applications for Enrollment of Choctaw Newborn
Act of 1905   Volume XVII

AFFIDAVIT OF ATTENDING PHYSICIAN OR MID-WIFE.

UNITED STATES OF AMERICA, Indian Territory,
Western   DISTRICT.

I, Mary Bohannon, a midwife, on oath state that I attended on Mrs. Louisa Terrell, wife of Houston Terrell on the 9th day of October, 1904; that there was born to her on said date a male child; that said child was living March 4, 1905, and is said to have been named Jesse James Terrell

                her
           Mary x Bohannon
Witnesses To Mark: mark
   { B J Spring
    Alexander Johnson

Subscribed and sworn to before me this 20 day of April, 1905

(Name Illegible)
Notary Public.

My commission expires March 4th 1907

AFFIDAVIT OF ATTENDING PHYSICIAN OR MIDWIFE

UNITED STATES OF AMERICA
INDIAN TERRITORY
Western   DISTRICT

I, Mary Bohannon a citizen of Choctaw Nation on oath state that I attended on Mrs. Louisa James Terrell wife of Houston Terrell on the 9 day of October, 1904, that there was born to her on said date a male child, that said child is now living, and is said to have been named Jesse James Terrell

              her
           Mary x Bohannon
           mark

Subscribed and sworn to before me this, the 17th day of January 1905

L.D. Allen   Notary Public.

WITNESSETH:
Must be two witnesses { Joseph Bohannon
who are citizens   Frank Coley

Applications for Enrollment of Choctaw Newborn
Act of 1905   Volume XVII

We hereby certify that we are well acquainted with   Mary Bohannon   a   midwife   and know   her   to be reputable and of good standing in the community.

   Joseph Bohannon

   Frank Coley

NEW-BORN AFFIDAVIT.

   Number..........

...Choctaw Enrolling Commission...

IN THE MATTER OF THE APPLICATION FOR ENROLLMENT, as a citizen of the Choctaw   Nation, of   Jessie[sic] James Terrel[sic]

born on the 9   day of ___Oct_____ 190 4

Name of father   Houston Terrel   a citizen of   Choctaw
Nation final enrollment No. 8054
Name of mother   Louisa Terrel   James   a citizen of   Choctaw
Nation final enrollment No. 8428

       Postoffice   Kinta I.T.

AFFIDAVIT OF MOTHER.

UNITED STATES OF AMERICA
INDIAN TERRITORY
Western   DISTRICT

  I   Louise Terrel   nee James   , on oath state that I am   17   years of age and a citizen by   Blood   of the   Choctaw   Nation, and as such have been placed upon the final roll of the   Choctaw   Nation, by the Honorable Secretary of the Interior my final enrollment number being   8454[sic] ; that I am the lawful wife of   Houston Terrel   , who is a citizen of the   Choctaw   Nation, and as such has been placed upon the final roll of said Nation by the Honorable Secretary of the Interior, his final enrollment number being   8054   and that a   Male   child was born to me on the   9th   day of   Oct   190 4; that said child has been named Jessie James Terrell[sic] and is now living.

Witnesseth.
 Must be two
 Witnesses who   Joseph Bohannon
 are Citizens.   Frank Coley

Applications for Enrollment of Choctaw Newborn
Act of 1905   Volume XVII

Subscribed and sworn to before me this   17   day of   Jan   190 5

L.D. Allen
Notary Public.

My commission expires: Feby 27-1907

(Letter below typed as given.)

INDIAN LAND AND MONEY
LFS-2-3-40
Birth Affidavit,
Jesse James Terrell,   February 3, 1940.
Choctaw New Born 1113.

Mr. E. O. Clark,
Stigler, Oklahoma.

Dear Mr. Clark,

telephone call of Miss John Rogers today, we are enclosing a certified copy of birth affidavit showing that Jesse James Terrell, Choctaw New Born 1113, was born October 9, 1904, the affidavit executed by his mother, Louisa Terrell, on April 20, 1903. Certified copies of records on file in this office are not sent out unless paid,for,hence we are sending the birth affidavit to you with the request that you have Jesse James Terrell forward the money, $1.50 the usual fee, for this affidavit, by you. You will find enclosed an envelope requiring no postage for remittance of the $1.50. payable to J. S. Fulton.

J. T. Wilkinson

John Rogers, Stigler
(Phone)
For E.O. Clark
B.A. Jesse James Terrell.
Choc N B 1113
$1⁵⁰ to JDF

1 copy.
Land #419
J.S. Fulton

Applications for Enrollment of Choctaw Newborn
Act of 1905   Volume XVII

Choctaw New Born 1254
    Ione Wallace
    (Born Feb. 18, 1903)

NEW-BORN AFFIDAVIT.

Number................

...Choctaw Enrolling Commission...

IN THE MATTER OF THE APPLICATION FOR ENROLLMENT, as a citizen of the Choctaw Nation, of Ione Wallace born on the 18 day of February 190 3

Name of father Robert Wallace   a citizen of Choctaw Nation
Nation final enrollment No. 304 (nee Beagles)
Name of mother Myrtle Wallace   a citizen of Choctaw
Nation final enrollment No. 9341

                     Postoffice   Archibald I.T.

AFFIDAVIT OF MOTHER.

UNITED STATES OF AMERICA
INDIAN TERRITORY
  Central   DISTRICT

I Myrtle Wallace, on oath state that I am 20 years of age and a citizen by blood of the Choctaw Nation, and as such have been placed upon the final roll of the Choctaw Nation, by the Honorable Secretary of the Interior my final enrollment number being 9341 ; that I am the lawful wife of Robert Wallace, who is a citizen of the Choctaw Nation, and as such has been placed upon the final roll of said Nation by the Honorable Secretary of the Interior, his final enrollment number being 304 and that a female child was born to me on the 18 day of February 190 3; that said child has been named Ione Wallace, and is now living.

                               Myrtle Wallace

Witnesseth.
  Must be two Witnesses who are Citizens. } Alfred W McClure
                       Robert Wallace

Applications for Enrollment of Choctaw Newborn
Act of 1905 Volume XVII

Subscribed and sworn to before me this 16 day of Jan 190 5

(Name Illegible)
Notary Public.

My commission expires:
Nov 15-1905

7-9341
BIRTH AFFIDAVIT.

DEPARTMENT OF THE INTERIOR.
COMMISSION TO THE FIVE CIVILIZED TRIBES.

IN RE APPLICATION FOR ENROLLMENT, as a citizen of the Choctaw Nation, of Ione Wallace, born on the 18 day of February, 1903

Name of Father: Robert Wallace   a citizen of the Choc Nation.
Name of Mother: Myrtle Wallace   a citizen of the Choc Nation.

Postoffice Ashland, I.T.

AFFIDAVIT OF MOTHER.

UNITED STATES OF AMERICA, Indian Territory, }
Central   DISTRICT.

I, Myrtle Wallace, on oath state that I am 21 years of age and a citizen by blood, of the Choc Nation; that I am the lawful wife of Robert Wallace, who is a citizen, by intermarriage of the Choctaw Nation; that a female child was born to me on 18 day of February, 1903; that said child has been named Ione Wallace, and was living March 4, 1905.

Myrtle Wallace

Witnesses To Mark:

Subscribed and sworn to before me this 25 day of April, 1905

OL Johnson
Notary Public.

Applications for Enrollment of Choctaw Newborn
Act of 1905 Volume XVII

AFFIDAVIT OF ATTENDING PHYSICIAN OR MID-WIFE.

UNITED STATES OF AMERICA, Indian Territory,
Central   DISTRICT.

I, Annie Hurt, a midwife, on oath state that I attended on Mrs. Myrtle Wallace, wife of Robert Wallace on the 18 day of February, 1903; that there was born to her on said date a female child; that said child was living March 4, 1905, and is said to have been named Ione Wallace

Annie Hurt

Witnesses To Mark:

Subscribed and sworn to before me this 25 day of April, 1905

OL Johnson
Notary Public.

AFFIDAVIT OF ATTENDING PHYSICIAN OR MIDWIFE

UNITED STATES OF AMERICA
INDIAN TERRITORY
Central   DISTRICT

I, Annie Hurt   a   midwife on oath state that I attended on Mrs. Myrtle Wallace wife of Robert Wallace on the 18 day of February, 190 3, that there was born to her on said date a female child, that said child is now living, and is said to have been named Ione Wallace

Annie Hurt

Subscribed and sworn to before me this, the 16 day of January   190 5

(Name Illegible)   Notary Public.

WITNESSETH:
Must be two witnesses who are citizens
{ Alfred W McClure
  Robert Wallace

We hereby certify that we are well acquainted with Annie Hurt a midwife and know her to be reputable and of good standing in the community.

_____   Alfred W McClure

_____   Robert Wallace

Applications for Enrollment of Choctaw Newborn
Act of 1905   Volume XVII

Choctaw New Born 1255
    Martha Jane Ott
    (Born April 9, 1903)

HARTSHORNE, INDIAN TERRITORY,)
)
CENTRAL DISTRICT.)

I, Melvina Nelson, being duly sworn, on oath state that I am 24 twenty-four years of age and a resident of Higgins, Indian Territory; that to my personal knowledge a female child was born to Alfred and Lizzie Ott on the 9th day of April, 1903; that the said female child was living on the 4th day of March, 1905, and is living yet and has been named Martha Jane Ott.

                                                        Melvina Nelson

    Subscribed and sworn to before me at Hartshorne, Indian Territory, this the 1rth[sic] day of June, 1905.
                                                        Wm J Hulsey
                                                        Notary Public.

7-9100-1.
                    DEPARTMENT OF THE INTERIOR,
              COMMISSION TO THE FIVE CIVILIZED TRIBES.
        SOUTH McALESTER, I.T.   APRIL 25, 1905.

    In the matter of the application for the enrollment of Martha Jane Ott as a citizen by blood of the Choctaw Nation.

Mose Willis being first duly sworn testifies as follows;

    EXAMINATION BY THE COMMISSION:

Q What is your name? A Mose Willis.
Q What is your age? A Forty-five.
Q What is your post office address? A Deamon[sic].
Q Are you acquainted with Alfred Ott and Lizzie Ott who have this day made application for the enrollment of their child Martha Jane Ott as a citizen by blood of the Choctaw Nation.[sic] [sic]
Q How far from Mr. Ott do you live? A About six miles.
Q Do you know when Martha Jane Ott was born? A Yes, sir.
Q When was this child born? A 1903, April 9th.
Q Who attended Mrs. Ott when this child Martha Jane was born?
A My wife.
Q Is she living at the present time? A no, sir.
                                                Witness excused.

Applications for Enrollment of Choctaw Newborn
Act of 1905 Volume XVII

Alfred Ott being first duly sworn testifies as follows:

EXAMINATION BY THE COMMISSION:

Q What is your name? A Alfred Ott.
Q How old are you? A Forty-seven.
Q What is your post office address? A Higgins.
Q You have this day made application for the enrollment of your child Martha Jane Ott as a citizen of the Choctaw Nation; when was Martha Jane born? A 1903, April 9th.
Q Is she living at this date? A Yes, sir.
Q Who attended your wife when this baby was born? A Mary Willis.
Q Is she living at this time? A Dead

Witness excused.

Chas. T. Difendafer being first duly sworn states that the above and foregoing is a full, true and correct transcript of his stenographic notes taken in said cause on said date.

Chas T. Difendafer

Subscribed and sworn to before me this 25th day of April 1905.

OL Johnson
Notary Public.

7- 9101
9100
BIRTH AFFIDAVIT.

DEPARTMENT OF THE INTERIOR.
COMMISSION TO THE FIVE CIVILIZED TRIBES.

IN RE APPLICATION FOR ENROLLMENT, as a citizen of the Choctaw Nation, of Martha Jane Ott, born on the 9 day of April, 1903

Name of Father: Alfred Ott   a citizen of the Choctaw Nation.
Name of Mother: Lizzie Ott   a citizen of the Choctaw Nation.

Postoffice   Higgins Ind Ter.

AFFIDAVIT OF MOTHER.

UNITED STATES OF AMERICA, Indian Territory,
Central   DISTRICT.

I, Lizzie Ott, on oath state that I am 35 years of age and a citizen by blood, of the Choctaw Nation; that I am the lawful wife of Alfred Ott,

Applications for Enrollment of Choctaw Newborn
Act of 1905 Volume XVII

who is a citizen, by blood of the Choctaw Nation; that a female child was born to me on 9th day of April, 1903; that said child has been named Martha Jane Ott, and was living March 4, 1905.

                                      her
                              Lizzie x Ott
Witnesses To Mark: mark
  { OL Johnson
    Chas T Difendafer

Subscribed and sworn to before me this 25th day of April, 1905

                              OL Johnson
                                  Notary Public.

(The testimony from April 25, 1905, above, given again.)

                                           7-NB-1255.
                Sub
              Muskogee, Indian Territory, June 3, 1905.

Alfred Ott,
     Higgins, Indian Territory.

Dear Sir:

     Referring to the application for the enrollment of your infant child, Martha Jane Ott, born April 9, 1903, it is noted from the testimony taken on April 25, 1905, that the midwife, who attended upon your wife at the time of birth of the applicant, is dead.

     In this event it will be necessary that the affidavits of two persons, who are disinterested and not related to the applicant, who have actual knowledge of the facts that the child was born, the date of her birth; that she was living on March 4, 1905, and that Lizzie Ott is her mother, be filed in this office.

     The testimony of Mose Willis, to the above facts, is on file in this office. It will, therefore, be necessary that you secure the affidavit of another person to the same facts. Before any further action can be taken in this matter this affidavit must be filed with the Commission.

                                   Respectfully,

                                   Commissioner in Charge.

Applications for Enrollment of Choctaw Newborn
Act of 1905   Volume XVII

7 NB 1255

Muskogee, Indian Territory, June 17, 1905.

Alfred Ott,
    Higgins, Indian Territory.

Dear Sir:

    Receipt is hereby acknowledged of the affidavits of Melvina Nelson to the birth of Martha Jane Ott, daughter of Alfred and Lizzie Ott, April 9, 1903, and the same has been filed with the records in this case.

Respectfully,

Chairman.

7- NB 1255

Muskogee, Indian Territory, September 1, 1905.

Alfred Ott,
    Higgins, Indian Territory.

Dear Sir:

    I am in receipt of your letter of August 27th, requesting to be notified when the enrollment of your child, Martha Jane, is approved.

    In reply to your letter you are advised that on August 22, 1905, the Secretary of the Interior approved the enrollment of your minor child, Martha Jane Ott as a citizen by blood of the Choctaw Nation and the name of the child appears upon the new-born roll of citizens by blood of the Choctaw Nation opposite number 1435.

Respectfully,

Commissioner.

Applications for Enrollment of Choctaw Newborn
Act of 1905 Volume XVII

Choctaw New Born 1256
Pearl Marshall
(Born Nov. 17, 1902)

NEW-BORN AFFIDAVIT.

Number..............

Choctaw Enrolling Commission.

IN THE MATTER OF THE APPLICATION FOR ENROLLMENT, as a citizen of the Choctaw Nation, of   Pearl Marshall

born on the 17th day of November 190 2

Name of father   William Henry Marshall   a citizen of   Choctaw
Nation final enrollment No   15757
Name of mother   Annie Palmer Marshall   a citizen of   Choctaw
Nation final enrollment No   1240

Postoffice   Coalgate I.T.

AFFIDAVIT OF MOTHER.

UNITED STATES OF AMERICA,
INDIAN TERRITORY,
Central   DISTRICT

I   Annie Palmer Marshall   on oath state that I am   24   years of age and a citizen by   Marriage   of the   Choctaw   Nation, and as such have been placed upon the final roll of the   Choctaw   Nation, by the Honorable Secretary of the Interior my final enrollment number being   1240   ; that I am the lawful wife of   William Henry Marshall   , who is a citizen of the   Choctaw   Nation, and as such has been placed upon the final roll of said Nation by the Honorable Secretary of the Interior, his final enrollment number being   15757   and that a   Female   child was born to me on the   17th day of   November   190 2 ; that said child has been named   Pearl Marshall   , and is now living.

WITNESSETH: Annie Palmer Marshall
Must be two Witnesses who are Citizens.   John Gibson
   Rebecca Billey

Subscribed and sworn to before me this   15   day of   November[sic]   190 5

C.M. Threadgill
Notary Public.

My commission expires   11 Feb 1907

Applications for Enrollment of Choctaw Newborn
Act of 1905 Volume XVII

Affidavit of Attending Physician or Midwife.

UNITED STATES OF AMERICA
INDIAN TERRITORY
Central DISTRICT

I, W.J. Conley M.D. a Physician on oath state that I attended on Mrs. Annie Palmer Marshall wife of William Henry Marshall on the 17th day of November , 190 2 , that there was born to her on said date a female child, that said child is now living, and is said to have been named Pearl Marshall

W.J. Conley, M.D.

Subscribed and sworn to before me this, the 15 day of March 190 5

C.M. Threadgill
Notary Public.

WITNESSETH:
Must be two witnesses who are citizens and know the child.

John Gibson
Rebecca Billey

We hereby certify that we are well acquainted with W.J. Conley M.D. a Physician and know him to be reputable and of good standing in the community.

John Gibson
Rebecca Billey

BIRTH AFFIDAVIT.

DEPARTMENT OF THE INTERIOR.
COMMISSION TO THE FIVE CIVILIZED TRIBES.

IN RE APPLICATION FOR ENROLLMENT, as a citizen of the Choctaw Nation, of Pearl Marshall , born on the 17th day of November , 1902

Name of Father: William Henry Marshall   a citizen of the Choctaw Nation.
Name of Mother: Annie Palmer Marshall   a citizen of the Choctaw (Inter-Mariage[sic]

Postoffice Coalgate Ind. Ter.

Applications for Enrollment of Choctaw Newborn
Act of 1905   Volume XVII

AFFIDAVIT OF MOTHER.

UNITED STATES OF AMERICA, Indian Territory, }
Central   DISTRICT.

I, Annie Palmer Marshall, on oath state that I am 23 years of age and a citizen by intermarriage, of the Choctaw Nation; that I am the lawful wife of William Henry Marshall, who is a citizen, by blood of the Choctaw Nation; that a female child was born to me on 17th day of November, 1902; that said child has been named Pearl Marshall, and was living March 4, 1905.

Annie Palmer Marshall

Witnesses To Mark:

Subscribed and sworn to before me this 25th day of April, 1905

W.H. Angell
Notary Public.

AFFIDAVIT OF ATTENDING PHYSICIAN OR MID-WIFE.

UNITED STATES OF AMERICA, Indian Territory, }
Central   DISTRICT.

I, William J. Conley, a Physician, on oath state that I attended on Mrs. Annie Palmer Marshall, wife of William Henry Marshall on the 17th day of November, 1902; that there was born to her on said date a female child; that said child was living March 4, 1905, and is said to have been named Pearl Marshall

William J. Conley M.D.

Witnesses To Mark:

Subscribed and sworn to before me this 24th day of March, 1905

Geo A Fooshee
Notary Public.

Applications for Enrollment of Choctaw Newborn
Act of 1905 Volume XVII

Choctaw New Born 1257
    Agnes Taylor
    (Born Sept. 3[sic], 1904)

BIRTH AFFIDAVIT.

DEPARTMENT OF THE INTERIOR.
COMMISSION TO THE FIVE CIVILIZED TRIBES.

IN RE APPLICATION FOR ENROLLMENT, as a citizen of the Choctaw Nation, of Agnes Taylor, born on the 8th day of September, 1904

Name of Father: Wilburn Taylor   a citizen of the Choctaw Nation.
Name of Mother: Lottie Jones   a citizen of the Choctaw Nation.

Postoffice   Howe, Ind. Ter.

AFFIDAVIT OF MOTHER.

UNITED STATES OF AMERICA, Indian Territory,
    Central   DISTRICT.

I, Lottie Jones, on oath state that I am 24 years of age and a citizen by blood, of the Choctaw Nation; that I am ~~not~~ the lawful wife of Wilburn Taylor, who is a citizen, by blood of the Choctaw Nation; that a female child was born to me on 8th day of September, 1904; that said child has been named Agnes Taylor, and was living March 4, 1905.

                          Lottie Jones

Witnesses To Mark:
{

Subscribed and sworn to before me this 27th day of March, 1905

                          Wirt Franklin
                          Notary Public.

AFFIDAVIT OF ATTENDING PHYSICIAN OR MID-WIFE.

UNITED STATES OF AMERICA, Indian Territory,
    Central   DISTRICT.

I, Celizzie Jones, a Midwife, on oath state that I attended on Mrs. Lottie Jones, ~~wife of~~ on the 8th day of September,

Applications for Enrollment of Choctaw Newborn
Act of 1905   Volume XVII

1904; that there was born to her on said date a   Female   child; that said child was living March 4, 1905, and is said to have been named   Agnes Taylor

                                          her
                                Celizzie x Jones

Witnesses To Mark: mark
   { Sidney Amos
     E Lee

     Subscribed and sworn to before me this   1   day of   April   , 1905

                                      Robert E. Lee
                                          Notary Public.
My com expires Jan 11 - 1906

Lottie Jones is Choctaw by blood, Enroll No. 2566.

NEW BORN AFFIDAVIT

                                   No

CHOCTAW ENROLLING COMMISSION

IN THE MATTER OF THE APPLICATION FOR ENROLLMENT as a citizen of the   Choctaw   Nation, of   Agnes Taylor   born on the   8   day of   Sept   190 4

     Name of father   Wilburn Taylor   a citizen of   Choctaw   Nation, final enrollment No.
     Name of mother   Lottie Jones   a citizen of   Choctaw   Nation, final enrollment No.   2566

                                   Howe I.T.   Postoffice.

AFFIDAVIT OF MOTHER

UNITED STATES OF AMERICA
    INDIAN TERRITORY
DISTRICT   Central

    I   Lottie Jones   , on oath state that I am   22   years of age and a citizen by   blood   of the   Choctaw   Nation, and as such have been placed upon the final roll of the   Choctaw   Nation, by the Honorable Secretary of the Interior my final enrollment number being   2566   ; that I am ~~the lawful wife of~~ *not married* Wilburn Taylor

Applications for Enrollment of Choctaw Newborn
Act of 1905 Volume XVII

Father of child, who is a citizen of the Choctaw Nation, and as such has been placed upon the final roll of said Nation by the Honorable Secretary of the Interior, his final enrollment number being — and that a female child was born to me on the 8 day of September 190 4; that said child has been named Agnes Taylor, and is now living.

WITNESSETH: Lottie Jones

Must be two witnesses { Charles T. Perry
who are citizens   { Buckner Collin

Subscribed and sworn to before me this, the 16 day of Feb., 190 5

James Bower
Notary Public.

My Commission Expires:
Sept 23-1907

Affidavit of Attending Physician or Midwife

UNITED STATES OF AMERICA, }
   INDIAN TERRITORY,   }
Central   DISTRICT   }

I, Celissie[sic] Jones a midwife on oath state that I attended on Mrs. Lottie Jones ~~wife of~~ *father of child Wilburn Taylor* on the 8 day of Sept, 190 4, that there was born to her on said date a female child, that said child is now living, and is said to have been named Agnes Taylor

                              her
                    Celissie x Jones   *Midwife*
                              mark
Subscribed and sworn to before me this the 23 day of February 1905

Robert E Lee
My com expires Jan 11-1906   Notary Public.

WITNESSETH:
Must be two witnesses   { Charles T. Perry
who are citizens and   {
know the child.   { Buckner Collin

We hereby certify that we are well acquainted with Cellissie[sic] Jones a midwife and know her to be reputable and of good standing in the community.

Must be two citizen { Charles T. Perry
witnesses.   { Buckner Collin

43

Applications for Enrollment of Choctaw Newborn
Act of 1905 Volume XVII

Choctaw New Born 1258
    Saleyan Ben
    (Born May 6, 1904)

NEW-BORN AFFIDAVIT.

Number..............

...Choctaw Enrolling Commission...

IN THE MATTER OF THE APPLICATION FOR ENROLLMENT, as a citizen of the Choctaw Nation, of Saleyan Ben

born on the 6th day of __May__ 190 4

Name of father James Ben   a citizen of Choctaw Nation final enrollment No. 13401   *Com Roll)*
Name of mother Bettie Ben   *(Collin Dawes*   a citizen of Choctaw Nation final enrollment No. 2934

                     Postoffice   Kullituklo IT

AFFIDAVIT OF MOTHER.

UNITED STATES OF AMERICA
INDIAN TERRITORY
  Central   DISTRICT

         I   Bettie Ben *(Collin Dawes Com Roll)* , on oath state that I am 24 years of age and a citizen by blood of the Choctaw Nation, and as such have been placed upon the final roll of the Choctaw Nation, by the Honorable Secretary of the Interior my final enrollment number being 2934 ; that I am the lawful wife of James Ben , who is a citizen of the Choctaw Nation, and as such has been placed upon the final roll of said Nation by the Honorable Secretary of the Interior, his final enrollment number being 13401 and that a female child was born to me on the 6th day of May 190 4; that said child has been named Saleyan Ben , and is now living.

                                                  her
                               Bettie x Ben *Collin Dawes Com Roll*
Witnesseth.   mark
   Must be two   } Levi Stewart
   Witnesses who
   are Citizens.   Nicey Allen

Applications for Enrollment of Choctaw Newborn
Act of 1905 Volume XVII

Subscribed and sworn to before me this 21 day of Jan 190 5

W.A. Shoney
Notary Public.

My commission expires: Jan 10, 1909

AFFIDAVIT OF ATTENDING PHYSICIAN OR MIDWIFE

UNITED STATES OF AMERICA
INDIAN TERRITORY
 Central DISTRICT

I, James Ben a *midwife Dead* Attendant on oath state that I attended on Mrs. Bettie Ben *(Collin)* wife of James Ben on the 6th day of May , 190 4, that there was born to her on said date a female child, that said child is now living, and is said to have been named Saleyan Ben

his
James x Ben
mark

Subscribed and sworn to before me this, the 21st day of Jan 190 5

W.A. Shoney Notary Public.

WITNESSETH:
Must be two witnesses who are citizens and know the child.
{ Levi Stewart
  Nicey Allen

We hereby certify that we are well acquainted with James Ben a Attendant and know him to be reputable and of good standing in the community.

Levi Stewart _____

Nicey Allen _____

Applications for Enrollment of Choctaw Newborn
Act of 1905   Volume XVII

7- NB 1258
BIRTH AFFIDAVIT.

DEPARTMENT OF THE INTERIOR.
COMMISSION TO THE FIVE CIVILIZED TRIBES.

IN RE APPLICATION FOR ENROLLMENT, as a citizen of the   Choctaw   Nation, of Saleyan Ben   , born on the 6   day of   May   , 1904

Name of Father: James Ben   a citizen of the   Choctaw   Nation.
Name of Mother: Bettie Ben nee Collin   a citizen of the   Choctaw   Nation.

Postoffice   Kullituklo Ind Ter

AFFIDAVIT OF MOTHER.

UNITED STATES OF AMERICA, Indian Territory, }
Central   DISTRICT. }

I,   Bettie Ben (Roll 2934)   , on oath state that I am   24   years of age and a citizen by   blood   , of the   Choctaw   Nation; that I am the lawful wife of James Ben Roll 13401   , who is a citizen, by   blood   of the   Choctaw   Nation; that a   female   child was born to me on   6   day of   May   , 1904; that said child has been named   Saleyan Ben   , and was living March 4, 1905.

Bettie Ben

Witnesses To Mark:
{ Silas Lewis
{ Aaron Hampton

Subscribed and sworn to before me this   5   day of   October   , 1905

F M Fuller
My commission expires April 18th 1908   Notary Public.

AFFIDAVIT OF ATTENDING PHYSICIAN OR MID-WIFE.

UNITED STATES OF AMERICA, Indian Territory, }
Central   DISTRICT. }

we are acquainted with
We,...........................and a ...., on oath state that I attended on Mrs.   Bettie Ben   , wife of   James Ben   and that on or about the   6   day of   May   , 1904; that there was born to her on said date a   female   child; that said child was living March 4, 1905, and is said to have been named   Saleyan Ben, that we are not related to the applicant

Applications for Enrollment of Choctaw Newborn
Act of 1905 Volume XVII

Witnesses To Mark:
- Silas Lewis
- Aaron x Hampton

Subscribed and sworn to before me this 5 day of October, 1905

F M Fuller
Notary Public.

BIRTH AFFIDAVIT.

DEPARTMENT OF THE INTERIOR.
COMMISSION TO THE FIVE CIVILIZED TRIBES.

IN RE APPLICATION FOR ENROLLMENT, as a citizen of the Choctaw Nation, of Saleyan Ben, born on the 6th day of May, 1904, 1

Name of Father: James Ben — a citizen of the Choctaw Nation.
Name of Mother: Bettie Ben, nee Collins[sic] — a citizen of the Choctaw Nation.

Postoffice Kullituklo, Ind Ter

AFFIDAVIT OF MOTHER.

UNITED STATES OF AMERICA, Indian Territory,
Central DISTRICT.

I, Bettie Ben, nee Collins, on oath state that I am 24 years of age and a citizen by blood, of the Choctaw Nation; that I am the lawful wife of James Ben Roll 13401, who is a citizen, by blood of the Choctaw Nation; that a female child was born to me on 6th day of May, 1904; that said child has been named Saleyan Ben, and was living March 4, 1905.

her
Bettie x Ben
mark

Witnesses To Mark:
- JH Adams
- *(Name Illegible)*

Subscribed and sworn to before me this 22 day of July, 1905

R.E. Rowells
Notary Public.

Applications for Enrollment of Choctaw Newborn
Act of 1905   Volume XVII

Department of the Interior,
COMMISSION TO THE FIVE CIVILIZED TRIBES.

In the matter of the death of   Salyan[sic] Ben   a citizen of the   Choctaw Nation, who formerly resided at or near   Nashoba   , Ind. Ter., and died on the   10   day of   August   , 1905

AFFIDAVIT OF RELATIVE.

UNITED STATES OF AMERICA,
INDIAN TERRITORY,
Central   District.

I,   Betty Ben   , on oath state that I am   28   years of age and a citizen by Blood   , of the   Choctaw   Nation; that my postoffice address is   Nashoba   , Ind. Ter.; that I am   the mother   of   Salyan Ben   who was a citizen, by   Blood   , of the   Choctaw   Nation and that said   Salyan Ben   died on the   10   day of   August   , 1905

Bettie Ben

Witnesses To Mark:
{ Silas Lewis
  O.G. Lewis

Subscribed and sworn to before me this   5   *day of*   October   , 190 5

F. M. Fuller
Notary Public.

AFFIDAVIT OF ACQUAINTANCE.

UNITED STATES OF AMERICA,
INDIAN TERRITORY,
Central   District.

I,   Aaron Hampton   , on oath state that I am   45   years of age, and a citizen by Blood   of the   Choctaw   Nation; that my postoffice address is   Nashoba   , Ind. Ter.; that I was personally acquainted with   Salyan Ben   who was a citizen, by Blood   , of the   Choctaw   Nation; and that said   Salyan Ben   died on the   10th   day of   August   , 1905

his
Aaron x Hampton
mark

Witnesses To Mark:
{ Silas Lewis
  O.G. Lewis

Applications for Enrollment of Choctaw Newborn
Act of 1905   Volume XVII

Subscribed and sworn to before me this   5   *day of*   October   , 190 5

F. M. Fuller
My commission expires April 18th 1908   Notary Public.

United States of America }
   Indian Territory   } ss
Central Judicial District   }

    Silas Lewis being by me first duly sworn on oath states that I am 27 years of age, and a citizen by blood of the Choctaw Nation, and that I was well acquainted with Saleyan Ben, that she was the daughter of James Ben and Bettie Ben nee Collin that she was born May 6, 1904, that she was living on March 4th 1905, that I am not related to either of the above named parties nor am I in any way interested in the claim of the said Saleyan Ben.

                                                            Silas Lewis

Subscribed and sworn to before me this 30 day of August 1905

                                                   RD Francis
My commission expires Jan 8-1908   Notary Public.

United States of America }
   Indian Territory   }
Central Judicial District   }

            I, Robinson Short[sic] being by me first sworn on oath states that I am 23 years of age, and a citizen by blood of the Choctaw Nation, and that I was well acquainted with Saleyan Ben that she was the daughter of James Ben and Bettie Ben nee Collin, that she was born on the 6th day of May 1904 that she was living on March 4th 1905 that I am not related to either of above named parties, nor am I in any way interested in the claim of the said Saleyan Ben

                                                          his
Witness   Robinson x Shoate
GH Adams   mark
AM Funkhouser

Subscribed and sworn to before me this 30th day of August 1905

                                                   RD Francis
                                                   Notary Public.

Applications for Enrollment of Choctaw Newborn
Act of 1905 Volume XVII

7-NB-1258

Muskogee, Indian Territory, June 1, 1905.

James Ben,
    Kullituklo, Indian Territory.

Dear Sir:

    There is enclosed herewith for execution application for the enrollment of your infant child, Saleyan Ben, born May 6, 1904.

    The affidavits heretofore filed with the Commission show the child was living on January 21, 1905. It is necessary, for the child to be enrolled, that she was living on March 4, 1905.

    It further appears from the affidavits heretofore filed in this case that you attended your wife at the birth of this child. If this is correct, then you are advised that before said child can be finally enrolled, it will be necessary that you furnish the Commission with the affidavits of two disinterested witnesses to the effect that said child was born on May 6, 1904 and was living on March 4, 1905.

    In having these affidavits executed care should be exercised to see that all names are written in full, as they appear in the body of the affidavit, and in the event that either of the persons signing the affidavit are unable to write, signatures by mark must be attested by two witnesses. Each affidavit must be executed before a Notary Public and the notarial seal and signature of the officer must be attached to each separate affidavit.

                  Respectfully,

                  Chairman.

Enc.
FVK-1

7-NB-1258

Muskogee, Indian Territory, July 25, 1905.

James Ben,
    Kullitulko[sic], Indian Territory.

Dear Sir:

    Your attention is called to a communication addressed to you by the Commission to the Five Civilized Tribes under date of June 1, 1905, with which there was inclosed

Applications for Enrollment of Choctaw Newborn
Act of 1905   Volume XVII

application to be executed in the matter of the enrollment of your infant child, Saleyan Ben, born May 6, 1904.

In said letter you were advised that the affidavits heretofore filed with the Commission to the Five Civilized Tribes, in the matter of the enrollment of your child, show that she was living on January 21, 1905, and that it was necessary for her to be enrolled that she was living March 4, 1905, and that in the event that you attended upon your wife at the time of the birth of the applicant, it was necessary that you file the affidavits of two disinterested persons who have actual knowledge of the facts, that the child was born, the date of her birth, that she was living March 4, 1905, and that Bittie[sic] Ben was her mother. No reply to this letter has been received.

There is inclosed you herewith affidavits to be executed by your wife, Bittie Ben, and two disinterested witnesses, in conformity with requirements above stated, and you are requested to return same to this office immediately, when properly executed, as no further action can be taken relative to the enrollment of said child until the evidence requested is supplied.

Respectfully,

LM 25/4 Commissioner.

7-NB-1258.

Muskogee, Indian Territory, September 5, 1905.

James Ben,
    Kullitucklo, Indian Territory.

Dear Sir:

Receipt is hereby acknowledged of the affidavits of Bettie ben, the mother, Silas Lewis and Rollinson[sic] Shoate witnesses to the birth of your infant child, Saleyan Ben, born May 6, 1904, offered in support of the application for the enrollment of said child as a citizen by blood of the Choctaw Nation.

Said affidavits have been filed with the record in this case.

Respectfully,

Acting Commissioner.

Applications for Enrollment of Choctaw Newborn
Act of 1905 Volume XVII

Choctaw N B 1258

Muskogee, Indian Territory, October 4, 1905.

Thomas J. Sanford,
    Attorney at Law,
        Ardmore, Indian Territory.

Dear Sir:

Receipt is hereby acknowledged of your letter of September 29, relative to the status of the enrollment of Saleyan Ben, child of James and Bittie[sic] Ben, and you are advised that the name of this child has not yet been placed upon a schedule of citizens by blood of the Choctaw Nation for forwarding to the Secretary of the Interior.

Respectfully,

Commissioner.

7-NB-1258

Muskogee, Indian Territory, October 16, 1905.

Thomas J. Sanford,
    Attorney at Law,
        Ardmore, Indian Territory.

Dear Sir:

Receipt is hereby acknowledged of your letter of October 11, 1905, asking if further evidence is necessary to support the application of Saleyan Ben for enrollment as a citizen of the Choctaw Nation.

In reply to your letter you are advised that it is not believed that further evidence will be necessary in support of the application for the enrollment of the above named child. In event further evidence should be desired you will be duly advised.

Respectfully,

Commissioner.

Applications for Enrollment of Choctaw Newborn
Act of 1905   Volume XVII

7-NB-1258

Muskogee, Indian Territory, January 1?, 1906.

A. M. Funkhouser,
    Tuskahoma, Indian Territory.

Dear Sir:

    Receipt is hereby acknowledged of your letter of January 10, 1906, in which you ask the status of the application for the enrollment of Saleyan Ben, daughter of James and Betty Ben.

    In reply to your letter you are advised that the name of Saleyan ben has not yet been placed upon a schedule of citizens by blood of the Choctaw Nation prepared for forwarding to the Secretary of the Interior, but in event further evidence is necessary to enable this office to determine the right of this child to enrollment you will be duly advised.

                      Respectfully,

                                        Commissioner.

7-NB-1258

Muskogee, Indian Territory, February 7, 1906.

James Ben,
    Tuskahoma, Indian Territory.

Dear Sir:

    Receipt is hereby acknowledged of your letter of January 28, 1906, asking if your child Saleyan Ben has been enrolled and approved.

    In reply to your letter you are advised that the name of your child Saleyan Ben has been placed upon a schedule of new born citizens of the Choctaw Nation which has been forwarded the Secretary of the Interior and you will be notified when her enrollment is approved by the Department.

                      Respectfully,

                                    Acting Commissioner.

Applications for Enrollment of Choctaw Newborn
Act of 1905   Volume XVII

Choctaw New Born 1259
    Carlison Christie
    (Born Feb. 28, 1904)

NEW BORN AFFIDAVIT

No ....

CHOCTAW ENROLLING COMMISSION

IN THE MATTER OF THE APPLICATION FOR ENROLLMENT as a citizen of the Choctaw Nation, of   Carlison Christie   born on the 28th day of   February   190 4

Name of father   Jesse Christie   a citizen of   Choctaw   Nation, final enrollment No.   3180
Name of mother   Elizabeth James   a citizen of   Choctaw   Nation, final enrollment No. ....

Rufe, Ind. Ter.   Postoffice.

AFFIDAVIT OF MOTHER

UNITED STATES OF AMERICA }
    INDIAN TERRITORY
DISTRICT   Central

I   Elizabeth James   , on oath state that I am   18   years of age and a citizen by   blood   of the   Choctaw   Nation, and as such have been placed upon the final roll of the   Choctaw   Nation, by the Honorable Secretary of the Interior my final enrollment number being .... ; that I am the lawful wife of   Jesse L Christie   , who is a citizen of the   Choctaw   Nation, and as such has been placed upon the final roll of said Nation by the Honorable Secretary of the Interior, his final enrollment number being   3180   and that a   Male   child was born to me on the   28th day of   February   190 4; that said child has been named   Carlison Christie   , and is now living.

                              her
WITNESSETH: Elizabeth x James
Must be two witnesses { William Tellio   mark
who are citizens   { Levi James

54

Applications for Enrollment of Choctaw Newborn
Act of 1905   Volume XVII

Subscribed and sworn to before me this, the 20th day of March , 190 5

W A Shoney
Notary Public.

My Commission Expires: Jan 10, 1909

AFFIDAVIT OF ATTENDING PHYSICIAN OR MIDWIFE

UNITED STATES OF AMERICA
INDIAN TERRITORY
  Central   DISTRICT

I, Winnie James   a   midwife on oath state that I attended on Mrs. Elizabeth James wife of Jesse L Christie on the 28th day of February , 190 4, that there was born to her on said date a male child, that said child is now living, and is said to have been named Carlison Christie

Winnie James   M.D.

WITNESSETH:

Must be two witnesses who are citizens and know the child.
{ William Tellio
  Levi James

Subscribed and sworn to before me this, the   20th   day of March   190 5

W A Shoney   Notary Public.

We hereby certify that we are well acquainted with   Winnie James   a   midwife   and know   her   to be reputable and of good standing in the community.

{ William Tellio
  Levi James

Choctaw New Born 1260
   Sherman Merryman
   (Born April 29, 1903)
   Grace Ella Merryman
   (Born March 3, 1905)

Applications for Enrollment of Choctaw Newborn
Act of 1905   Volume XVII

BIRTH AFFIDAVIT.

DEPARTMENT OF THE INTERIOR.
COMMISSION TO THE FIVE CIVILIZED TRIBES.

IN RE APPLICATION FOR ENROLLMENT, as a citizen of the Choctaw Nation, of Sherman Merryman, born on the 29th day of April, 1903

Name of Father: Gibson V. Merryman   a citizen of the Choctaw Nation.
Name of Mother: Paralee Merryman   a citizen of the Choctaw Nation.

Postoffice   Wilburton, I.T.

AFFIDAVIT OF MOTHER.

UNITED STATES OF AMERICA, Indian Territory,
Central   DISTRICT.

I, Paralee Merryman, on oath state that I am 30 years of age and a citizen by intermarriage, of the Choctaw Nation; that I am the lawful wife of Gibson V. Merryman, who is a citizen, by blood of the Choctaw Nation; that a male child was born to me on 29th day of April, 1905[sic]; that said child has been named Sherman Merryman, and was living March 4, 1905.

Paralee Merryman

Witnesses To Mark:
  Sophronia Nead
  James A Nead

Subscribed and sworn to before me this 27 day of April, 1905.

Chas H Hudson
Notary Public.

AFFIDAVIT OF ATTENDING PHYSICIAN OR MID-WIFE.

UNITED STATES OF AMERICA, Indian Territory,
Central   DISTRICT.

I, Florentine Sisimoore, a midwife, on oath state that I attended on Mrs. Paralee Merryman, wife of Gibson V. Merryman on the 29 day of April, 1903; that there was born to her on said date a male child; that said child was living March 4, 1905, and is said to have been named Sherman Merryman

her
Florentine x Sisimoore
mark

Applications for Enrollment of Choctaw Newborn
Act of 1905   Volume XVII

Witnesses To Mark:
- Ester Sizemore
- *(Name Illegible)*

Subscribed and sworn to before me this 27 day of April, 1905

My com expires 1/11/1909   Chas H Hudson
                                        Notary Public.

BIRTH AFFIDAVIT.

DEPARTMENT OF THE INTERIOR.
COMMISSION TO THE FIVE CIVILIZED TRIBES.

IN RE APPLICATION FOR ENROLLMENT, as a citizen of the Choctaw Nation, of Sherman Merryman, born on the 29 day of April, 1903

Name of Father: Gipson[sic] V. Merryman   a citizen of the Choctaw Nation.
Name of Mother: Pairlee[sic] Merryman   a citizen of the Choctaw Nation.

Postoffice   Wilburton, Ind Ter

AFFIDAVIT OF MOTHER.

UNITED STATES OF AMERICA, Indian Territory,
Central   DISTRICT.

I, Pairlee Merryman, on oath state that I am 30 years of age and a citizen by intermarriage, of the Choctaw Nation; that I am the lawful wife of Gipson V. Merryman, who is a citizen, by blood of the Choctaw Nation; that a male child was born to me on 29 day of April, 1903; that said child has been named Sherman Merryman, and was living March 4, 1905.

                                        Pairlee Merryman
Witnesses To Mark:

Subscribed and sworn to before me this 5 day of July, 1905

                                        Chas H Hudson
                                        Notary Public.

Applications for Enrollment of Choctaw Newborn
Act of 1905 Volume XVII

AFFIDAVIT OF ATTENDING PHYSICIAN OR MID-WIFE.

UNITED STATES OF AMERICA, Indian Territory, } DISTRICT.

I, Clorentine[sic] Sisimoore , a midwife , on oath state that I attended on Mrs. Pairlee Merryman , wife of Gipson V. Merryman on the 29 day of April , 1903; that there was born to her on said date a male child; that said child was living March 4, 1905, and is said to have been named Sherman Merryman

                 her
            Clorentine x Sisimoore
Witnesses To Mark: mark
{ Maud Wilcox
{ Lydia Mai Hudson

Subscribed and sworn to before me this 5th day of July , 1905

            Chas H Hudson
             Notary Public.

NEW-BORN AFFIDAVIT.

    Number..................

...Choctaw Enrolling Commission...

IN THE MATTER OF THE APPLICATION FOR ENROLLMENT, as a citizen of the Choctaw Nation, of Sherman Merryman

born on the 29th day of ___April___ 190 3

Name of father Gibson V Merryman   a citizen of Choctaw
Nation final enrollment No. 8513
Name of mother Pairlee Merryman   a citizen of Choctaw
Nation final enrollment No. 734

           Postoffice   Wilburton IT

AFFIDAVIT OF MOTHER.

UNITED STATES OF AMERICA
INDIAN TERRITORY
  Central   DISTRICT

     I   Pairlee Merryman , on oath state that I am 30 years of age and a citizen by intermarriage of the Choctaw Nation, and as such have been placed upon the final roll of the Choctaw Nation, by the

Applications for Enrollment of Choctaw Newborn
Act of 1905 Volume XVII

Honorable Secretary of the Interior my final enrollment number being 734 ; that I am the lawful wife of Gibson V Merryman , who is a citizen of the Choctaw Nation, and as such has been placed upon the final roll of said Nation by the Honorable Secretary of the Interior, his final enrollment number being 8513 and that a Male child was born to me on the 29th day of April 190 3; that said child has been named Sherman Merryman , and is now living.

Pairlee Merryman

Witnesseth.

Must be two Witnesses who are Citizens. } Ed Riddle
Richard R Riddle

Subscribed and sworn to before me this 20' day of Feb 190 5

Chas H Hudson
Notary Public.

My commission expires:

AFFIDAVIT OF ATTENDING PHYSICIAN OR MIDWIFE

UNITED STATES OF AMERICA
INDIAN TERRITORY
Central DISTRICT

I, Clorentine Moore[sic] a midwife on oath state that I attended on Mrs. Pairlee Merryman wife of Gibson V Merryman on the 29th day of April , 190 3 , that there was born to her on said date a Male child, that said child is now living, and is said to have been named Sherman Merryman

Mrs Clorentine x Moore ~~M.D.~~
her
mark

Subscribed and sworn to before me this, the 15 day of Feb 190 5

Chas H Hudson
Notary Public.

WITNESSETH:

Must be two witnesses who are citizens and know the child. { Ed Riddle
Richard R Riddle

We hereby certify that we are well acquainted with Clorentine Moore a midwife and know her to be reputable and of good standing in the community.

Ed Riddle
Richard R Riddle

Applications for Enrollment of Choctaw Newborn
Act of 1905 Volume XVII

BIRTH AFFIDAVIT.

DEPARTMENT OF THE INTERIOR.
COMMISSION TO THE FIVE CIVILIZED TRIBES.

IN RE APPLICATION FOR ENROLLMENT, as a citizen of the Choctaw Nation, of Grace Ella Merryman, born on the 3rd day of March, 1905

Name of Father: Gibson V. Merryman   a citizen of the Choctaw Nation.
Name of Mother: Paralee Merryman   a citizen of the Choctaw Nation.

Postoffice   Wilburton, I.T.

AFFIDAVIT OF MOTHER.

UNITED STATES OF AMERICA, Indian Territory,
Central   DISTRICT.

I, Paralee Merryman, on oath state that I am 30 years of age and a citizen by intermarriage, of the Choctaw Nation; that I am the lawful wife of Gibson v. Merryman, who is a citizen, by blood of the Choctaw Nation; that a Female child was born to me on 3rd day of March, 1905; that said child has been named Grace Ella Merryman, and was living March 4, 1905.

                                             Paralee Merryman

Witnesses To Mark:
    (Name Illegible)
    James A Nead

Subscribed and sworn to before me this 27 day of April, 1905

                                             Chas H Hudson
                                             Notary Public.

AFFIDAVIT OF ATTENDING PHYSICIAN OR MID-WIFE.

UNITED STATES OF AMERICA, Indian Territory,
Central   DISTRICT.

I, Saphronia Need, a midwife, on oath state that I attended on Mrs. Paralee Merryman, wife of Gibson V. Merryman on the 3rd day of March, 1905; that there was born to her on said date a Female child; that said child was living March 4, 1905, and is said to have been named Grace Ella Merryman

                                             Saphronia Need

Applications for Enrollment of Choctaw Newborn
Act of 1905   Volume XVII

Witnesses To Mark:
{ FT Vaught
{ James A Need

Subscribed and sworn to before me this 27 day of   April   , 1905

My com expires 1/11/1909   Chas H Hudson
                                           Notary Public.

<del>7-2894</del>.
𝑛.𝐵. 1260

Muskogee, Indian Territory, May 5, 1905.

Charles H. Hudson,
    Wilburton, Indian Territory.

Dear Sir:

    Receipt is hereby acknowledged of your letter of April 27, enclosing the affidavits of Paralee Merryman and Florentine Sisimoore to the birth of Sherman Merryman; also the affidavits of Paralee Merryman and Saphronia Nead to the birth of Grace Ella Merryman, children of Gibson V. and Paralee Merryman, April 29, 1903 and March 3, 1905, and the same have been filed with our records as applications for the enrollment of said children.

                                      Respectfully,

                                        Commissioner in Charge.

7-NB-1260

Muskogee, Indian Territory, July 10, 1905.

Gipson B[sic]. Merryman,
    Wilburton, Indian Territory.

Dear Sir:

    Receipt is hereby acknowledged of the affidavits of Pairlee Merryman and Clemintine[sic] Wizmore[sic] to the birth of Sherman Merryman, son of Gipson V. and Pairlee Merryman, April 29, 1903, and the same have been filed with the records of this office in the matter of the enrollment of said child.

                                        Respectfully,

                                        Commissioner.

Applications for Enrollment of Choctaw Newborn
Act of 1905 Volume XVII

7-NB-1260.

Muskogee, Indian Territory, June 29, 1905.

Gipson V. Merryman,
    Wilburton, Indian Territory.

Dear Sir:

    There is herewith enclosed for execution application for the enrollment of your infant child, Sherman Merryman. The midwife, in her affidavit of April 27, 1905 heretofore filed in this office, gives the date of the applicant's birth as April 29, 1903, while the mother in her affidavit of the same date gives the date of birth as April 29, 1905.

    In the enclosed application the date of birth is left blank. Please insert the correct date, and when the affidavits are properly executed return them to this office.

    In having these affidavits executed care should be exercised to see that all names are written in full, as they appear in the body of the affidavit, and if either of the persons signing the affidavits are unable to write, signatures by mark must be attested by two witnesses. Each affidavit must be executed before a Notary Public and the notarial seal and signature of the officer must be attached to each separate affidavit.

    You are requested to give this matter your immediate attention as no further action can be taken until these affidavits are filed with the Commission.

    Respectfully,

    Chairman.

DeB--1/29.

7-NB-1260

Muskogee, Indian Territory, August 4, 1905.

Gibson B[sic]. Merryman,
    Wilburton, Indian Territory.

Dear Sir:

    Receipt is hereby acknowledged of your letter of July ??, 1905, asking when you can file for your children Sherman and Grace Ella Merryman.

Applications for Enrollment of Choctaw Newborn
Act of 1905 Volume XVII

In reply to your letter you are advised that the names of your children Sherman and Grace Ella Merryman have been placed upon schedules of citizens by blood of the Choctaw Nation which have been forwarded the Secretary of the Interior and you will be notified when their enrollment is approved by the Department. Pending the approval of their enrollment, however, no selection of allotment could be made in their behalf.

Respectfully,

Commissioner.

7-NB-589
7-NB-1260

Muskogee, Indian Territory, July 25, 1905.

Mary J. F. Graham,
Bengal, Indian Territory.

Dear Madam:

Replying to that portion of your letter of July 18, 1905, in which you ask the status of the enrollment of Lawrence Graham and Grace Ella, Marion Francis and Benjamin C. Merryman, you are advised that the enrollment of Benjamin C. and Marion Francis Merryman as citizens by blood of the Choctaw Nation was on June 30, 1905, approved by the Secretary of the Interior.

The names of Lawrence Graham and Grace Ella Merryman has been placed upon a schedule of citizens by blood of the Choctaw Nation which has been forwarded the Secretary of the Interior, and you will be notified when their enrollment is approved.

Respectfully,

Commissioner.

(The letter above given again, only with the date of July 27, 1905.)

Applications for Enrollment of Choctaw Newborn
Act of 1905 Volume XVII

7-NB-1260

Muskogee, Indian Territory, September 11, 1905.

G. V. Merryman,
    Wilburton, Indian Territory.

Dear Sir:

    Replying to your letter of August 30th, you are advised that on August 22, 1905, the Secretary of the Interior approved the enrollment of your minor child, Sherman Merryman, as a citizen of the Choctaw Nation, and the name of said child appears upon the final roll of new-born citicens[sic] by blood of the Choctaw Nation, opposite number 1436.

    The child is now entitled to an allotment and selection thereof should be made without delay at the land office for the nation in which the prospective allotment is located.

                        Respectfully,

                                    Acting Commissioner.

Choctaw New Born 1261
    William E. Folsom
    (Born May 17, 1903)
    Cletus A. Folsom
    (Born Aug. 24, 1904)

Certificate of Marriage

This is to certify that on this 21st day of August 1902 at my office in Gaines County Choctaw Nation Indian Territory
I H.F. Battle County Judge in and for said County Have this day united in the bonds of Matrimony Mr William W. Folsom a citizen of the Choctaw Nation and Miss Rosa L Thatcher a citizen of the United States according to all the laws customs and usage of the Choctaw Nation.
Given under my hand and seal as such County Judge the day and year before named

                                Frank Battle
                County Judge Gaines County Choctaw Nation

Applications for Enrollment of Choctaw Newborn
Act of 1905 Volume XVII

File in the Clerk office this the 25 day of August A.D. 1902

    Marcus Battice
        Clerk of Gaines County C.N.

This is the certified copy of William W. Folsom Rosa L. Thatcher Marriage Certificate has been Recorded in Gaines County Record Book Page 42

    Given under my hand and seal this the 6th day of July A.D. 1905

seal   Eastman W Nelson
E.W.N.   Clerk of Gaines County C.N.

BIRTH AFFIDAVIT.

DEPARTMENT OF THE INTERIOR.
COMMISSION TO THE FIVE CIVILIZED TRIBES.

IN RE APPLICATION FOR ENROLLMENT, as a citizen of the Choctaw Nation, of Cletus A Folsom, born on the 24 day of August, 1904

Name of Father: William W Folsom   a citizen of the Choctaw Nation.
Name of Mother: Rosie L Folsom   a citizen of the Choctaw Nation.

            Postoffice   Chambers IT

AFFIDAVIT OF MOTHER.

UNITED STATES OF AMERICA, Indian Territory, ⎫
    Central   DISTRICT. ⎭

    I, Rosie L Folsom, on oath state that I am 22 years of age and a citizen by Inter-M, of the Choctaw Nation; that I am the lawful wife of William W Folsom, who is a citizen, by blood of the Choctaw Nation; that a female child was born to me on 24th day of August, 1904; that said child has been named Cletus A Folsom, and was living March 4, 1905.

                                    Rosie L Folsom

Witnesses To Mark:
   { OP Folsom
     Zenobia V Jones

Applications for Enrollment of Choctaw Newborn
Act of 1905   Volume XVII

Subscribed and sworn to before me this 20th day of   April   , 1905

                    W.T. Culbertson
                    Notary Public.

AFFIDAVIT OF ATTENDING PHYSICIAN OR MID-WIFE.

UNITED STATES OF AMERICA, Indian Territory, }
   Central   DISTRICT.

    I,   A.G. Jones   , a   Physician   , on oath state that I attended on Mrs.   Rosie L Folsom   , wife of   William W Folsom   on the 24th day of Aug   , 1904; that there was born to her on said date a   Female   child; that said child was living March 4, 1905, and is said to have been named   Cletus A Folsom

                    A.G. Jones M.D.

Witnesses To Mark:
{ OP Folsom
{ Zenobia V Jones

Subscribed and sworn to before me this 20th day of   April   , 1905

                    W.T. Culbertson
                    Notary Public.

Affidavit of Attending Physician or Midwife

UNITED STATES OF AMERICA, }
    INDIAN TERRITORY,
    ....DISTRICT

    I,   A G Jones   a   Physician   on oath state that I attended on Mrs. Rosa Folsom   wife of   Wm W. Folsom   on the   24 day of   Aug , 190 4, that there was born to her on said date a   Female   child, that said child is now living, and is said to have been named   Cletus A Folsom

              A G Jones   M. D.

Subscribed and sworn to before me this the   16th   day of   Feb   1905

              GE Bell
                Notary Public.

WITNESSETH:
Must be two witnesses { OP Folsom
who are citizens and
know the child.   { W.S. Folsom

Applications for Enrollment of Choctaw Newborn
Act of 1905 Volume XVII

We hereby certify that we are well acquainted with   Dr A.G. Jones   a   Physician   and know   him   to be reputable and of good standing in the community.

Must be two citizen witnesses. { Eliza Fulton / Alie H Folsom

NEW BORN AFFIDAVIT

No ....

CHOCTAW ENROLLING COMMISSION

IN THE MATTER OF THE APPLICATION FOR ENROLLMENT as a citizen of the Choctaw Nation, of   Cletus A Folsom   born on the 24 day of August   190 4

Name of father Wm W. Folsom   a citizen of Choctaw Nation, final enrollment No. 12619

Name of mother Rose Folsom   a citizen of Choctaw Nation, final enrollment No. ....

Chambers IT   Postoffice.

AFFIDAVIT OF MOTHER

UNITED STATES OF AMERICA }
INDIAN TERRITORY }
DISTRICT Central }

I   Rose Folsom   , on oath state that I am 22 years of age and a citizen by Inter M of the Choctaw Nation, and as such have been placed upon the final roll of the not enrolled Nation, by the Honorable Secretary of the Interior my final enrollment number being ~~12619~~ ; that I am the lawful wife of William w Folsom , who is a citizen of the Choctaw Nation, and as such has been placed upon the final roll of said Nation by the Honorable Secretary of the Interior, his final enrollment number being 12619 and that a Female child was born to me on the 24th day of August   190 4; that said child has been named Cletus A Folsom , and is now living.

Rosa Folsom

WITNESSETH:
Must be two witnesses who are citizens { OP Folsom / W.S. Folsom

Applications for Enrollment of Choctaw Newborn
Act of 1905 Volume XVII

Subscribed and sworn to before me this, the 9th day of Feby, 1905

W.T. Culbertson
Notary Public.

My Commission Expires:
Sept 22 - 1907

BIRTH AFFIDAVIT.

DEPARTMENT OF THE INTERIOR.
COMMISSION TO THE FIVE CIVILIZED TRIBES.

IN RE APPLICATION FOR ENROLLMENT, as a citizen of the Choctaw Nation, of William E Folsom, born on the 17th day of May, 1903

Name of Father: William W Folsom   a citizen of the Choctaw Nation.
Name of Mother: Rosie L Folsom   a citizen of the Choctaw Nation.

Postoffice   Chambers IT

AFFIDAVIT OF MOTHER.

UNITED STATES OF AMERICA, Indian Territory,
Central   DISTRICT.

I, Rosie L Folsom, on oath state that I am 22 years of age and a citizen by Inter-M, of the Choctaw Nation; that I am the lawful wife of William W Folsom, who is a citizen, by blood of the Choctaw Nation; that a male child was born to me on 17th day of May, 1903; that said child has been named William E Folsom, and was living March 4, 1905.

Rosie L Folsom

Witnesses To Mark:
{ Zenobia V Jones
{ Eliza Fulton

Subscribed and sworn to before me this 20th day of April, 1905

W.T. Culbertson
Notary Public.

Applications for Enrollment of Choctaw Newborn
Act of 1905 Volume XVII

AFFIDAVIT OF ATTENDING PHYSICIAN OR MID-WIFE.

UNITED STATES OF AMERICA, Indian Territory, }
Central   DISTRICT. }

    I, Mrs O.P. Folsom , a midwife , on oath state that I attended on Mrs. Rosie E Folsom , wife of William W Folsom on the 17th day of May , 1903; that there was born to her on said date a male child; that said child was living March 4, 1905, and is said to have been named William E Folsom

                                O.P. Folsom

Witnesses To Mark:
  { Zenobia V Jones
    Eliza Fulton

    Subscribed and sworn to before me this 20th day of April , 1905

                             W.T. Culbertson
                                Notary Public.

NEW BORN AFFIDAVIT

                    No ....

CHOCTAW ENROLLING COMMISSION

    IN THE MATTER OF THE APPLICATION FOR ENROLLMENT as a citizen of the Choctaw Nation, of William E Folsom born on the 17th day of May 190 3

    Name of father W^m W Folsom a citizen of Choctaw Nation, final enrollment No. 12619
    Name of mother Rose Folsom a citizen of Choctaw Nation, final enrollment No. not enrolled

                            Chambers IT   Postoffice.

Applications for Enrollment of Choctaw Newborn
Act of 1905 Volume XVII

AFFIDAVIT OF MOTHER

UNITED STATES OF AMERICA
INDIAN TERRITORY
DISTRICT Central

I Rose Folsom , on oath state that I am 22 years of age and a citizen by Inter-M of the Choctaw Nation, and as such have been placed upon the final roll of the not enrolled Nation, by the Honorable Secretary of the Interior my final enrollment number being................. ; that I am the lawful wife of William W Folsom , who is a citizen of the Choctaw Nation, and as such has been placed upon the final roll of said Nation by the Honorable Secretary of the Interior, his final enrollment number being 12619 and that a Male child was born to me on the 17th day of May 190 3; that said child has been named William E , and is now living.

WITNESSETH:
Must be two witnesses who are citizens { W.S. Folsom
Lillie P. Folsom

Rosa Folsom

Subscribed and sworn to before me this, the 9th day of Feby , 190 5

W.T. Culbertson
Notary Public.

My Commission Expires:
Sept 22-1909

Affidavit of Attending Physician or Midwife

UNITED STATES OF AMERICA,
INDIAN TERRITORY,
Central   DISTRICT

I, O.P. Folsom a Midwife on oath state that I attended on Mrs. Rose Folsom wife of Wm W. Folsom on the 17th day of May , 190 3, that there was born to her on said date a male child, that said child is now living, and is said to have been named William E

O.P. Folsom   M. D.

Subscribed and sworn to before me this the 9th day of Feby 1905

W.T. Culbertson
Notary Public.

WITNESSETH:
Must be two witnesses who are citizens and know the child. { W.S. Folsom
Lillie P Folsom

Applications for Enrollment of Choctaw Newborn
Act of 1905   Volume XVII

We hereby certify that we are well acquainted with   Mrs O P Folsom
a   Midwife   and know   her   to be reputable and of good standing in the community.

Must be two citizen⎧ *(Name Illegible)*
witnesses.   ⎩ T.J. Ryan

7-4406.

Muskogee, Indian Territory, April 27, 1905.

William W. Folsom,
    Chambers, Indian Territory.

Dear Sir:

    Receipt is hereby acknowledged of the affidavits or Rosie L. Folsom and O. P. Folsom to the birth of William E. Folsom, son of William W. and Rosie L. Folsom, May 17, 1903: also affidavits of Rosie L. Folsom and A. G. Jones to the birth of Cletus A. Folsom, daughter of William W. and Rosie L. Folsom, August 24, 1904, and the same have been filed with our records as an application for the enrollment of said children.

Respectfully,

Chairman.

7-NB-1261.

Muskogee, Indian Territory, June 2, 1905.

William W. Folsom,
    Chambers, Indian Territory.

Dear Sir:

    Referring to the application for the enrollment of your infant child, Cletus A. Folsom, born August 24, 1905, it is noted from the affidavits heretofore filed in this office that the applicant claims through you.

    Before this matter can be finally determined it will be necessary for you to file in this office either the original or a certified copy of the license and certificate of your marriage to the applicant's mother, Rosie L. Folsom.

Respectfully,

[sic]

Applications for Enrollment of Choctaw Newborn
Act of 1905 Volume XVII

7-4555
7-NB-1261

Muskogee, Indian Territory, July 18, 1905.

William W. Folsom,
    Chambers, Indian Territory.

Dear Sir:

Receipt is hereby acknowledged of your letter of July 8, 1905, transmitting marriage certificate between yourself and Rosa L. Thatcher which you forwarded in the matter of the enrollment of your children William E. and Cletus A. Folsom and also request that your wife be enrolled as an intermarried citizen of the Choctaw Nation.

In reply to your letter you are advised that it does not appear from the records of this office that application was made to the Commission to the Five Civilized Tribes for the enrollment of your wife Rosa Folsom as an intermarried citizen of the Choctaw Nation, and there is now no provision for the reception of original applications for enrollment in the Choctaw and Chickasaw Nations.

Respectfully,

Commissioner.

Choctaw New Born 1262
    Evelynn Crutchfield
    (Born Dec. 3, 1902)

BIRTH AFFIDAVIT.
DEPARTMENT OF THE INTERIOR.
COMMISSION TO THE FIVE CIVILIZED TRIBES.

IN RE APPLICATION FOR ENROLLMENT, as a citizen of the Choctaw Nation, of Evelynn Crutchfield, born on the 3rd day of December, 1902

Name of Father: John W Crutchfield Roll ?.w. 749 a citizen of the Choctaw Nation.
Name of Mother: Gertrude Crutchfield Roll 11018 a citizen of the Choctaw Nation.

Postoffice   Caddo I.T.

Applications for Enrollment of Choctaw Newborn
Act of 1905   Volume XVII

AFFIDAVIT OF MOTHER.

UNITED STATES OF AMERICA, Indian Territory,
.... DISTRICT.

I, ..., on oath state that I am .... years of age and a citizen by ...., of the .... Nation; that I am the lawful wife of ...., who is a citizen, by .... of the .... Nation; that a .... child was born to me on .... day of ...., 1......, that said child has been named ...., and was living March 4, 1905.

Witnesses To Mark:
{ ....
  .... }

Subscribed and sworn to before me this .... day of ...., 1905.

....
Notary Public.

AFFIDAVIT OF ATTENDING PHYSICIAN OR MID-WIFE.

UNITED STATES OF AMERICA, Indian Territory,
.... DISTRICT.

I, W.J. Melton, a physician, on oath state that I attended on Mrs. Gertrude Crutchfield, wife of John W Crutchfield on the 3rd day of December, 1902; that there was born to her on said date a female child; that said child was living March 4, 1905, and is said to have been named Evelynn Crutchfield

W.J. Melton

Witnesses To Mark:
{

Subscribed and sworn to before me this 30th day of Jany, 1905

(Name Illegible)
Notary Public.

Applications for Enrollment of Choctaw Newborn
Act of 1905 Volume XVII

Affidavit of Attending Physician or Midwife

UNITED STATES OF AMERICA, }
INDIAN TERRITORY,
Central   DISTRICT

I, W.J. Melton a Practicing Physician on oath state that I attended on Mrs. Gertrude Crutchfield wife of John W Crutchfield on the 3rd day of December, 190 2, that there was born to her on said date a Female child, that said child is now living, and is said to have been named Evelynn Crutchfield

W. J. Melton   M. D.

Subscribed and sworn to before me this the 11th day of Feby 1905

A.E. Folsom
Notary Public.

WITNESSETH:
Must be two witnesses who are citizens and know the child. { F Manning
AF Manning

We hereby certify that we are well acquainted with W.J. Melton a Physician and know him to be reputable and of good standing in the community.

Must be two citizen witnesses. { F. Manning
A.F Manning

NEW BORN AFFIDAVIT

No ....

CHOCTAW ENROLLING COMMISSION

IN THE MATTER OF THE APPLICATION FOR ENROLLMENT as a citizen of the Choctaw Nation, of Evelynn Crutchfield born on the 3^{d} day of December 190 2

Name of father John W Crutchfield a citizen of Choctaw Nation, final enrollment No. 749
Name of mother Gertrude Crutchfield a citizen of Choctaw Nation, final enrollment No. 11018

74

Applications for Enrollment of Choctaw Newborn
Act of 1905   Volume XVII

Caddo I.T.   Postoffice.

AFFIDAVIT OF MOTHER

UNITED STATES OF AMERICA
INDIAN TERRITORY
DISTRICT   Central

I   Gertrude Crutchfield   , on oath state that I am   21   years of age and a citizen by   blood   of the   Choctaw   Nation, and as such have been placed upon the final roll of the   Choctaw   Nation, by the Honorable Secretary of the Interior my final enrollment number being   11018   ; that I am the lawful wife of   John W. Crutchfield   , who is a citizen of the   Choctaw   Nation, and as such has been placed upon the final roll of said Nation by the Honorable Secretary of the Interior, his final enrollment number being   749   and that a   Female   child was born to me on the   3^d day of   December   190 2; that said child has been named   Evelynn Crutchfield   , and is now living.

Gertrude Crutchfield

WITNESSETH:

Must be two witnesses who are citizens { F Manning
AF Manning

Subscribed and sworn to before me this, the   8th day of   February   , 190 5

A.E. Folsom
Notary Public.

My Commission Expires:
Jan 9th 1909

BIRTH AFFIDAVIT.

DEPARTMENT OF THE INTERIOR.
COMMISSION TO THE FIVE CIVILIZED TRIBES.

IN RE APPLICATION FOR ENROLLMENT, as a citizen of the   Choctaw   Nation, of   Evelynn Crutchfield   , born on the   3ed[sic]   day of   December   , 1902

Name of Father: John W. Crutchfield   a citizen of the   Choctaw   Nation.
Name of Mother: Gertrude Crutchfield   a citizen of the   Choctaw   Nation.

Postoffice   Caddo Indian Territory

Applications for Enrollment of Choctaw Newborn
Act of 1905   Volume XVII

AFFIDAVIT OF MOTHER.

UNITED STATES OF AMERICA, Indian Territory, }
    Central   DISTRICT. }

I, Gertrude Crutchfield, on oath state that I am 22 years of age and a citizen by Blood, of the Choctaw Nation; that I am the lawful wife of John W. Crutchfield, who is a citizen, by marraige[sic] of the Choctaw Nation; that a female child was born to me on 3ed day of December, 1902; that said child has been named Evelynn Crutchfield, and was living March 4, 1905.

                                      Gertrude Crutchfield

Witnesses To Mark:
{

    Subscribed and sworn to before me this 27th day of April, 1905

                                  JL Rappolee
                                  Notary Public.

AFFIDAVIT OF ATTENDING PHYSICIAN OR MID-WIFE.

UNITED STATES OF AMERICA, Indian Territory, }
    Central   DISTRICT. }

I, W. J. Melton, a Physician, on oath state that I attended on Mrs. Gertrude Crutchfield, wife of John W. Crutchfield on the 3ed day of December, 1905[sic]; that there was born to her on said date a female child; that said child was living March 4, 1905, and is said to have been named Evelynn Crutchfield

                                    W.J. Melton

Witnesses To Mark:
{

    Subscribed and sworn to before me this 27th day of April, 1905

                                  JL Rappolee
                                  Notary Public.

Applications for Enrollment of Choctaw Newborn
Act of 1905 Volume XVII

7-3923.

Muskogee, Indian Territory, December 12, 1902.

J.W. Crutchfield,
    Caddo, Indian Territory.

Dear Sir:

    Receipt is hereby acknowledged of your letter of the 5th inst., in which you ask if you can have your infant child, born December 2[sic], 1902, enrolled as a citizen of the Choctaw Nation.

    You are advised that the Commission is without authority to enroll this child as a citizen of the Choctaw Nation, it appearing that said child was born December 2, 1902, subsequent to the ratification by the citizens of the Choctaw and Chickasaw Nations on September 25, 1902, of an act of Congress approved July 1, 1902 (32 Stats., 641).

    Section twenty-eight thereof provides as follows:

    "The names of all persons living on the date of the final ratification of this agreement entitled to be enrolled as provided in section 27 hereof shall be placed upon the rolls made by said Commission; and no child born thereafter to a citizen or freedman and no person intermarried thereafter to a citizen shall be entitled to enrollment or to participate in the distribution of the tribal property of the Choctaws and Chickasaws."

    Respectfully,

    Acting Chairman.

7--3923.

Muskogee, Indian Territory, May 5, 1905.

John W. Crutchfield,
    Caddo, Indian Territory.

Dear Sir:

    Receipt is hereby acknowledged of the affidavits of Gertrude Crutchfield and W. J. Melton to the birth of Evelynn Crutchfield, daughter of John W. and Gertrude Crutchfield, December 3, 1902, and the same have been filed with our records as an application for the enrollment of said child.

Applications for Enrollment of Choctaw Newborn
Act of 1905   Volume XVII

Respectfully,

Commissioner in Charge.

───────

7 NB 1262

Muskogee, Indian Territory, June 8, 1905.

John A. Crutchfield,
    Caddo, Indian Territory.

Dear Sir:

    Receipt is hereby acknowledged of the affidavit of W. J. Melton to the birth of Evelynn Crutchfield, daughter of John and Gertrude Crutchfield, December 3, 1902, and the same has been filed in the matter of the enrollment of said child.

Respectfully,

Chairman.

───────

7--NB--1262

Muskogee, Indian Territory, June 2, 1905.

John W. Crutchfield,
    Caddo, Indian Territory.

Dear Sir:

    There is enclosed you herewith affidavit to be executed in support of the application for the enrollment of your infant child, Evelynn Crutchfield.

    In the affidavit of the mother of this applicant dated April 27, 1905, the date of her birth is given as December 3, 1902, while in the affidavit of the attending physician dated April 27, 1905, this date is given as December 3, 1905. In the enclosed affidavit the date of birth is left blank. Please insert the correct date and when the affidavit is properly executed return to this office.

    In having the affidavit executed care should be exercised to see that all names are written in full, as they appear in the body of the affidavit, and in the event the person signing the affidavit is unable to write, signatures by mark must be attested by two witnesses. The affidavit must be executed before a Notary Public and the notarial seal and signature of the officer must be attached thereto.

Applications for Enrollment of Choctaw Newborn
Act of 1905   Volume XVII

This matter should receive your immediate attention as no further action can be taken relative to the enrollment of said child until the Commission has been furnished this affidavit.

                          Respectfully,

                                      Commissioner in Charge.

Enc-FVK-11

Choctaw New Born 1263
    Emeline Edward
    (Born March 22, 1904)

BIRTH AFFIDAVIT.

DEPARTMENT OF THE INTERIOR.
COMMISSION TO THE FIVE CIVILIZED TRIBES.

IN RE APPLICATION FOR ENROLLMENT, as a citizen of the Choctaw Nation, of Emeline Edwards[sic]   , born on the 22nd day of March , 1904

Name of Father: Wesley Edwards   a citizen of the Choctaw Nation.
Name of Mother: Sealy Edwards   a citizen of the Choctaw Nation.

                      Postoffice   Finley, Ind. Ter.

AFFIDAVIT OF MOTHER.

UNITED STATES OF AMERICA, Indian Territory,
   Central   DISTRICT.

I, Sealy Edwards , on oath state that I am about 40 years of age and a citizen by blood , of the Choctaw Nation; that I am the lawful wife of Wesley Edwards , who is a citizen, by blood of the Choctaw Nation; that a female child was born to me on 22nd day of March , 1904; that said child has been named Emeline Edwards , and was living March 4, 1905.

                                   her
                         Sealy x Edwards
Witnesses To Mark: mark
   { Robert Anderson
     Vester W Rose

Applications for Enrollment of Choctaw Newborn
Act of 1905 Volume XVII

Subscribed and sworn to before me this 26th day of April , 1905

Wirt Franklin
Notary Public.

AFFIDAVIT OF ATTENDING PHYSICIAN OR MID-WIFE.

UNITED STATES OF AMERICA, Indian Territory, }
Central DISTRICT. }

I, Siney Billy , a mid-wife , on oath state that I attended on Mrs. Sealy Edwards , wife of Wesley Edwards on the 22nd day of March , 1904; that there was born to her on said date a female child; that said child was living March 4, 1905, and is said to have been named Emeline Edwards

her
Siney x Billy
mark

Witnesses To Mark:
{ Robert Anderson
{ Vester W Rose

Subscribed and sworn to before me this 26th day of April , 1905

Wirt Franklin
Notary Public.

Affidavit of Attending Physician or Midwife

UNITED STATES OF AMERICA, }
INDIAN TERRITORY, }
Central DISTRICT }

I, Wesley Edward a ....
on oath state that I attended on Mrs. Cely[sic] Edward wife of Wesley Edward on the 22nd day of March , 190 4, that there was born to her on said date a Female child, that said child is now living, and is said to have been named Emeline Edward

Wesley Edward M. D.

Subscribed and sworn to before me this the 20th day of Jan 1905

Su Finley
Notary Public.

WITNESSETH:
Must be two witnesses { Goodman McKinzie
who are citizens and {
know the child.   { Stephen Battiest

Applications for Enrollment of Choctaw Newborn
Act of 1905   Volume XVII

We hereby certify that we are well acquainted with a Stephen Battiest and know them Goodman McKinzie to be reputable and of good standing in the community.

Must be two citizen witnesses. { Mack McKenzie   Wesley Sherred

NEW-BORN AFFIDAVIT.

Number..................

Choctaw Enrolling Commission.

IN THE MATTER OF THE APPLICATION FOR ENROLLMENT, as a citizen of the Choctaw   Nation, of   Emeline Edward

born on the   22nd   day of   March   190 4

Name of father   Wesley Edward   a citizen of   Choctaw
Nation final enrollment No   5135
Name of mother   Cely[sic] Edward   a citizen of   Choctaw
Nation final enrollment No   5136

Postoffice   Finley Ind Ter

AFFIDAVIT OF MOTHER.

UNITED STATES OF AMERICA,
INDIAN TERRITORY,
Central   DISTRICT

I   Cely Edward   on oath state that I am 35 years of age and a citizen by   Blood   of the   Choctaw   Nation, and as such have been placed upon the final roll of the   Choctaw   Nation, by the Honorable Secretary of the Interior my final enrollment number being   5136   ; that I am the lawful wife of   Wesley Edward   , who is a citizen of the   Choctaw   Nation, and as such has been placed upon the final roll of said Nation by the Honorable Secretary of the Interior, his final enrollment number being   5135   and that a   Female   child was born to me on the   22nd   day of   March   190 4 ; that said child has been named   Emeline Edward   , and is now living.

her
Cely x Edward
mark

WITNESSETH:
Must be two Witnesses who are Citizens. } Stephen Battiest
Goodman McKenzie

Applications for Enrollment of Choctaw Newborn
Act of 1905 Volume XVII

Subscribed and sworn to before me this 20th day of Jan 190 5

Su Finley
Notary Public.

My commission expires May 1908

Choctaw New Born 1264
    Winnona Dyer
    (Born July 19, 1903)

NEW-BORN AFFIDAVIT.

Number

Choctaw Enrolling Commission.

IN THE MATTER OF THE APPLICATION FOR ENROLLMENT, as a citizen of the Choctaw   Nation, of   Winnona Dyer

born on the 19th day of July 190 3

Name of father   Elliston E. Dyer   a citizen of   Choctaw
Nation final enrollment No   1259
Name of mother   Nancy J Dyer   a citizen of   Choctaw
Nation final enrollment No   503

Postoffice   Durant I T

AFFIDAVIT OF MOTHER.

UNITED STATES OF AMERICA,
   INDIAN TERRITORY,
  Central   DISTRICT

I   Nancy J Dyer   on oath state that I am 29 years of age and a citizen by intermarriage of the Choctaw Nation, and as such have been placed upon the final roll of the Choctaw Nation, by the Honorable Secretary of the Interior my final enrollment number being 503 ; that I am the lawful wife of   Elliston E Dyer   , who is a citizen of the Choctaw Nation, and as such has been placed upon the final roll of said Nation by the Honorable Secretary of the Interior, his final enrollment number being 1259 and that a female child was born to me on the 19th day of July 190 3 ; that said child has been named Winnona Dyer   , and is now living.

Applications for Enrollment of Choctaw Newborn
Act of 1905 Volume XVII

Nancy J Dyer

WITNESSETH:

Must be two Witnesses who are Citizens. } EM Wilson
C.A. Woodward

Subscribed and sworn to before me this 14 day of Jan 190 5

W A Shoney
Notary Public.

My commission expires Jan 10, 1909

Affidavit of Attending Physician or Midwife.

UNITED STATES OF AMERICA
INDIAN TERRITORY
Central   DISTRICT

I, T L Crisman[sic]   a   Physician on oath state that I attended on Mrs. Nancy J Dyer   wife of Elliston E Dyer on the 19th day of July , 190 3 , that there was born to her on said date a female child, that said child is now living, and is said to have been named Winnona Dyer

T.L. Crissman   M.D.

Subscribed and sworn to before me this, the 18 day of January 190 5

Jess Johnson
Notary Public.

WITNESSETH:

Must be two witnesses who are citizens and know the child. { J.J. Gardner
Z W Durant

We hereby certify that we are well acquainted with Dr T.L. Crisman[sic] a physician and know him to be reputable and of good standing in the community.

{ C.A. Woodward
J.J. Gardner

Applications for Enrollment of Choctaw Newborn
Act of 1905   Volume XVII

BIRTH AFFIDAVIT.

DEPARTMENT OF THE INTERIOR.
COMMISSION TO THE FIVE CIVILIZED TRIBES.

IN RE APPLICATION FOR ENROLLMENT, as a citizen of the Choctaw Nation, of Winnona Dyer, born on the 19th day of July, 1903

Name of Father: Elliston E Dyer.   a citizen of the Choctaw Nation.
Name of Mother: Nancy J Dyer.   a citizen of the Choctaw Nation.

Postoffice   Durant Ind Terr.

AFFIDAVIT OF MOTHER.

UNITED STATES OF AMERICA, Indian Territory,
Central   DISTRICT.

I, Nancy J Dyer, on oath state that I am 29 years of age and a citizen by inter-marriage, of the Choctaw Nation; that I am the lawful wife of Elliston E Dyer., who is a citizen, by blood of the Choctaw Nation; that a female child was born to me on 19th day of July, 1903; that said child has been named Winnona Dyer, and was living March 4, 1905.

Nancy J Dyer

Witnesses To Mark:
{

Subscribed and sworn to before me this 27th day of April, 1905

T.B. Wilkins
Notary Public.

AFFIDAVIT OF ATTENDING PHYSICIAN OR MID-WIFE.

UNITED STATES OF AMERICA, Indian Territory,
Central   DISTRICT.

I, T.L. Crissman, M.D., a Physician & Surgeon, on oath state that I attended on Mrs. Mrs. Nancy J. Dyer, wife of Elliston E. Dyer on the 19th day of July, 1903; that there was born to her on said date a female child; that said child was living March 4, 1905, and is said to have been named Winnona Dyer

T.L. Crissman M.D.

Witnesses To Mark:
{

Applications for Enrollment of Choctaw Newborn
Act of 1905 Volume XVII

Subscribed and sworn to before me this 27th day of April , 1905

                    T. B. Wilkins
                          Notary Public.

                          7-567.

           Muskogee, Indian Territory, May 4, 1905.

Elliston E. Dyer,
    Durant, Indian Territory.

Dear Sir:

    Receipt is hereby acknowledged of the affidavits of Nancy J. Dyer and T. L. Crissman to the birth of Winnona Dyer, daughter of Elliston E. and Nancy J. Dyer, July 19, 1903, and the same have been filed with our records as an application for the enrollment of said child.

                    Respectfully,

                                    Chairman.

Choctaw New Born 1265
    Push-Ma-Ta-Ha F. Ellis
    (Born Sept. 29, 1904)

BIRTH AFFIDAVIT.
                  DEPARTMENT OF THE INTERIOR.
          COMMISSION TO THE FIVE CIVILIZED TRIBES.

    IN RE APPLICATION FOR ENROLLMENT, as a citizen of the Choctaw Nation, of Pushmataha F. Ellis , born on the 29th day of September , 1904

Name of Father: Chas. V. Ellis   a citizen of the Choctaw Nation.
Name of Mother: Delphine Ellis (nee Mugler)   a citizen of the Choctaw Nation.

                    Postoffice   Caddo Indian Territory

Applications for Enrollment of Choctaw Newborn
Act of 1905   Volume XVII

AFFIDAVIT OF MOTHER.

UNITED STATES OF AMERICA, Indian Territory, }
    Central   DISTRICT.

I, Delphine Ellis (nee Mugler), on oath state that I am 20 years of age and a citizen by blood, of the Choctaw Nation; that I am the lawful wife of Chas. V. Ellis, who is a citizen, by marriage of the Choctaw Nation; that a male child was born to me on 29th day of September, 1904; that said child has been named Pushmataha F. Ellis, and was living March 4, 1905.

                                        Delphine Ellis

Witnesses To Mark:
{

Subscribed and sworn to before me this 1st day of May, 1905

                                        JL Rappolee
                                        Notary Public.

AFFIDAVIT OF ATTENDING PHYSICIAN OR MID-WIFE.

UNITED STATES OF AMERICA, Indian Territory, }
    Central   DISTRICT.

I, Bettie Guess, a midwife, on oath state that I attended on Mrs. Delphine Ellis (nee Mugler), wife of Chas. V. Ellis on the 29th day of September, 1904; that there was born to her on said date a male child; that said child was living March 4, 1905, and is said to have been named Pushmataha F. Ellis

                                        Bettie Guess

Witnesses To Mark:
{

Subscribed and sworn to before me this 1st day of May, 1905

                                        JL Rappolee
                                        Notary Public.

Applications for Enrollment of Choctaw Newborn
Act of 1905 Volume XVII

Affidavit of Attending Physician or Midwife

UNITED STATES OF AMERICA,
INDIAN TERRITORY,
Central   DISTRICT

I, Mrs. Bettie Guess   a   Mid Wife   on oath state that I attended on Mrs. Delphin[sic] Ellis   wife of Charles V Ellis   on the 29th day of September   , 190 4, that there was born to her on said date a   male   child, that said child is now living, and is said to have been named   Push-ma-taha Ellis

Bettie Guess   M. D.

Subscribed and sworn to before me this the   14th day of   February   1905

AE Folsom
Notary Public.

WITNESSETH:
Must be two witnesses who are citizens and know the child.
{ Theodolia Mugler
  Minnie Lee

We hereby certify that we are well acquainted with   Mrs Bettie Guess   a   mid wife   and know   her   to be reputable and of good standing in the community.

Must be two citizen witnesses.
{ Theodolia Mugler
  Minnie Lee

NEW BORN AFFIDAVIT

No _____

CHOCTAW ENROLLING COMMISSION

IN THE MATTER OF THE APPLICATION FOR ENROLLMENT as a citizen of the Choctaw Nation, of   Pushmataha Ellis   born on the 29th day   of   September   190 4

Name of father   Charles V Ellis   a citizen of   _____   Nation,
final enrollment No.   _____
Name of mother   Delphine Ellis   a citizen of   Choctaw   Nation,
final enrollment No.   10954

Caddo IT   Postoffice.

Applications for Enrollment of Choctaw Newborn
Act of 1905 Volume XVII

AFFIDAVIT OF MOTHER

UNITED STATES OF AMERICA
INDIAN TERRITORY
DISTRICT Central

I Delphine Ellis , on oath state that I am 20 years of age and a citizen by blood of the Choctaw Nation, and as such have been placed upon the final roll of the Choctaw Nation, by the Honorable Secretary of the Interior my final enrollment number being 10954 ; that I am the lawful wife of Charles V Ellis , who is a citizen of the ——— Nation, and as such has been placed upon the final roll of said Nation by the Honorable Secretary of the Interior, his final enrollment number being ——— and that a Male child was born to me on the 29th day of September 190 4; that said child has been named Push-ma-ta-ha Ellis , and is now living.

WITNESSETH:
Must be two witnesses who are citizens
{ Theodolia Mugler
  Minnie Lee

Delphine Ellis

Subscribed and sworn to before me this, the 11th day of February , 190 5

A.E. Folsom
Notary Public.

My Commission Expires:
Jan. 9-1909

Applications for Enrollment of Choctaw Newborn
Act of 1905 Volume XVII

No. 394

Certificate of Record of Marriages.

UNITED STATES OF AMERICA,
INDIAN TERRITORY, } SCT:
Central   DISTRICT.

I,   E.J. Fannin   , Clerk of the United States Court in the Indian Territory and District aforesaid, do hereby CERTIFY, that the License for and Certificate of the Marriage of

Mr.   Chas V Ellis   and

M iss Delphine Mugler   was

filed in my office in said Territory and District the 22 day of   October A.D., 190 3 and duly recorded in Book 1 of Marriage Record, Page   197

WITNESS my hand and seal of said Court, at   Durant   , this 22-   day of   October   A.D. 190 3

E.J. Fannin
Clerk.
By   W.B. Stone   *Deputy.*

DEPARTMENT OF THE INTERIOR,
Commission to the Five Civilized Tribes.

FILED

MAY 3 1905

Tams Bixby CHAIRMAN.

89

Applications for Enrollment of Choctaw Newborn
Act of 1905 Volume XVII

No. 986

MARRIAGE LICENSE

United States of America, The Indian Territory,
 CENTRAL DISTRICT, SS.

To any Person Authorized by Law to Solemnize Marriage, Greeting:

You are hereby commanded to Solemnize the Rite and publish the Banns of Matrimony between Mr.   Chas V. Ellis
of   Caddo   in the Indian Territory, aged   24   years,
and M iss Delphine Mugler   of   Caddo
in the Indian Territory., aged   -18-   years, according to law, and do you officially sign and return this License to the parties therein named.

WITNESS my hand and official seal, this   -15th-   day
of   October   A. D. 190 3

 E.J. Fannin
SEAL.   Clerk of the United States Court.

 W.B. Stone   Deputy

Certificate of Marriage.

United States of America,
The Indian Territory, } ss.
Central   District.

I,   F.F Thredgill Minister
a   of the Gospel   , do hereby certify, that on the   -18-   day of
October   A. D. 190 3   , I did, duly and according to law, as commanded in the foregoing License, solemnize the Rite and publish the Banns of Matrimony between the parties therein named.

Witness my hand, this   -18-   day of   October   A. D. 190 3

My credentials are recorded in the office of the Clerk of
the United States Court in the Indian Territory,
Central District, Book   C   , Page   54   }   F F Thredgill

 a

Note—This License and Certificate of Marriage must be returned to the Office of the Clerk of the United States Court of the Indian Territory, from whence it was issued, within sixty days from the date thereof, or the party to whom the License was issued will be liable in the amount of the One Hundred Dollars ($100.00)

Applications for Enrollment of Choctaw Newborn
Act of 1905   Volume XVII

7 N.B. 1265

Muskogee, Indian Territory, May 4m[sic] 1905.

Charles V. Ellis,
    Caddo, Indian Territory.

Dear Sir:

    Receipt is hereby acknowledged of a certified copy of the marriage license and certificate between Charles V. Ellis and Delphine Mugler, which you offer in support of the application for the enrollment of your child, Push-ma-ta-ha Ellis, and the same has been filed with the records in this case.

Respectfully,

Chairman.

Choctaw New Born 1266
    Louie Fobb
    (Born June 23, 1904)

DEPARTMENT OF THE INTERIOR,
COMMISSION TO THE FIVE CIVILIZED TRIBES.

    IN THE MATTER OF THE APPLICATION FOR THE ENROLLMENT OF LOUIE FOBB AS A CITIZEN BY BLOOD OF THE CHOCTAW NATION.
7-NB-*1266*.

Applications for Enrollment of Choctaw Newborn
Act of 1905 Volume XVII

NEW-BORN AFFIDAVIT.

Number..................

...Choctaw Enrolling Commission...

IN THE MATTER OF THE APPLICATION FOR ENROLLMENT, as a citizen of the Choctaw Nation, of Louie Fobb

born on the 23rd day of ___June___ 190 4

Name of father Eastman Fobb   a citizen of Choctaw
Nation final enrollment No. 3664
Name of mother Sallie Fobb   a citizen of Choctaw
Nation final enrollment No. 3237

Postoffice Goodwater I.T.

AFFIDAVIT OF MOTHER.

UNITED STATES OF AMERICA
INDIAN TERRITORY
Central   DISTRICT

I   Sallie Fobb   , on oath state that I am 35 years of age and a citizen by blood of the Choctaw Nation, and as such have been placed upon the final roll of the Choctaw Nation, by the Honorable Secretary of the Interior my final enrollment number being 3664[sic] ; that I am the lawful wife of Eastman Fobb , who is a citizen of the Choctaw Nation, and as such has been placed upon the final roll of said Nation by the Honorable Secretary of the Interior, his final enrollment number being 3237 and that a Male child was born to me on the 23rd day of June 190 4; that said child has been named Louie Fobb , and is now living.

                                          her
                                  Sallie x Fobb

Witnesseth.   mark
  Must be two ⎫   W.S. Ward
  Witnesses who ⎬
  are Citizens. ⎭   William Barnett

Subscribed and sworn to before me this 21 day of Jan 190 5

                              W A Shoney
                                        Notary Public.

My commission expires: Jan 10, 1909

Applications for Enrollment of Choctaw Newborn
Act of 1905 Volume XVII

AFFIDAVIT OF ATTENDING PHYSICIAN OR MIDWIFE

UNITED STATES OF AMERICA
INDIAN TERRITORY
   Central   DISTRICT

    I, Winsie Lewis a midwife on oath state that I attended on Mrs. Sallie Fobb wife of Eastman Fobb on the 23rd day of June, 190 4, that there was born to her on said date a male child, that said child is now living, and is said to have been named Louie Fobb

                                                          her
                                           Winsie x Lewis
                                              mark

        Subscribed and sworn to before me this, the   21st day of Jan 190 5

WITNESSETH: W.A. Shoney   Notary Public.
  Must be two witnesses   {   W.S. Ward
  who are citizens
                         William Barnett

    We hereby certify that we are well acquainted with   Winsie Lewis a midwife and know her to be reputable and of good standing in the community.

    W.S. Ward   _____

    William Barnett   _____

DEPARTMENT OF THE INTERIOR,
COMMISSIONER TO THE FIVE CIVILIZED TRIBES.

Mena, Arkansaw[sic], May 31, 1906.

    In the matter of the application for the enrollment of Louie Fobb, Choctaw Card Number 1266. *N B*

    Testimony taken one mile west of Goodwater, Indian Territory, on May 5th, 1906.

    EASTMAN FOBB, being duly sworn, testified as follows:

        Through Interpreter Jacob Homer.

Applications for Enrollment of Choctaw Newborn
Act of 1905   Volume XVII

BY THE COMMISSIONER:

Q What is your name? A Eastman Fobb.
Q How old are you? A About 28.
Q What is your post office address? A Goodwater, I. T?[sic]
Q Are you a citizen by blood of the Choctaw Nation? A Yes.

    Witness is identified as a Choctaw by blood, Roll Number 2664.

Q Was Sallie Fobb your wife in 1904? A Yes, sir.
Q Were you the lawful husband of Sallie Fobb in the year 1904? A Yes, sir.
Q Did you have a child by Sallie Fobb; if so, what was its name? A Louie.
Q When was the child born? A It was in the month of June, 1904.
Q Was the child living March 4, 1905? A No, it was dead.
Q When did it die?
A It died the 23rd day of February, 1905.

    Witness Excused.

    Testimony taken one mile west of Goodwater, Indian Territory, on May 5, 1906.

    SIMEON BYINGTON, being duly sworn, testified as follows:
through interpreter Jacob Homer:

BY THE COMMISSIONER:

Q What is your name? A Simeon Byington.
Q How old are you? A 23.
Q What is your post office address? A Goodwater, I.T.
Q Are you a citizen by blood of the Choctaw Nation? A Yes.
Q Were you acquainted with Louie Fobb? A Yes sir.
Q Who was his father? A Eastman Fobb.
Q Who was the mother of Louie Fobb? A Sallie Fobb.
Q Was Sallie Fobb the legal wife of Eastman Fobb when Louie Fobb was born?
A Yes, sir.
Q When was the child born? A In the month of June 1904.
Q Was the child living March 4, 1905? A No, sir.
Q When did Louie Fobb die?
A The 23rd day of February, 1905.
Q Did you attend the burial of this child? A Yes.
Q Have you a record of the child's death? A No, sir.
Q How near did you live to this child at the time of its death?
A About half a mile.
Q Were you related to the child? [sic] No.
Q You state upon oath and as a matter of fact the Louie Fobb died the 23rd day of February, 1905. A Yes, sir.

Applications for Enrollment of Choctaw Newborn
Act of 1905   Volume XVII

Witness Excused.

W.P.covington[sic], being duly sworn, states that the above and foregoing is a full, true and correct transcript of his stenographic notes taken in the preceding case on date and at place mentioned.

W.P. Covington

Subscribed and sworn to before me, this 9th day of   June   1906.

Lacey P. Bobo
Notary Public.

7-NB-1196[sic].
O.L.J.

DEPARTMENT OF THE INTERIOR,
COMMISSION TO THE FIVE CIVILIZED TRIBES.

In the matter of the application for the enrollment of Louie Fobb as a citizen by blood of the Choctaw Nation.

---oOo---

It appears from the record herein that on April 25, 1905, application was made to the Commission to the Five Civilized Tribes for the enrollment of Louie Fobb as a citizen by blood of the Choctaw Nation.

It further appears from the record herein and from the records of the Commission to the Five Civilized Tribes that the applicant was born on June 23, 1904; that he is a son of Eastman Fobb, a recognized and enrolled citizen by blood of the Choctaw Nation, whose name appears as number 3664 upon the final roll of citizens by blood of the Choctaw Nation, approved by the Secretary of the Interior, December 12, 1902, and Sallie Fobb, a recognized and enrolled citizen by blood of the Choctaw Nation, whose name (as Sallie Dyer) appears as number 3237 upon the final roll of citizens by blood of the Choctaw Nation, approved by the Secretary of the Interior, December 12, 1902, and that said applicant died February 23, 1905.

The Act of Congress approved March 3, 1905 (33 Stats. 1070), provides:

"That the Commission to the Five Civilized Tribes is authorized for sixty days after the date of the approval of this act to receive and consider applications for enrollment of children born subsequent to September twenty-fifth, nineteen hundred and two, and prior to March fourth, nineteen hundred and five, and who were living on said latter date, to citizens by blood of the Choctaw and Chickasaw tribes of Indians whose enrollment has been approved by the Secretary of the Interior prior to the date of the approval of this act; and to enroll and make allotments to such children."

Applications for Enrollment of Choctaw Newborn
Act of 1905 Volume XVII

It is therefore ordered that the application for the enrollment of Louie Fobb as a citizen by blood of the Choctaw Nation be, and the same is hereby dismissed.

Muskogee, Indian Territory.
AUG 9 1906

Tams Bixby Commissioner.

7-N.B.-1266 **COPY**

Muskogee, Indian Territory, August 9, 1906.

Eastman Fobb,
    Goodwater, Indian Territory.

Dear Sir:

    Inclosed herewith you will find a copy of the order of the Commissioner to the Five Civilized Tribes, dated August 9, 1906, dismissing the application for the enrollment of your minor child, Louie Fobb as a citizen by blood of the Choctaw Nation.

Respectfully,
SIGNED

Tams Bixby
Commissioner.

Registered.
Incl. 7-N.B.-1266

7-N.B.-1266 **COPY**

Muskogee, Indian Territory, August 9, 1906.

Mansfield, McMurray & Cornish,
    Attorneys for Choctaw and Chickasaw Nations,
        South McAlester, Indian Territory.

Gentlemen:

    Inclosed herewith you will find a copy of the order of the Commissioner to the Five Civilized Tribes, dated August 9, 1906, dismissing the application for the enrollment of Louie Fobb as a citizen by blood of the Choctaw Nation.

Respectfully,
SIGNED

Tams Bixby
Commissioner.

Incl. 7-N.B.-1266

Applications for Enrollment of Choctaw Newborn
Act of 1905   Volume XVII

NEW BORN AFFIDAVIT

NUMBER_____

CHOCTAW ENROLLING COMMISSION.

IN THE MATTER OF THE APPLICATION FOR ENROLLMENT as a citizen of the Choctaw Nation, of LOUIE FOBB, born on the 23rd day of JUNE 1904.
Name of father EASTMAN FOBB a citizen of the CHOCTAW Nation, final enrollment No. 3664.
Name of mother SALLIE FOBB a citizen of CHOCTAW Nation; final enrollment No. 3237.

Postoffice GOODWATER, I. T.

AFFIDAVIT OF MOTHER

UNITED STATES OF AMERICA

INDIAN TERRITORY

CENTRAL DISTRICT.

    I SALLIE FOBB, on oath state that I am 35 years of age and a citizen by blood of the Choctaw Nation BLOOD, of the CHOCTAW Nation, by the Honorable Secretary of the Interior my final enrollment No. being 3664; that I [sic] the lawful wife of EASTMAN FOBB who is a citizen of the CHOCTAW Nation, and as such has been placed upon the final roll of said Nation by the Honorable Secretary of the Interior, his final enrollment No. being 3237 and that a MALE child was born to me on the 23rd day of JUNE 1904; that said child has been named LOUIE FOBB, and is now living.

Witnesseth:	her Sallie x Fobb mark
must be two (W. S. Ward witnesses who (are citizens. (William Barnett	

Subscribed and sworn to before me this 24 day of Jan 1905.

(SEAL)   W. A. Shoney

My commission Expires: Jan 10 1909   Notary Public

Applications for Enrollment of Choctaw Newborn
Act of 1905   Volume XVII

AFFIDAVIT OF ATTENDING PHYSICIAN OR MIDWIFE.

UNITED STATES OF AMERICA
INDIAN TERRITORY
CENTRAL DISTRICT.

I, WINSIE LEWIS a MIDWIFE on oath state that I attended on Mrs. SALLIE FOBB, wife of EASTMAN FOBB, on the 23rd day of JUNE 1904, that there was born to her on said date a MALE child that said child is now living and is said to have been named LOUIE FOBB

            her
         Winsie X Lewis
           mark

(SEAL)   Subscribed and sworn to before me this the 21st day of
         JAN 1905

Witnesseth: W. A. Shoney NOTARY PUBLIC.
       W. S. Ward
Must be two witnesses (
who are citizens.   (William Barnnett[sic]

We hereby certify that we are well acquainted with WINSIE LEWIS a MIDWIFE and know HER to be reputable and of good standing in the community.

W. S. WARD

WILLIAM BARNETT

Choctaw New Born 1267
  Stella Gardner
  (Born Feb. 1, 1903)
  Eliner[sic] Gardner
  (Born Nov. 20, 1904)

Applications for Enrollment of Choctaw Newborn
Act of 1905 Volume XVII

BIRTH AFFIDAVIT.

DEPARTMENT OF THE INTERIOR.
COMMISSION TO THE FIVE CIVILIZED TRIBES.

IN RE APPLICATION FOR ENROLLMENT, as a citizen of the Choctaw Nation, of Stella Gardner, born on the 1 day of February, 1903

Name of Father: J B Gardner   a citizen of the US ~~Nation~~.
Name of Mother: Malinda Belt now Gardner   a citizen of the Choctaw Nation.

Postoffice Kiowa IT

AFFIDAVIT OF MOTHER.

UNITED STATES OF AMERICA, Indian Territory, }
Cent   DISTRICT.

I, Malinda Belt now Gardner, on oath state that I am 29 years of age and a citizen by Blood, of the Choctaw Nation; that I am the lawful wife of J B Gardner, who is a citizen, ~~by~~ —— of the US ~~Nation~~; that a Female child was born to me on 1 day of February, 1903; that said child has been named Stella Gardner, and was living March 4, 1905.

Malinda Belt now Gardner

Witnesses To Mark:
{

Subscribed and sworn to before me this 1 day of May, 1905

H.B. Rowley
Notary Public.

AFFIDAVIT OF ATTENDING PHYSICIAN OR MID-WIFE.

UNITED STATES OF AMERICA, Indian Territory, }
Cent   DISTRICT.

I, Annie Gardner, a midwife, on oath state that I attended on Mrs. Malinda Gardner, wife of J B Gardner on the 1 day of February, 1903; that there was born to her on said date a Female child; that said child was living March 4, 1905, and is said to have been named Stella Gardner

her
Annie x Gardner
mark

Applications for Enrollment of Choctaw Newborn
Act of 1905 Volume XVII

Witnesses To Mark:
{ J C Farley
Charles F Gill

Subscribed and sworn to before me this 1 day of May, 1905

HB Rowley
Notary Public.

NEW BORN AFFIDAVIT

No

CHOCTAW ENROLLING COMMISSION

IN THE MATTER OF THE APPLICATION FOR ENROLLMENT as a citizen of the Choctaw Nation, of Stella Gardner born on the 1st day of February 190 3

Name of father J B Gardner a citizen of US Nation, final enrollment No. X as Gardner

Name of mother Malinda Belt *now known* a citizen of Choctaw Nation, final enrollment No. 11255

Kiowa I.T. Postoffice.

AFFIDAVIT OF MOTHER

UNITED STATES OF AMERICA
INDIAN TERRITORY
DISTRICT Central

I Malinda Belt *now known as Gardner*, on oath state that I am 28 years of age and a citizen by Blood of the Choctaw Nation, and as such have been placed upon the final roll of the Choctaw Nation, by the Honorable Secretary of the Interior my final enrollment number being 11255 ; that I am the lawful wife of J B Gardner, who is a citizen of the US Nation, and as such has been placed upon the final roll of said Nation by the Honorable Secretary of the Interior, his final enrollment number being x and that a Female child was born to me on the 1st day of February 190 3; that said child has been named Stella Gardner , and is now living.

Malinda Gardner

Applications for Enrollment of Choctaw Newborn
Act of 1905   Volume XVII

WITNESSETH:

Must be two witnesses who are citizens { M.E. Crisp
Dixon Sexton

Subscribed and sworn to before me this, the 15 day of Feby , 190 5

H B Rowley
Notary Public.

My Commission Expires: Nov 22nd 1905

Affidavit of Attending Physician or Midwife

UNITED STATES OF AMERICA,
INDIAN TERRITORY,
Cent   DISTRICT

I, Annie Gardner a Midwife on oath state that I attended on Mrs. Malinda Gardner wife of J B Gardner on the 1st day of Feby , 190 3, that there was born to her on said date a Female child, that said child is now living, and is said to have been named Stella Gardner

her
Annie x Gardner   ~~M. D.~~ Midwife
mark

Subscribed and sworn to before me this the 15 day of Feby   1905

HB Rowley
Notary Public.

WITNESSETH:

Must be two witnesses who are citizens and know the child. { M.E. Crisp
Dixon Sexton

We hereby certify that we are well acquainted with Annie Gardner a midwife and know her to be reputable and of good standing in the community.

Must be two citizen witnesses. { M.E. Crisp
Dixon Sexton

Applications for Enrollment of Choctaw Newborn
Act of 1905 Volume XVII

BIRTH AFFIDAVIT.

DEPARTMENT OF THE INTERIOR.
COMMISSION TO THE FIVE CIVILIZED TRIBES.

IN RE APPLICATION FOR ENROLLMENT, as a citizen of the Choctaw Nation, of Elmer Gardner, born on the 20 day of November, 1904

Name of Father: J B Gardner a citizen of the US ~~Nation~~.
Name of Mother: Malinda Belt now Gardner a citizen of the Choctaw Nation.

Postoffice Kiowa I.T.

AFFIDAVIT OF MOTHER.

UNITED STATES OF AMERICA, Indian Territory,
Central DISTRICT.

I, Malinda Belt now Gardner, on oath state that I am 29 years of age and a citizen by Blood, of the Choctaw Nation; that I am the lawful wife of J B Gardner, who is a citizen, ~~by~~ of the US ~~Nation~~; that a Male child was born to me on 20 day of November, 1904; that said child has been named Elmer Gardner, and was living March 4, 1905.

Malinda Belt now Gardner

Witnesses To Mark:

Subscribed and sworn to before me this 1st day of May, 1905

H.B. Rowley
Notary Public.

AFFIDAVIT OF ATTENDING PHYSICIAN OR MID-WIFE.

UNITED STATES OF AMERICA, Indian Territory,
Central DISTRICT.

I, S W Jackson, a Physician, on oath state that I attended on Mrs. Malinda Gardner, wife of J B Gardner on the 20 day of November, 1904; that there was born to her on said date a Male child; that said child was living March 4, 1905, and is said to have been named Elmer Gardner

S.W. Jackson M.D.

Applications for Enrollment of Choctaw Newborn
Act of 1905 Volume XVII

Witnesses To Mark:

{

Subscribed and sworn to before me this 1st day of May , 1905

HB Rowley
Notary Public.

Affidavit of Attending Physician or Midwife

UNITED STATES OF AMERICA,
    INDIAN TERRITORY,
Cent   DISTRICT

I, S W Jackson a Physician on oath state that I attended on Mrs. Malinda Gardner wife of J B Gardner on the 20 day of November , 190 4, that there was born to her on said date a male child, that said child is now living, and is said to have been named Elmer Gardner

S.W. Jackson   M. D.

Subscribed and sworn to before me this the 15 day of Feby 1905

HB Rowley
Notary Public.

WITNESSETH:

Must be two witnesses who are citizens and know the child. { M.E. Crisp
Dixon Sexton

We hereby certify that we are well acquainted with SW Jackson a Physician and know him to be reputable and of good standing in the community.

Must be two citizen witnesses. { M.E. Crisp
Dixon Sexton

Applications for Enrollment of Choctaw Newborn
Act of 1905 Volume XVII

NEW BORN AFFIDAVIT

No ....

CHOCTAW ENROLLING COMMISSION

IN THE MATTER OF THE APPLICATION FOR ENROLLMENT as a citizen of the Choctaw Nation, of   Elmer Gardner   born on the   20" day of   November   190 4

Name of father   J B Gardner   a citizen of   US   ~~Nation~~,
final enrollment No.   X   *as Gardner*

Name of mother   Malinda Belt *now known*   a citizen of   Choctaw   Nation,
final enrollment No.   11255

Kiowa I.T.   Postoffice.

AFFIDAVIT OF MOTHER

UNITED STATES OF AMERICA
   INDIAN TERRITORY
DISTRICT   Centl

I   Malinda Belt *now known as Gardner* , on oath state that I am   28   years of age and a citizen by   Blood   of the   Choctaw   Nation, and as such have been placed upon the final roll of the   Choctaw   Nation, by the Honorable Secretary of the Interior my final enrollment number being   11255   ; that I am the lawful wife of   J B Gardner , who is a citizen of the   U.S.   ~~Nation~~, and as such has been placed upon the final roll of said Nation by the Honorable Secretary of the Interior, his final enrollment number being   x   and that a   male   child was born to me on the   20   day of   November   190 4; that said child has been named   Elmer Gardner , and is now living.

                             Malinda Gardner

WITNESSETH:
  Must be two witnesses { M.E. Crisp
  who are citizens   Dixon Sexton

Subscribed and sworn to before me this, the   15   day of   Feby   , 190 5

                         H B Rowley
                              Notary Public.

My Commission Expires:
    Nov 22nd 1905

Applications for Enrollment of Choctaw Newborn
Act of 1905 Volume XVII

7-4017

Muskogee, Indian Territory, May 8, 1905.

J. B. Gardner,
    Kiowa, Indian Territory.

Dear Sir:

    Receipt is hereby acknowledged of the affidavits of Malinda Belt now Gardner and Annie Gardner to the birth of Stella Gardner, daughter of J. B. and Malinda Gardner, February 1, 1903; also affidavits of Malinda Belt now Gardner and S. W. Jackson, to the birth of Elmer Gardner, son of J. B. and Malinda Gardner, November 20, 1904, and the same have been filed with our records as an application for the enrollment of said children.

                  Respectfully,

                  Commissioner in Charge.

Choctaw New Born 1268
    Jack Griffin Gardner
    (Born April 4, 1904)

NEW-BORN AFFIDAVIT.

    Number............

Choctaw Enrolling Commission.

    IN THE MATTER OF THE APPLICATION FOR ENROLLMENT, as a citizen of the Choctaw Nation, of   Jack Griffin Gardner

born on the 4th day of April 190 4

Name of father   Daniel H. Gardner   a citizen of   Choctaw
Nation final enrollment No   10743
Name of mother   *mother not enrolled*   a citizen of   Choctaw
Nation final enrollment No............

                Postoffice   Bokchito I.T.

Applications for Enrollment of Choctaw Newborn
Act of 1905   Volume XVII

AFFIDAVIT OF MOTHER.

UNITED STATES OF AMERICA,
    INDIAN TERRITORY,
Cent Jud.   DISTRICT

I   Minnie Gardner   on oath state that I am 28 years of age and a citizen by non of the _____ Nation, and as such have been placed upon the final roll of the Choctaw Nation, by the Honorable Secretary of the Interior my final enrollment number being —— ; that I am the lawful wife of Daniel H. Gardner, who is a citizen of the Choctaw Nation, and as such has been placed upon the final roll of said Nation by the Honorable Secretary of the Interior, his final enrollment number being 10743 and that a male child was born to me on the 4 day of April 190 4 ; that said child has been named Jack Griffin Gardner, and is now living.

                              Minnie Gardner

WITNESSETH:
Must be two Witnesses who are Citizens. } Rhoda Cochnauer
                  David W Cochnauer

Subscribed and sworn to before me this 23^d day of Jany 190 5

                        (Name Illegible)
                        Notary Public.

My commission expires _____

Affidavit of Attending Physician or Midwife.

State of Missouri
City of St Louis

I, J.J. Breaker a Physician on oath state that I attended on Mrs. Minnie Gardner wife of Daniel H. Gardner on the 4 day of April , 190 4 , that there was born to her on said date a Male child, that said child is now living, and is said to have been named Jack Griffin Gardner

                      J.J. Breaker   M.D.

Subscribed and sworn to before me this, the 27th day of January 190 5
My com expires April 10-1908

                      Sarah J Guyre
                      Notary Public.

WITNESSETH:
Must be two witnesses who are citizens and know the child. } Rhoda Cochnauer
                  David W Cochnauer

Applications for Enrollment of Choctaw Newborn
Act of 1905   Volume XVII

We hereby certify that we are well acquainted with J.J. Breaker a Physician and know him to be reputable and of good standing in the community.

{ D.W. Cochnauer

T. J. Impson

BIRTH AFFIDAVIT.

DEPARTMENT OF THE INTERIOR.
COMMISSION TO THE FIVE CIVILIZED TRIBES.

IN RE APPLICATION FOR ENROLLMENT, as a citizen of the Choctaw Nation, of Jeck[sic] Griffin Gardner, born on the 4th day of April, 1904

Name of Father: Daniel H Gardner   a citizen of the Choctaw Nation.
Name of Mother: Minnie Gardner   a citizen of the Choctaw Nation.

Postoffice   Bokchito, I.T.

AFFIDAVIT OF MOTHER.

UNITED STATES OF AMERICA, Indian Territory,
Central   DISTRICT.

I, Minnie Gardner, on oath state that I am 28 years of age and a citizen by Intermarriage, of the Choctaw Nation; that I am the lawful wife of Daniel H Gardner, who is a citizen, by Blood of the Choctaw Nation; that a male child was born to me on 4th day of April, 1904; that said child has been named Joch[sic] Griffin Gardner, and was living March 4, 1905.

Minnie Gardner

Witnesses To Mark:

Subscribed and sworn to before me this 29th day of April, 1905

W C Caudill
Notary Public.

Applications for Enrollment of Choctaw Newborn
Act of 1905   Volume XVII

AFFIDAVIT OF ATTENDING PHYSICIAN OR MID-WIFE.

UNITED STATES OF AMERICA, Indian Territory,　}
　Central　　　　　　　DISTRICT.

I, J J Breaker, a Physician, on oath state that I attended on Mrs. Minnie Gardner, wife of Daniel H Gardner on the 4th day of April, 1904; that there was born to her on said date a male child; that said child was living March 4, 1905, and is said to have been named Joch[sic] Griffin Gardner

　　　　　　　　　　　　　　J.J. Breaker

Witnesses To Mark:
{

Subscribed and sworn to before me this 29th day of April, 1905

　　　　　　　　　　　W C Caudill
　　　　　　　　　　　Notary Public.

Choctaw New Born 1269
　　Earnest J. Gibson
　　(Born Oct. 18, 1904)

NEW-BORN AFFIDAVIT.

　　　　Number............

...Choctaw Enrolling Commission...

IN THE MATTER OF THE APPLICATION FOR ENROLLMENT, as a citizen of the Choctaw　　Nation, of　　Ernest[sic] J. Gibson

born on the 18 day of October 190 4

Name of father   Thenton Gibson　　　a citizen of   Choctaw
Nation final enrollment No.   13190
Name of mother   Sallie Gibson　　　a citizen of   Choctaw
Nation final enrollment No.   985

　　　　　　　　　Postoffice   Featherston I.T.

Applications for Enrollment of Choctaw Newborn
Act of 1905 Volume XVII

AFFIDAVIT OF MOTHER.

UNITED STATES OF AMERICA
INDIAN TERRITORY
Central   DISTRICT

I   Sallie Gibson   , on oath state that I am 20 years of age and a citizen by marriage of the Choctaw Nation, and as such have been placed upon the final roll of the Choctaw Nation, by the Honorable Secretary of the Interior my final enrollment number being   985 ; that I am the lawful wife of   Thenton Gibson   , who is a citizen of the   Choctaw   Nation, and as such has been placed upon the final roll of said Nation by the Honorable Secretary of the Interior, his final enrollment number being   13190   and that a   Male   child was born to me on the 18   day of   October   190 4; that said child has been named   Ernest J Gibson   , and is now living.

Sallie Gibson

Witnesseth.

Must be two Witnesses who are Citizens.   Sam Gibson
Willie Jones

Subscribed and sworn to before me this   17   day of   March   190 5

James Bower
Notary Public.

My commission expires:
Sept 23-1907

AFFIDAVIT OF ATTENDING PHYSICIAN OR MIDWIFE

UNITED STATES OF AMERICA
INDIAN TERRITORY
Central   DISTRICT

I,   Cillian Gibson   a   Midwife on oath state that I attended on Mrs.   Sallie Gibson   wife of   Thenton Gibson on the 18   day of   October   , 190 4, that there was born to her on said date a   male child, that said child is now living, and is said to have been named   Ernest J Gibson

her
Cillian x Gibson   M.D.
mark

WITNESSETH:
Must be two witnesses who are citizens and know the child.   Sam Gibson
Willie Jones

Subscribed and sworn to before me this, the   17   day of March   190 5

James Bower   Notary Public.

Applications for Enrollment of Choctaw Newborn
Act of 1905 Volume XVII

We hereby certify that we are well acquainted with Cillian Gibson a midwife and know her to be reputable and of good standing in the community.

{ Sam Gibson
  Willie Jones

BIRTH AFFIDAVIT.

DEPARTMENT OF THE INTERIOR.
COMMISSION TO THE FIVE CIVILIZED TRIBES.

IN RE APPLICATION FOR ENROLLMENT, as a citizen of the Choctaw Nation, of Earnest J Gibson, born on the 18 day of Oct, 1904

Name of Father: Thenton Gibson   a citizen of the Choctaw Nation.
Name of Mother: Sallie Gibson   a citizen of the Choctaw Nation.

Postoffice   Featherston Ind Ter

AFFIDAVIT OF MOTHER.

UNITED STATES OF AMERICA, Indian Territory, }
Central   DISTRICT.

I, Sallie Gibson, on oath state that I am Twenty years of age and a citizen by marriage, of the Choctaw Nation; that I am the lawful wife of Thenton Gibson, who is a citizen, by Blood of the Choctaw Nation; that a male child was born to me on 18 day of October, 1904; that said child has been named Earnest J Gibson, and was living March 4, 1905.

Sallie Gibson

Witnesses To Mark:
{

Subscribed and sworn to before me this First day of May, 1905

My commission expires   JC Hubert
Nov 25 1908   Notary Public.

Applications for Enrollment of Choctaw Newborn
Act of 1905   Volume XVII

AFFIDAVIT OF ATTENDING PHYSICIAN OR MID-WIFE.

UNITED STATES OF AMERICA, Indian Territory, }
   Central   DISTRICT. }

      I, Sillen[sic] Gibson, a midwife, on oath state that I attended on Mrs. Sallie Gibson, wife of Thenton Gibson on the 18 day of October, 1904; that there was born to her on said date a male child; that said child was living March 4, 1905, and is said to have been named Earnest J Gibson

                                                                   her
                                                         Sillen x Gibson
Witnesses To Mark: mark
  { Sam Gibson
  { P McCullough

      Subscribed and sworn to before me this First day of May, 1905

                                      JC Hubert
My commission   Notary Public.
    expires Nov 25 1908

                                                                                       Choctaw 4775.

                           Muskogee, Indian Territory, May 4, 1905.

Thenton Gibson,
    Featherston, Indian Territory.

Dear Sir:

      Receipt is hereby acknowledged of the affidavits of Sallie Gibson and Sillen Gibson to the birth of Earnest J. Gibson, son of Thenton and Sallie Gibson, October 18, 1904, and the same have been filed with our records as an application for the enrollment of said child as a citizen of the Choctaw Nation.

                                   Respectfully,

                                           Chairman.

Applications for Enrollment of Choctaw Newborn
Act of 1905 Volume XVII

Choctaw New Born 1270
    Charley James
    (Born Dec. 5, 1903)

NEW-BORN AFFIDAVIT.

Number..............

...Choctaw Enrolling Commission...

IN THE MATTER OF THE APPLICATION FOR ENROLLMENT, as a citizen of the Choctaw Nation, of Charley James

born on the 5th day of December 190 3

Name of father William James   a citizen of Choctaw
Nation final enrollment No. 2151
Name of mother Annie Woolery   a citizen of Choctaw
Nation final enrollment No. 3764

                                                  Postoffice   Valliant, I.T.

AFFIDAVIT OF MOTHER.

UNITED STATES OF AMERICA
INDIAN TERRITORY
    Central   DISTRICT

I Annie Woolery, on oath state that I am 19 years of age and a citizen by blood of the Choctaw Nation, and as such have been placed upon the final roll of the Choctaw Nation, by the Honorable Secretary of the Interior my final enrollment number being 3764 ; that I am the lawful wife of William James , who is a citizen of the Choctaw Nation, and as such has been placed upon the final roll of said Nation by the Honorable Secretary of the Interior, his final enrollment number being 2151 and that a Male child was born to me on the 5th day of December 190 3; that said child has been named Charley James , and is now living.

                                                 Annie Woolery

Witnesseth.
Must be two Witnesses who are Citizens.   L E Baken
                       David Nakishi

Applications for Enrollment of Choctaw Newborn
Act of 1905 Volume XVII

Subscribed and sworn to before me this 22 day of Feb 190 5

W A Shoney
Notary Public.

My commission expires: Jan 10, 1909

AFFIDAVIT OF ATTENDING PHYSICIAN OR MIDWIFE

UNITED STATES OF AMERICA
INDIAN TERRITORY
Central DISTRICT

I, Nancy Woolery a midwife on oath state that I attended on Mrs. Annie Woolery wife of Willie James on the 5th day of December , 190 3, that there was born to her on said date a male child, that said child is now living, and is said to have been named Charley James

          her
      Nancy x Woolery ~~M.D~~.
          mark

WITNESSETH:

Must be two witnesses who are citizens and know the child.
{ L.E. Baken
  David Nakishi

Subscribed and sworn to before me this, the 22 day of Feb 190 5

W A Shoney Notary Public.

We hereby certify that we are well acquainted with Nancy Woolery a midwife and know her to be reputable and of good standing in the community.

{ L.E. Baken
  David Nakishi

BIRTH AFFIDAVIT.

DEPARTMENT OF THE INTERIOR.
COMMISSION TO THE FIVE CIVILIZED TRIBES.

IN RE APPLICATION FOR ENROLLMENT, as a citizen of the Choctaw Nation, of Charley James , born on the 5th day of December , 1903

Name of Father: William James *Roll 2151* a citizen of the Choctaw Nation.

Name of Mother: Annie James *nee Woolery* *Roll* *3764* a citizen of the Choctaw Nation.

Applications for Enrollment of Choctaw Newborn
Act of 1905 Volume XVII

Postoffice Valliant I.T.

AFFIDAVIT OF MOTHER.

UNITED STATES OF AMERICA, Indian Territory, }
..................................DISTRICT. }

I, Annie James *nee Woolery*, on oath state that I am 19 years of age and a citizen by blood, of the Choctaw Nation; that I am the lawful wife of William James, who is a citizen, by blood of the Choctaw Nation; that a male child was born to me on 5th day of December, 1903; that said child has been named Charley James, and was living March 4, 1905.

Annie James *nee Woolery Roll 3764*

Witnesses To Mark:
{

Subscribed and sworn to before me this 3rd day of August, 1905

(Name Illegible)
Notary Public.

AFFIDAVIT OF ATTENDING PHYSICIAN OR MID-WIFE.

UNITED STATES OF AMERICA, Indian Territory, }
..................................DISTRICT. }

I, Nancy Woolery, a midwife, on oath state that I attended on Mrs. Annie James *nee Woolery*, wife of William James on the 5th day of December, 1903; that there was born to her on said date a male child; that said child was living March 4, 1905, and is said to have been named Charley James

her
Nancy x Woolery
mark

Witnesses To Mark:
{ *(Name Illegible)* Valliant I.T.
{ *(Name Illegible)* Lehigh I.T.

Subscribed and sworn to before me this 3rd day of August, 1905

(Name Illegible)
Notary Public.

Applications for Enrollment of Choctaw Newborn
Act of 1905 Volume XVII

7--NB--1270

Muskogee, Indian Territory, June 1, 1905.

Annie Woolery,
    Valliant, Indian Territory.

Dear Madam:

    There is enclosed you herewith for execution application for the enrollment of your infant child, Charley James, born December 5, 190 3

    The affidavits heretofore filed with the Commission show the child was living on February 22, 1905. It is necessary, for the child to be enrolled, that he was living on March 4, 1905.

    In having these affidavits executed care should be exercised to see that all names are written in full, as they appear in the body of the affidavit, and in the event either of the persons signing the affidavit are unable to write, signatures by mark must be attested by two witnesses. Each affidavit must be executed before a Notary Public and the notarial seal and signature of the officer must be attached to each separate affidavit.

Respectfully,

Chairman.

Enc. FVK-8

7-NB-1270

Muskogee, Indian Territory, July 25, 1905.

Annie Woolery,
    Valliant, Indian Territory.

Dear Madam:

    Your attention is called to a communication addressed to you by the Commission to the Five Civilized Tribes, under date of June 1, 1905, with which there was inclosed for execution application for the enrollment of your infant child, Charley James Woolery, born December 5, 1903.

    In said letter you were advised that the affidavits heretofore filed with the Commission to the Five Civilized Tribes show that the child was living on February 22, 1905, and that it was lecessary[sic] for him to be enrolled, that he was living on March 4, 1905. No reply to this letter has been received.

Applications for Enrollment of Choctaw Newborn
Act of 1905   Volume XVII

You are requested to have the affidavits properly executed immediately, as no further action can be taken relative to the enrollment of said child until the information requested has been supplied.

Respectfully,

Commissioner.

7-NB-1270

Muskogee, Indian Territory, August 8, 1905.

Mrs. Annie James,
    Valliant, Indian Territory.

Dear Madam:

Receipt is hereby acknowledged of the affidavits of Annie James nee Woolery and Nancy Woolery to the birth of Charley James, son of William James and Annie James nee Woolery, December 5, 1903, and the same have been filed with the records of this office in the matter of the enrollment of said child.

Respectfully,

Acting Commissioner.

Choc. New Born 1271
    Sylma Kendrick
    (Born Oct. 5, 1904)

Central District
    Ind. Ty.
Duplicate of Marriage Certificate

This is to certify that I J.E. Potts a minister of the gospel did on the 8 Day of December 1903, according to the Choctaw laws solemnize the rites of matrimony between Mr W W Kendrick of Hugo I.T. age 21 & Miss Lester Brittinham of Hugo age 18.

This 19 Day of June 1905   L E Potts
Witness to marriage
    Amanda Potts
    P.O. Hugo I.T.

Applications for Enrollment of Choctaw Newborn
Act of 1905 Volume XVII

Personally appeared before me the undersigned authority, J E Potts a minister of the Gospel who makes oath that the statements herein made are true & correct also Amanda Potts who makes oath that she was present & a witness to said marriage

This 19 day June 1905

    W.T. Glenn
    Notary Public
    Central District
    Ind. Ty.

NEW-BORN AFFIDAVIT.

Number ....

Choctaw Enrolling Commission.

IN THE MATTER OF THE APPLICATION FOR ENROLLMENT, as a citizen of the Choctaw Nation, of   Sylma Kendrick

born on the 5 day of October 190 4

Name of father   William W Kendrick   a citizen of   Choctaw Nation final enrollment No 3911
Name of mother   Lester Kendrick   a citizen of   ———
Nation final enrollment No ....

    Postoffice   Hugo I.T.

AFFIDAVIT OF MOTHER.

UNITED STATES OF AMERICA, ⎫
 INDIAN TERRITORY, ⎬
 Central   DISTRICT ⎭

I   Lester Kendrick   on oath state that I am 19 years of age and a citizen by ——— of the ——— Nation, and as such have been placed upon the final roll of the ——— Nation, by the Honorable Secretary of the Interior my final enrollment number being ——— ; that I am the lawful wife of   William W Kendrick , who is a citizen of the   Choctaw   Nation, and as such has been placed upon the final roll of said Nation by the Honorable Secretary of the Interior, his final enrollment number being 3911   and that a   Female   child was born to me on the 5 day of   October   190 4 ; that said child has been named   Sylma Kendrick , and is now living.

          Lester Kendrick

WITNESSETH:
 Must be two ⎫ Isaac Spring
 Witnesses who ⎬
 are Citizens. ⎭ Willie Spring

Applications for Enrollment of Choctaw Newborn
Act of 1905   Volume XVII

Subscribed and sworn to before me this 19 day of January   190 5

W.T. Glenn
Notary Public.

My commission expires 1907

Affidavit of Attending Physician or Midwife.

UNITED STATES OF AMERICA
INDIAN TERRITORY
Central   DISTRICT

I,   T. W. Simmons   a   Practicing Physician on oath state that I attended on Mrs. Lester Kendrick   wife of   William W Kendrick on the   5   day of   October   , 190 4 , that there was born to her on said date a Female child, that said child is now living, and is said to have been named Sylma Kendrick

Thomas W Simmons   M.D.

Subscribed and sworn to before me this, the   19 day of   Jany   190 5

W.T. Glenn
Notary Public.

WITNESSETH:
Must be two witnesses who are citizens and know the child.
- Isaac Spring
- Willie Spring

We hereby certify that we are well acquainted with T.W. Simmons a Practicing Physician   and know him   to be reputable and of good standing in the community.

- Isaac Spring
- Willie Spring

BIRTH AFFIDAVIT.

DEPARTMENT OF THE INTERIOR.
COMMISSION TO THE FIVE CIVILIZED TRIBES.

IN RE APPLICATION FOR ENROLLMENT, as a citizen of the   Choctaw   Nation, of Sylma Kendrick   , born on the 5th day of October , 1904

Roll

Name of Father: William W Kendrick   3911   a citizen of the   Choctaw   Nation.
Name of Mother: Lester Kendrick   a citizen of the   Choctaw   Nation.

Applications for Enrollment of Choctaw Newborn
Act of 1905 Volume XVII

Postoffice   Hugo I.T.

AFFIDAVIT OF MOTHER.

UNITED STATES OF AMERICA, Indian Territory, } DISTRICT.

I, Lester Kendrick, on oath state that I am 19 years of age and a citizen ~~by~~ , of the United States Nation; that I am the lawful wife of William W Kendrick, who is a citizen, by blood of the Choctaw Nation; that a Female child was born to me on 5th day of October , 1904; that said child has been named Sylma Kendrick, and was living March 4, 1905.

Lester Kendrick

Witnesses To Mark:
{

Subscribed and sworn to before me this 15 day of June , 1905

W.T. Glenn
Notary Public.

AFFIDAVIT OF ATTENDING PHYSICIAN OR MID-WIFE.

UNITED STATES OF AMERICA, Indian Territory, } DISTRICT.

I, Thomas W Simmons , a physician , on oath state that I attended on Mrs. William W Kendrick , wife of William W Kendrick on the 5th day of October , 1904; that there was born to her on said date a female child; that said child was living March 4, 1905, and is said to have been named Sylma Kendrick

Thos W Simmons M.D.

Witnesses To Mark:
{

Subscribed and sworn to before me this 15 day of June , 1905

W.T. Glenn
Notary Public.

Applications for Enrollment of Choctaw Newborn
Act of 1905 Volume XVII

7--NB--1271

Muskogee, Indian Territory, June 1, 1905.

William W. Kendrick,
    Hugo, Indian Territory.

Dear Sir:

    There is enclosed you herewith for execution application for the enrollment of your infant child, Sylma Kendrick, born October 5, 1904.

    The affidavits heretofore filed with the Commission show the child was living on January 19, 1905. It is necessary, for the child to be enrolled, that she was living on March 4, 1905.

    In having these affidavits executed care should be exercised to see that all names are written in full, as they appear in the body of the affidavit, and in the event that either of the persons signing the affidavit are unable to write, signatures by mark must be attested by two witnesses. Each affidavit must be executed before a Notary Public and the notarial seal and signature of the officer must be attached to each separate affidavit.

    It further appears from the application for the enrollment of said child heretofore filed with this Commission that this applicant claims through you.

    In this event it will be necessary for you to file in this office, either the original or a certified copy of the license and certificate of your marriage to the applicant's mother, Lester Kendrick.

    Respectfully,

    Chairman.

FVK-10

---

7 NB 1271

Muskogee, Indian Territory, June 23, 1905.

William W. Kendrick,
    Hugo, Indian Territory.

Dear Sir:

    Receipt is hereby acknowledged of the affidavits of Lester Kendrick and Thomas W. Simmons to the birth of Sylma Kendrick, daughter of William A[sic]. and Lester Kendrick, October 5, 1904, and the same have been filed with our records in the matter of the enrollment of said child.

Applications for Enrollment of Choctaw Newborn
Act of 1905   Volume XVII

Receipt is also acknowledged of the affidavit of J. E. Potts to the marriage between W. W. Kendrick and Lester Brittinham and the same have been filed with the record in this case.

Respectfully,

Chairman.

Choc. New Born 1272
    Jack Evelyn King
    (Born Sep. 16, 1904)

NEW-BORN AFFIDAVIT.

Number................

...Choctaw Enrolling Commission...

IN THE MATTER OF THE APPLICATION FOR ENROLLMENT, as a citizen of the Choctaw Nation, of Jack Evelyn King

born on the 16th day of ___September___ 190 4

Name of father   Luther King   a citizen of   ———
Nation final enrollment No. Entermarried[sic] white
Name of mother   Mamy[sic] Taylor *now King*   a citizen of   Chocktaw[sic]
Nation final enrollment No.   8417

                                          Postoffice   Russel Ville I.T.

AFFIDAVIT OF MOTHER.

UNITED STATES OF AMERICA
INDIAN TERRITORY
  Western   DISTRICT

      I   Mamy Taylor now King   , on oath state that I am 22   years of age and a citizen by   blood   of the   Chocktaw   Nation, and as such have been placed upon the final roll of the   Chocktaw   Nation, by the Honorable Secretary of the Interior my final enrollment number being   8417 ; that I am the lawful wife of   Luther King white   , who is a citizen of the   white   Nation, and as such has been placed upon the final roll of said Nation by the Honorable Secretary of the Interior, his final enrollment number being .... and that a   Female   child was born to

Applications for Enrollment of Choctaw Newborn
Act of 1905 Volume XVII

me on the 16th day of September 190 4; that said child has been named Jack Evelyn King , and is now living.

Mamie King

Witnesseth.
Must be two Witnesses who are Citizens. T. D. Dyer
T.J. Walls

Subscribed and sworn to before me this 4 day of Jan 190 5

John M Long
Notary Public.

My commission expires: Nov 27 1907

AFFIDAVIT OF ATTENDING PHYSICIAN OR MIDWIFE

UNITED STATES OF AMERICA
INDIAN TERRITORY
Western DISTRICT

I, James M Turner a Physician on oath state that I attended on Mrs. Mamy King wife of Luther King on the 16th day of June[sic] , 190 4, that there was born to her on said date a Female child, that said child is now living, and is said to have been named Jack Evelyn King

JM Turner M.D.

Subscribed and sworn to before me this, the 7th day of January 190 5

WITNESSETH:
Must be two witnesses who are citizens T. D. Dyer
T.J. Walls

Guy A Curry Notary Public.

We hereby certify that we are well acquainted with James M Turner a Physician and know him to be reputable and of good standing in the community.

T. D. Dyer _____

T. J. Walls _____

Applications for Enrollment of Choctaw Newborn
Act of 1905   Volume XVII

BIRTH AFFIDAVIT.

DEPARTMENT OF THE INTERIOR.
COMMISSION TO THE FIVE CIVILIZED TRIBES.

IN RE APPLICATION FOR ENROLLMENT, as a citizen of the Choctaw Nation, of Jack Evelyn King, born on the 16th day of September, 1904

Name of Father: L. L. King   a citizen of the _____ Nation.
Name of Mother: Mamie King, nee Taylor   a citizen of the Choctaw Nation.

Postoffice   Russellville, I. T.

AFFIDAVIT OF MOTHER.

UNITED STATES OF AMERICA, Indian Territory, }
Western   DISTRICT.   }

I, Mamie King, nee Taylor, on oath state that I am 23 years of age and a citizen by blood, of the Choctaw Nation; that I am the lawful wife of L. L. King, who is a citizen, by ------ of the _____ Nation; that a Female child was born to me on 16th day of September, 1904; that said child has been named Jack Evelyn King, and was living March 4, 1905.

Mamie King

Witnesses To Mark:
{

Subscribed and sworn to before me this 24th day of May, 1905.

Guy A. Curry
Notary Public.

AFFIDAVIT OF ATTENDING PHYSICIAN OR MID-WIFE.

UNITED STATES OF AMERICA, Indian Territory, }
Western   DISTRICT.   }

I, J. M. Turner, a Physcian[sic], on oath state that I attended on Mrs. Mamie King, wife of L. L. King on the 16th day of September, 1904; that there was born to her on said date a Female child; that said child was living March 4, 1905, and is said to have been named Jack Evelyn King

J.M. Turner M.D.

Applications for Enrollment of Choctaw Newborn
Act of 1905 Volume XVII

Witnesses To Mark:
- D.A. Billington
- J.H. Vaughan

Subscribed and sworn to before me this 24 day of May, 1905

John M Lentz
Notary Public.

BIRTH AFFIDAVIT.

DEPARTMENT OF THE INTERIOR.
COMMISSION TO THE FIVE CIVILIZED TRIBES.

IN RE APPLICATION FOR ENROLLMENT, as a citizen of the Choctaw Nation, of Jack Evelyn King, born on the 16 day of September, 1904

Name of Father: L. L. King   a citizen of the U.S. ~~Nation~~.

Name of Mother: Mamie King, nee Taylor Roll 8417 a citizen of the Choctaw Nation.

Postoffice Russellville, I.T.

AFFIDAVIT OF MOTHER.

UNITED STATES OF AMERICA, Indian Territory, DISTRICT.

I, ..., on oath state that I am .... years of age and a citizen by ...., of the .... Nation; that I am the lawful wife of ...., who is a citizen, by .... of the .... Nation; that a .... child was born to me on .... day of ...., 1......, that said child has been named ...., and was living March 4, 1905.

Witnesses To Mark:

Subscribed and sworn to before me this .... day of ...., 1905.

Notary Public.

Applications for Enrollment of Choctaw Newborn
Act of 1905   Volume XVII

AFFIDAVIT OF ATTENDING PHYSICIAN OR MID-WIFE.

UNITED STATES OF AMERICA, Indian Territory,
Western DISTRICT.

I, J. M. Turner, a Physician, on oath state that I attended on Mrs. Mamie King, wife of L. L. King on the 16 day of September, 1904; that there was born to her on said date a female child; that said child was living March 4, 1905, and is said to have been named Jack Evelyn King

J.M. Turner M.D.

Witnesses To Mark:

Subscribed and sworn to before me this 12 day of June, 1905
my commission expires Nov 27 1907

John M Lentz
Notary Public.

7--NB--1272

Muskogee, Indian Territory, June 2, 1905.

Luther King,
   Russellville, Indian Territory.

Dear Sir:

There is enclosed herewith for execution affidavit in support of the application for the enrollment of your infant child, Jack Evelyn King.

In the affidavit of the mother of this applicant dated January 4, 1905, the date of her birth is given as September 16, 1904, while in the affidavit of the attending physician executed January 7, 1905, the date of the birth of the applicant is given as June 16, 1904. In the enclosed affidavit the date of birth is left blank. Please insert the correct date and when the affidavit is properly executed return to this office.

In having the affidavit executed care should be exercised to see that all names are written in full, as they appear in the body of the affidavit, and in the event the person signing the same is unable to write, signatures by mark must be attested by two witnesses. The affidavit must be executed before a Notary Public and the notarial seal and signature of the officer must be attached thereto.

This matter should receive your immediate attention as no further action can be taken relative to the enrollment of said child until the Commission has been furnished this affidavit.

Applications for Enrollment of Choctaw Newborn
Act of 1905   Volume XVII

Respectfully,

Commissioner in Charge.

Enc-FVK-10

7 NB 1272

Muskogee, Indian Territory, June 17, 1905.

L. L. King,
    Russellville, Indian Territory.

Dear Sir:

    Receipt is hereby acknowledged of the affidavit of J. M. Turner to the birth of Jack Evelyn King, daughter of L. L. King and Mamie King nee Taylor, September 16, 1904, and the same has been filed with our records in the matter of the enrollment of said child.

Respectfully,

Chairman.

Choc. New Born 1273
    Eddie Randell
    (Born Apr. 10, 1904)

BIRTH AFFIDAVIT.

DEPARTMENT OF THE INTERIOR.
COMMISSION TO THE FIVE CIVILIZED TRIBES.

IN RE APPLICATION FOR ENROLLMENT, as a citizen of the Choctaw Nation, of Eddie Randell, born on the 10th day of April, 1904

Name of Father: Gus Randell   a citizen of the United States ~~Nation~~.
Name of Mother: Mattie Randell   a citizen of the Choctaw Nation.

Postoffice   Finley, Ind. Ter.

Applications for Enrollment of Choctaw Newborn
Act of 1905   Volume XVII

AFFIDAVIT OF MOTHER.

UNITED STATES OF AMERICA, Indian Territory, }
Central   DISTRICT.

I,   Mattie Randell   , on oath state that I am   25   years of age and a citizen by   blood   , of the   Choctaw   Nation; that I am the lawful wife of   Gus Randell   , who is a citizen, ~~by~~ .... of the   United States   ~~Nation~~; that a   male   child was born to me on   10th   day of   April   , 1904; that said child has been named   Eddie Randell   , and was living March 4, 1905.

Mattie Randell

Witnesses To Mark:
{

Subscribed and sworn to before me this   26th   day of   April   , 1905

Wirt Franklin
Notary Public.

AFFIDAVIT OF ATTENDING PHYSICIAN OR MID-WIFE.

UNITED STATES OF AMERICA, Indian Territory, }
Central   DISTRICT.

I,   Janey Randell   , a mid-wife   , on oath state that I attended on Mrs.   Mattie Randell   , wife of   Gus Randell   on the   10th day of   April   , 1904; that there was born to her on said date a   male   child; that said child was living March 4, 1905, and is said to have been named   Eddie Randell

Janey Randell

Witnesses To Mark:
{

Subscribed and sworn to before me this   26th   day of   April   , 1905

Wirt Franklin
Notary Public.

Applications for Enrollment of Choctaw Newborn
Act of 1905   Volume XVII

Choc. New Born 1274
    Amanda Owen
    (Born Jan. 14, 1904)

NEW BORN AFFIDAVIT

No ....

CHOCTAW ENROLLING COMMISSION

IN THE MATTER OF THE APPLICATION FOR ENROLLMENT as a citizen of the Choctaw Nation, of Amanda Owen born on the 14th day of January 190 4

Name of father   C. C. Owen   a citizen of   U.S.   ~~Nation~~, final enrollment No. ....

Name of mother   Martha Owen   a citizen of   Choctaw   Nation, final enrollment No. 4921

Antlers I.T.   Postoffice.

AFFIDAVIT OF MOTHER

UNITED STATES OF AMERICA
INDIAN TERRITORY
DISTRICT   Central

I   Martha Owen   , on oath state that I am   20   years of age and a citizen by   blood   of the   Choctaw   Nation, and as such have been placed upon the final roll of the   Choctaw   Nation, by the Honorable Secretary of the Interior my final enrollment number being   4921   ; that I am the lawful wife of   C C Owen   , who is a citizen of the   U. S.   ~~Nation~~, and as such has been placed upon the final roll of said Nation by the Honorable Secretary of the Interior, his final enrollment number being .... and that a   Female   child was born to me on the   14th   day of January 190 4; that said child has been named   Amanda Owen   , and is now living.

                                        Martha Owen

WITNESSETH:
   Must be two witnesses { Z.D. Anderson
   who are citizens   { J.J. Turner

Applications for Enrollment of Choctaw Newborn
Act of 1905 Volume XVII

Subscribed and sworn to before me this, the 22 day of Feby , 190 5

A.J. Arnote
Notary Public.

My Commission Expires:
May 16th 1907

Affidavit of Attending Physician or Midwife

UNITED STATES OF AMERICA,
   INDIAN TERRITORY,
Central   DISTRICT

I, I. D. Walker a Physician on oath state that I attended on Mrs. Martha Owen wife of C. C. Owen on the 14 day of January , 190 4, that there was born to her on said date a Female child, that said child is now living, and is said to have been named Amanda Owen

I.D. Walker   M. D.

Subscribed and sworn to before me this the 22 day of Feby 1905

A.J. Arnote
Notary Public.

WITNESSETH:

Must be two witnesses who are citizens and know the child. { Z.D. Anderson
J.J. Turner

We hereby certify that we are well acquainted with Dr. I. D. Walker a Physician and know him to be reputable and of good standing in the community.

Must be two citizen witnesses. { Z.D. Anderson
J.J. Turner

Applications for Enrollment of Choctaw Newborn
Act of 1905 Volume XVII

BIRTH AFFIDAVIT.

DEPARTMENT OF THE INTERIOR.
COMMISSION TO THE FIVE CIVILIZED TRIBES.

IN RE APPLICATION FOR ENROLLMENT, as a citizen of the Choctaw Nation, of Amanda Owen, born on the 14th day of January, 1904

Name of Father: C. C. Owen   a citizen of the United States ~~Nation~~.
Name of Mother: Martha Owen   a citizen of the Choctaw Nation.

Postoffice   Antlers, Ind. Ter.

AFFIDAVIT OF MOTHER.

UNITED STATES OF AMERICA, Indian Territory, }
Central   DISTRICT.

I, Martha Owen, on oath state that I am 20 years of age and a citizen by blood, of the Choctaw Nation; that I am the lawful wife of C. C. Owen, who is a citizen, ~~by~~ .... of the United States ~~Nation~~; that a female child was born to me on 14th day of January, 1904; that said child has been named Amanda Owen, and was living March 4, 1905.

Martha Owen

Witnesses To Mark:
{

Subscribed and sworn to before me this 25th day of April, 1905

Wirt Franklin
Notary Public.

AFFIDAVIT OF ATTENDING PHYSICIAN OR MID-WIFE.

UNITED STATES OF AMERICA, Indian Territory, }
Central   DISTRICT.

I, Martha P. Owen, a mid-wife, on oath state that I attended on Mrs. Martha Owen, wife of C. C. Owen on the 14th day of January, 1904; that there was born to her on said date a female child; that said child was living March 4, 1905, and is said to have been named Amanda Owen

her
Martha x P. Owen
mark

Applications for Enrollment of Choctaw Newborn
Act of 1905 Volume XVII

Witnesses To Mark:
- Robert Anderson
- Vester W Rose

Subscribed and sworn to before me this 25th day of April, 1905

Wirt Franklin
Notary Public.

Choc. New Born 1275
    Alma Mae McDaniel
    (Born Sep. 1, 1903)

BIRTH AFFIDAVIT.

DEPARTMENT OF THE INTERIOR.
COMMISSION TO THE FIVE CIVILIZED TRIBES.

IN RE APPLICATION FOR ENROLLMENT, as a citizen of the Choctaw Nation, of Alma Mae McDaniel, born on the 1st day of September, 1903

Name of Father: Thomas E. McDaniel   a citizen of the Choctaw Nation.
Name of Mother: Kate McDaniel   a citizen of the Choctaw Nation.

Postoffice   Atok[sic] Ind Ter

AFFIDAVIT OF MOTHER.

UNITED STATES OF AMERICA, Indian Territory,
   Central   DISTRICT.

    I, Kate McDaniel, on oath state that I am 25 years of age and a citizen by intermarriage, of the Choctaw Nation; that I am the lawful wife of Thomas McDaniel, who is a citizen, by blood of the Choctaw Nation; that a female child was born to me on 1st day of September, 1903; that said child has been named Alma Mae McDaniel, and was living March 4, 1905.

                           Kate McDaniel

Witnesses To Mark:

Applications for Enrollment of Choctaw Newborn
Act of 1905   Volume XVII

Subscribed and sworn to before me this 20 day of April, 1905

A.H. Crouthamel
Notary Public.

My com. Ex Feb. 3.1907

AFFIDAVIT OF ATTENDING PHYSICIAN OR MID-WIFE.

UNITED STATES OF AMERICA, Indian Territory,
Central DISTRICT.

I, J. F. Park, a Physician, on oath state that I attended on Mrs. Kate McDaniel, wife of Thomas E. McDaniel on the 1st day of September, 1903; that there was born to her on said date a Female child; that said child was living March 4, 1905, and is said to have been named Alma Mae McDaniel

J.F. Park M.D.

Witnesses To Mark:

Subscribed and sworn to before me this 25th day of April, 1905

F.M. Hinsley
Notary Public.
Central District, Indian Territory.

My commission expires
December 6th 1906

7-5394

Muskogee, Indian Territory, April 28, 1905.

Tom McDaniel,
   Atoka, Indian Territory.

Dear Sir:

   Receipt is hereby acknowledged of your letter of April 25, 1905, inclosing the affidavits of Kate McDaniel and J. F Park to the birth of Alma Mae McDaniel, daughter of Thomas E. McDaniel and Kate McDaniel, September 1, 1903, and the same have been filed in the matter of the application for the enrollment of said child.

                Respectfully,

                                        Chairman.

Applications for Enrollment of Choctaw Newborn
Act of 1905   Volume XVII

Choc. New Born 1276
    Ervin McMurry[sic]
    (Born May 13, 1904)

BIRTH AFFIDAVIT.

DEPARTMENT OF THE INTERIOR,
COMMISSION TO THE FIVE CIVILIZED TRIBES.

IN RE *Application for Enrollment*, as a citizen of the Choctaw Nation, of Ervin McMurray , born on the 13 day of May , 1904

Name of Father: O. M. McMurray   a citizen of the United States Nation.
Name of Mother: Beckey McMurray   a citizen of the Choctaw Nation.

Post-Office: Crowder City

AFFIDAVIT OF MOTHER.

UNITED STATES OF AMERICA,
   INDIAN TERRITORY.
Central   District.

I, Beckey McMurray , on oath state that I am 26 years of age and a citizen by Blood , of the Choctaw Nation; that I am the lawful wife of O.M. McMurray , who is a citizen, by .... of the United States Nation; that a Male child was born to me on 13 day of May , 1904 , that said child has been named Ervin McMurray , and is now living.

                                 Beckey McMurray
WITNESSES TO MARK:

Subscribed and sworn to before me this 24 day of April , 1905.

                                 R.B. Coleman
                                   NOTARY PUBLIC.

Applications for Enrollment of Choctaw Newborn
Act of 1905 Volume XVII

AFFIDAVIT OF ATTENDING PHYSICIAN OR MID-WIFE.

UNITED STATES OF AMERICA,
INDIAN TERRITORY.
Central District.

I, W.E. Abbott, a Physician, on oath state that I attended on Mrs. Beckey McMurray, wife of O. M. McMurray on the 13 day of May, 190 4; that there was born to her on said date a Male child; that said child is now living and is said to have been named Ervin McMurray

Dr W.E. Abbott

WITNESSES TO MARK:

Subscribed and sworn to before me this 24 day of April, 1905.

R.B. Coleman
NOTARY PUBLIC.

7-4818

Muskogee, Indian Territory, April 28, 1905.

O. M. McMurray,
    Crowder City, Indian Territory.

Dear Sir:

    Receipt is hereby acknowledged of the affidavits of Beckey McMurry[sic] and Dr. W. E. Abbott to the birth of Ervin McMurray, son of O. M. and Beckey McMurray, May 13, 1904, and the same have been filed with our records in the matter of the enrollment of said child.

Respectfully,

Chairman.

Applications for Enrollment of Choctaw Newborn
Act of 1905   Volume XVII

Choc. New Born 1277
    Salina Jefferson
    (Born Aug. 1, 1904)

        Cancelled and transferred to
           Chick. N. B. 519

1277

NEW BORN

Salina Jefferson
Born Aug. 1 1904

Choctaw Nation
(Act March 3 1905)

Cancelled and
Transferred to Chick.
N.B. 519

Choc. New Born 1278
    Douglas J. Pierce
    (Born Oct. 30, 1904)

NEW-BORN AFFIDAVIT.

        Number...............

Choctaw Enrolling Commission.

IN THE MATTER OF THE APPLICATION FOR ENROLLMENT, as a citizen of the Choctaw   Nation, of   Douglas J Pierce

born on the   30   day of   Oct   190 4

Name of father   Ed Pierce   a citizen of   Choctaw Nation final enrollment No   13786

Applications for Enrollment of Choctaw Newborn
Act of 1905 Volume XVII

Name of mother Belle Pierce   a citizen of   Choctaw
Nation final enrollment No   13787

                    Postoffice   Nelson, I.T.

AFFIDAVIT OF MOTHER.

UNITED STATES OF AMERICA,
   INDIAN TERRITORY,
  Central   DISTRICT

    I   Belle Pierce   on oath state that I am   34   years of age and a citizen by   Blood   of the   Choctaw   Nation, and as such have been placed upon the final roll of the   Choctaw   Nation, by the Honorable Secretary of the Interior my final enrollment number being   13787   ; that I am the lawful wife of   Ed Pierce   , who is a citizen of the   Choctaw   Nation, and as such has been placed upon the final roll of said Nation by the Honorable Secretary of the Interior, his final enrollment number being   13786   and that a   Male   child was born to me on the   30   day of   October   190 4 ; that said child has been named   Douglas J Pierce   , and is now living.

                                                Belle Pierce

WITNESSETH:
  Must be two   Henry Williams
  Witnesses who
  are Citizens.   Willy Griggs

      Subscribed and sworn to before me this   23   day of   Jan   190 5

                                  W.E. Larecy
                    My commission expires   Notary Public.
My commission expires   *July 9th, 1908.*

Affidavit of Attending Physician or Midwife

UNITED STATES OF AMERICA,
   INDIAN TERRITORY,
  Central   DISTRICT

    I,   Dr H Strachan   a   Physician   on oath state that I attended on Mrs. Bell[sic] Pierce   wife of   Ed Pierce   on the   Oct 30th   day of   1904   , 190 4, that there was born to her on said date a   Infant male   child, that said child is now living, and is said to have been named   Doglas[sic] J Pierce

                               H Strachan   M. D.

    Subscribed and sworn to before me this the   18   day of   January   1905

                                   H Morris
                                   Notary Public.

Applications for Enrollment of Choctaw Newborn
Act of 1905   Volume XVII

WITNESSETH:

Must be two witnesses who are citizens and know the child. { Willy Griggs
Mary Griggs

We hereby certify that we are well acquainted with D^r H Strachan a Physician and know him to be reputable and of good standing in the community.

Must be two citizen witnesses. { R.A. Woods
Henry Williams

BIRTH AFFIDAVIT.

DEPARTMENT OF THE INTERIOR.
COMMISSION TO THE FIVE CIVILIZED TRIBES.

IN RE APPLICATION FOR ENROLLMENT, as a citizen of the Choctaw Nation, of Douglas J. Pierce , born on the 30 day of Oct , 1904

Name of Father: Ed Pierce   a citizen of the Choctaw Nation.
Name of Mother: Belle Pierce   a citizen of the Choctaw Nation.

Postoffice   Soper Ind. Ter.

AFFIDAVIT OF MOTHER.

UNITED STATES OF AMERICA, Indian Territory, Central DISTRICT.

I, Belle Pierce , on oath state that I am 34 years of age and a citizen by blood , of the Choctaw Nation; that I am the lawful wife of Ed Pierce , who is a citizen, by blood of the Choctaw Nation; that a male child was born to me on 30 day of October , 1904; that said child has been named Douglas J. Pierce , and was living March 4, 1905.

Belle Pierce

Witnesses To Mark:

Subscribed and sworn to before me this 25th day of April , 1905

H. Morris
Notary Public.

Applications for Enrollment of Choctaw Newborn
Act of 1905   Volume XVII

AFFIDAVIT OF ATTENDING PHYSICIAN OR MID-WIFE.

UNITED STATES OF AMERICA, Indian Territory,
Central   DISTRICT.

I, H. Strachan, a Physician, on oath state that I attended on Mrs. Belle Pierce, wife of Ed Pierce on the 30th day of Oct., 1904; that there was born to her on said date a male child; that said child was living March 4, 1905, and is said to have been named Douglas J Pierce

H Strachan, M.D.

Witnesses To Mark:

Subscribed and sworn to before me this 25th day of April, 1905

H. Morris
Notary Public.

Choc. New Born 1279
  Houston Wesley
  (Born May 27, 1904)

NEW BORN AFFIDAVIT

No ....

CHOCTAW ENROLLING COMMISSION

IN THE MATTER OF THE APPLICATION FOR ENROLLMENT as a citizen of the Choctaw Nation, of Houston Wesley born on the 27th day of May 1904

Name of father   Edmond Wesley   a citizen of   Choctaw   Nation, final enrollment No. 4733
Name of mother   Rhoda Wesley   a citizen of   Choctaw   Nation, final enrollment No. 4734

Antlers   Postoffice.

Applications for Enrollment of Choctaw Newborn
Act of 1905   Volume XVII

AFFIDAVIT OF MOTHER

UNITED STATES OF AMERICA
INDIAN TERRITORY
DISTRICT   Central

I   Rhoda Wesley   , on oath state that I am   33   years of age and a citizen by   blood   of the   Choctaw   Nation, and as such have been placed upon the final roll of the   Choctaw   Nation, by the Honorable Secretary of the Interior my final enrollment number being   4734   ; that I am the lawful wife of   Edmond Wesley   , who is a citizen of the   Choctaw   Nation, and as such has been placed upon the final roll of said Nation by the Honorable Secretary of the Interior, his final enrollment number being   4733   and that a   Male   child was born to me on the   27th day of   May   190 4; that said child has been named   Houston Wesley   , and is now living.

Rhoda Wesley

WITNESSETH:
Must be two witnesses   { William Willis
who are citizens   Janey Willis

Subscribed and sworn to before me this, the   14   day of   Feby   , 190 5

A.J. Arnote
Notary Public.

My Commission Expires: May 16th 1907

Affidavit of Attending Physician or Midwife

UNITED STATES OF AMERICA,
INDIAN TERRITORY,
Central   DISTRICT

I,   Mulsie Nelson   a   Midwife on oath state that I attended on Mrs. Rhoda Wesley   wife of   Edmond Wesley on the   27th day of   May   , 190 4, that there was born to her on said date a   male   child, that said child is now living, and is said to have been named   Houston Wesley

Attest
S. P. Davenport

her
Mulsie x Nelson   *Midwife*
mark

Subscribed and sworn to before me this the   14   day of   Feby   1905

A.J. Arnote
Notary Public.

Applications for Enrollment of Choctaw Newborn
Act of 1905 Volume XVII

WITNESSETH:
Must be two witnesses who are citizens and know the child.
{ William Willis
  Janey Willis }

We hereby certify that we are well acquainted with Mulsie Nelson a Mid-wife and know her to be reputable and of good standing in the community.

Must be two citizen witnesses.
{ William Willis
  Janey Willis }

BIRTH AFFIDAVIT.

DEPARTMENT OF THE INTERIOR.
COMMISSION TO THE FIVE CIVILIZED TRIBES.

IN RE APPLICATION FOR ENROLLMENT, as a citizen of the Choctaw Nation, of Houston Wesley, born on the 27th day of May, 1904

Name of Father: Edmond Wesley   a citizen of the Choctaw Nation.
Name of Mother: Rhoda Wesley   a citizen of the Choctaw Nation.

Postoffice   Antlers, Ind. Ter.

AFFIDAVIT OF MOTHER.

UNITED STATES OF AMERICA, Indian Territory,
Central DISTRICT.

I, Rhoda Wesley, on oath state that I am 34 years of age and a citizen by blood, of the Choctaw Nation; that I am the lawful wife of Edmond Wesley, who is a citizen, by blood of the Choctaw Nation; that a male child was born to me on 27th day of May, 1904; that said child has been named Houston Wesley, and was living March 4, 1905.

           her
Rhoda x Wesley
      mark

Witnesses To Mark:
{ Robert Anderson
  Vester W Rose }

Subscribed and sworn to before me this 26th day of April, 1905.

             Wirt Franklin
                Notary Public.

Applications for Enrollment of Choctaw Newborn
Act of 1905   Volume XVII

AFFIDAVIT OF ATTENDING PHYSICIAN OR MID-WIFE.

UNITED STATES OF AMERICA, Indian Territory,
   Central   DISTRICT.

    I, Molsey[sic] Nelson, a mid-wife, on oath state that I attended on Mrs. Rhoda Wesley, wife of Edmond Wesley on the 27th day of May, 1904; that there was born to her on said date a male child; that said child was living March 4, 1905, and is said to have been named Houston Wesley

                                             her
                               Molsey x Nelson
Witnesses To Mark: mark
    { Robert Anderson
      Vester W Rose

    Subscribed and sworn to before me this 26th day of April, 1905

                               Wirt Franklin
                                Notary Public.

Choc. New Born 1280
    Bertha Elizabeth Nelson
    (Born Dec. 28, 1902)

BIRTH AFFIDAVIT.

DEPARTMENT OF THE INTERIOR.
COMMISSION TO THE FIVE CIVILIZED TRIBES.

    IN RE APPLICATION FOR ENROLLMENT, as a citizen of the Choctaw Nation, of Bertha Elizabeth Nelson, born on the 28th day of December, 1902

Name of Father: Eden Nelson   a citizen of the Choctaw Nation.
Name of Mother: Laura Nelson   a citizen of the Choctaw Nation.

                        Postoffice   Antlers, Ind. Ter.

Applications for Enrollment of Choctaw Newborn
Act of 1905   Volume XVII

AFFIDAVIT OF MOTHER.

UNITED STATES OF AMERICA, Indian Territory, }
Central   DISTRICT.

I, Laura Nelson, on oath state that I am 29 years of age and a citizen by blood, of the Choctaw Nation; that I am the lawful wife of Eden Nelson, who is a citizen, by blood of the Choctaw Nation; that a female child was born to me on 28th day of December, 1902; that said child has been named Bertha Elizabeth Nelson, and was living March 4, 1905.

                                       Laura Nelson

Witnesses To Mark:
{

Subscribed and sworn to before me this 26th day of April, 1905

                                       Wirt Franklin
                                       Notary Public.

AFFIDAVIT OF ATTENDING PHYSICIAN OR MID-WIFE.

UNITED STATES OF AMERICA, Indian Territory, }
Central   DISTRICT.

I, Lula Nelson, a mid-wife, on oath state that I attended on Mrs. Laura Nelson, wife of Eden Nelson on the 28th day of December, 1902; that there was born to her on said date a female child; that said child was living March 4, 1905, and is said to have been named Bertha Elizabeth Nelson
                                       her
                                  Lula x Nelson

Witnesses To Mark: mark
{ Vester W Rose
  Robert Anderson

Subscribed and sworn to before me this 26th day of April, 1905

                                       Wirt Franklin
                                       Notary Public.

Applications for Enrollment of Choctaw Newborn
Act of 1905 Volume XVII

Choc. New Born 1281
    Ollie Hampton
    (Born Aug. 28, 1904)

BIRTH AFFIDAVIT.

DEPARTMENT OF THE INTERIOR.
COMMISSION TO THE FIVE CIVILIZED TRIBES.

IN RE APPLICATION FOR ENROLLMENT, as a citizen of the Choctaw Nation, of Ollie Hampton, born on the 28th day of August, 1904

Name of Father: Johnson Hampton   a citizen of the Choctaw Nation.
Name of Mother: Frances Hampton   a citizen of the Choctaw Nation.

Postoffice   Antlers, Ind. Ter.

AFFIDAVIT OF MOTHER.

UNITED STATES OF AMERICA, Indian Territory,
Central   DISTRICT.

    I, Frances Hampton, on oath state that I am 30 years of age and a citizen by blood, of the Choctaw Nation; that I am the lawful wife of Johnson Hampton, who is a citizen, by blood of the Choctaw Nation; that a female child was born to me on 28th day of August, 1904; that said child has been named Ollie Hampton, and was living March 4, 1905.

                                 Frances Hampton

Witnesses To Mark:

    Subscribed and sworn to before me this 26th day of April, 1905

                                 Wirt Franklin
                                 Notary Public.

AFFIDAVIT OF ATTENDING PHYSICIAN OR MID-WIFE.

UNITED STATES OF AMERICA, Indian Territory,
Central   DISTRICT.

    I, Lucy Landis, a mid-wife, on oath state that I attended on Mrs. Frances Hampton, wife of Johnson Hampton on the 28th day of

Applications for Enrollment of Choctaw Newborn
Act of 1905 Volume XVII

August   , 1904; that there was born to her on said date a   female   child; that said child was living March 4, 1905, and is said to have been named Ollie Hampton

Lucy Landi

Witnesses To Mark:
{

Subscribed and sworn to before me this 26th day of   April   , 1905

Wirt Franklin
Notary Public.

Choc. New Born 1282
Olin Vernon Hoyt
(Born Sep. 5, 1903)

NEW-BORN AFFIDAVIT.

Number..................

...Choctaw Enrolling Commission...

IN THE MATTER OF THE APPLICATION FOR ENROLLMENT, as a citizen of the Choctaw   Nation, of   Olin V. Hoyt

born on the 6[sic]   day of   September   190 3

Name of father Milo A. Hoyt   a citizen of   Choctaw
Nation final enrollment No. 15434
Name of mother   Lizzie Hoyt   a citizen of   Choctaw
Nation final enrollment No. 917

Postoffice   Hoyt, I.T.

Applications for Enrollment of Choctaw Newborn
Act of 1905   Volume XVII

AFFIDAVIT OF MOTHER.

UNITED STATES OF AMERICA
INDIAN TERRITORY
Western   DISTRICT

I   Lizzie Hoyt   , on oath state that I am   28   years of age and a citizen by   Intermarriage   of the   Choctaw   Nation, and as such have been placed upon the final roll of the   Choctaw   Nation, by the Honorable Secretary of the Interior my final enrollment number being   917   ; that I am the lawful wife of   Milo A Hoyt   , who is a citizen of the   Choctaw   Nation, and as such has been placed upon the final roll of said Nation by the Honorable Secretary of the Interior, his final enrollment number being   15434   and that a   Male   child was born to me on the   6   day of   September   190 3; that said child has been named   Olin V. Hoyt   , and is now living.

Lizzie Hoyt

Witnesseth.

Must be two Witnesses who are Citizens.   J.D. Bench
Bettie Bench

Subscribed and sworn to before me this   4   day of   Jan   190 5

John M. Lentz
Notary Public.

My commission expires: Nov 27 1907

AFFIDAVIT OF ATTENDING PHYSICIAN OR MIDWIFE

UNITED STATES OF AMERICA
INDIAN TERRITORY
Western   DISTRICT

I,   T.B. Turner   a   Physician   on oath state that I attended on Mrs.   Lizzie Hoyt   wife of Milo A Hoyt on the   6th[sic]   day of   September   , 190 3 , that there was born to her on said date a male   child, that said child is now living, and is said to have been named   Olin Hoyt

T.B. Turner   M.D.

Subscribed and sworn to before me this, the   27   day of   February   190 5

WITNESSETH:
Must be two witnesses who are citizens   J.D. Bench
Bettie Bench

John M Lentz   Notary Public.

Applications for Enrollment of Choctaw Newborn
Act of 1905 Volume XVII

We hereby certify that we are well acquainted with T.B. Turner a Practicing Physician and know him to be reputable and of good standing in the community.

J.D. Bench _____

Sam Bench _____

BIRTH AFFIDAVIT.

DEPARTMENT OF THE INTERIOR.
COMMISSION TO THE FIVE CIVILIZED TRIBES.

IN RE APPLICATION FOR ENROLLMENT, as a citizen of the Choctaw Nation, of Olin Vernon Hoyt, born on the 5th day of September, 1903

Name of Father: Milo A. Hoyt   a citizen of the Choctaw Nation.
Name of Mother: Lizzie Hoyt   a citizen of the Choctaw Nation.

Postoffice Hoyt I.T.

AFFIDAVIT OF MOTHER.

UNITED STATES OF AMERICA, Indian Territory, }
Western DISTRICT. }

I, Lizzie Hoyt, on oath state that I am 29 years of age and a citizen by Marriage, of the Choctaw Nation; that I am the lawful wife of Milo A. Hoyt, who is a citizen, by Blood of the Choctaw Nation; that a Male child was born to me on the 5th day of September, 1903; that said child has been named Olin Vernon Hoyt, and was living March 4, 1905.

Lizzie Hoyt

Witnesses To Mark:
{ *(Name Illegible)*
{ J.N. Prince

Subscribed and sworn to before me this 22 day of April, 1905

my commission
Expires Nov 27 1907

John M Lentz
Notary Public.

Applications for Enrollment of Choctaw Newborn
Act of 1905 Volume XVII

AFFIDAVIT OF ATTENDING PHYSICIAN OR MID-WIFE.

UNITED STATES OF AMERICA, Indian Territory, }
Western DISTRICT.

I, T.B. Turner, a Physician, on oath state that I attended on Mrs. Lizzie Hoyt, wife of Milo A Hoyt on the 5 day of September, 1903; that there was born to her on said date a Male child; that said child was living March 4, 1905, and is said to have been named Olin Vernon Hoyt

T.B. Turner

Witnesses To Mark:
{ *(Name Illegible)*
{ J.N. Prince

Subscribed and sworn to before me this 22 day of April, 1905

my commission
Expires Nov 27 1907

John M Lentz
Notary Public.

BIRTH AFFIDAVIT.

DEPARTMENT OF THE INTERIOR.
COMMISSION TO THE FIVE CIVILIZED TRIBES.

IN RE APPLICATION FOR ENROLLMENT, as a citizen of the Choctaw Nation, of Olin Vernon Hoyt, born on the 5 day of September, 1903.

Name of Father: Milo A. Hoyt   *Roll 15434*   a citizen of the Choctaw Nation.
Name of Mother: Lizzie Hoyt   " *?.W.917*   a citizen of the Choctaw Nation.

Postoffice   Hoyt I.T.

AFFIDAVIT OF MOTHER.

UNITED STATES OF AMERICA, Indian Territory, }
Western DISTRICT.

I, Lizzie Hoyt, on oath state that I am 29 years of age and a citizen by marriage, of the Choctaw Nation; that I am the lawful wife of Milo A. Hoyt, who is a citizen, by Blood of the Choctaw Nation; that a Male child was born to me on the 5 day of September, 1903; that said child has been named Olin Vernon Hoyt, and was living March 4, 1905.

Lizzie Hoyt

Applications for Enrollment of Choctaw Newborn
Act of 1905   Volume XVII

Witnesses To Mark:
  { W.T. Carlton
  { H.B. Carlton

Subscribed and sworn to before me this 9 day of June, 1905

My commission
Expires Nov 27 1907

John M Lentz
Notary Public.

AFFIDAVIT OF ATTENDING PHYSICIAN OR MID-WIFE.

UNITED STATES OF AMERICA, Indian Territory,
  Western   DISTRICT.

I, T.B. Turner, a Physician, on oath state that I attended on Mrs. Lizzie Hoyt, wife of Milo A Hoyt on the 5 day of September, 1903; that there was born to her on said date a Male child; that said child was living March 4, 1905, and is said to have been named Olin Vernon Hoyt

T.B. Turner M.D.

Witnesses To Mark:
  { W.T. Carlton
  { H.B. Carlton

Subscribed and sworn to before me this 9 day of June, 1905

My commission
Expires Nov 27 1907

John M Lentz
Notary Public.

7-2990

Muskogee, Indian Territory, April 28, 1905.

Milo A. Hoyt,
  Hoyt, Indian Territory.

Dear Sir:

Receipt is hereby acknowledged of the affidavits of Lizzie Hoyt and T. B. Turner to the birth of Olin Vernon Hoyt, son of Milo A. and Lizzie Hoyt, September 5, 1903, and the same have been filed in the matter of the enrollment of said child.

Respectfully,

Chairman.

Applications for Enrollment of Choctaw Newborn
Act of 1905   Volume XVII

7-NB-1282

Muskogee, Indian Territory, June 2, 1905.

Milo A. Hoyt,
    Hoyt, Indian Territory.

Dear Sir:

    There is enclosed you herewith for execution application for the enrollment of your infant child, Olin Vernon Hoyt.

    In the affidavits of January 4, 1905, the date of the birth of the applicant is given as September 6, 1903, while in the affidavits dated April 22, 1905, this date is given as September 5, 1903. In the enclosed application the date of birth is left blank. Pleas insert the correct date and when the affidavits are properly executed return them to this office.

    In having the affidavits executed care should be exercised to see that all names are written in full, as they appear in the body of the affidavits and in the event that either of the persons signing the affidavit are unable to write, signatures by mark must be attested by two witnesses. Each affidavit must be executed before a Notary Public and the notarial seal and signature of the officer must be attached to each separate affidavit.

    This matter should receive your immediate attention as no further action can be taken relative to the enrollment of said child until the Commission has been furnished these affidavits.

        Respectfully,

        Commissioner in Charge.

Enc-FVK-9

---

7 NB 1282

Muskogee, Indian Territory, June 14, 1905

Milo A. Hoyt,
    Hoyt, Indian Territory.

Dear Sir:

    Receipt is hereby acknowledged of the affidavits of Lizzie Hoyt and T. B. Turner to the birth of Olin Vernon Hoyt, son of Milo A. and Lizzie Hoyt, September 5, 1903, and the same have been filed in the matter of the enrollment of said child.

        Respectfully,

        Chairman.

Applications for Enrollment of Choctaw Newborn
Act of 1905   Volume XVII

Choc. New Born 1283
    Frank Adkins
    (Born Dec. 1, 1902)
    Roscoe Adkins
    (Born Aug. 12, 1904)

Cleveland Co.
Norman, O.T.
Dec 12 - 1902

To whom it may concern -
this is to certify that I attended
Mrs. John Adkins in confinement
on the first day of Dec 1902 when
she was delivered of a male child
healthy & sound.
    R.D. Lowther M.D.

Subscribed and sworn to this 12th
day of Dec 1902
    (Name Illegible) N.P.
My com. Ex April 12, 1905

BIRTH AFFIDAVIT.

DEPARTMENT OF THE INTERIOR.
COMMISSION TO THE FIVE CIVILIZED TRIBES.

    IN RE APPLICATION FOR ENROLLMENT, as a citizen of the   Choctaw Nation Nation, of   Frank. Adkins.   , born on the   1st   day of December   , 1902

Name of Father: John A. Adkins.   a citizen of the   Choctaw   Nation.
Name of Mother: Tobitha. Adkins.   a citizen of the   Choctaw   Nation.

    Postoffice   Norman, Okla.

Applications for Enrollment of Choctaw Newborn
Act of 1905   Volume XVII

AFFIDAVIT OF MOTHER.

UNITED STATES OF AMERICA, Okla Territory, }
Cleveland   DISTRICT.

I, Tobitha. Adkins. , on oath state that I am twenty eight years of age and a citizen by blood , of the Choctaw Nation; that I am the lawful wife of John A. Adkins , who is a citizen, by marriage of the Choctaw Nation; that a male child was born to me on 1st day of December , 1902; that said child has been named Frank. Adkins. , and was living March 4, 1905.

Tobitha Adkins

Witnesses To Mark:
{ Wm Symoth
{ Lotin Jones

Subscribed and sworn to before me this 22nd day of April , 1905

8

(Name Illegible)
Notary Public.

AFFIDAVIT OF ATTENDING PHYSICIAN OR MID-WIFE.

UNITED STATES OF AMERICA, Okla Territory, }
Cleveland   DISTRICT.

I, R. D. Lowther. , a Physician , on oath state that I attended on Mrs. Tobitha. Adkins , wife of John A. Adkins. on the 1st day of December , 1905[sic]; that there was born to her on said date a male child; that said child was living March 4, 1905, and is said to have been named Frank. Adkins.

R.D. Lowther M.D.

Witnesses To Mark:
{

Subscribed and sworn to before me this 22nd day of April , 1905

(Name Illegible)
Notary Public.

Commission Expires April 22, 1908

Applications for Enrollment of Choctaw Newborn
Act of 1905 Volume XVII

BIRTH AFFIDAVIT.

DEPARTMENT OF THE INTERIOR.
COMMISSION TO THE FIVE CIVILIZED TRIBES.

IN RE APPLICATION FOR ENROLLMENT, as a citizen of the Choctaw Nation, of Roscoe. Adkins. , born on the 12th day of August , 1904

Name of Father: John A. Adkins. a citizen of the Choctaw Nation.
Name of Mother: Tobitha. Adkins. a citizen of the Choctaw Nation.

Postoffice Norman, Okla.

AFFIDAVIT OF MOTHER.

UNITED STATES OF AMERICA, Okla Territory, }
Cleveland County xxxxxxxx }

I, Tobitha. Adkins. , on oath state that I am twenty eight years of age and a citizen by blood , of the Choctaw Nation; that I am the lawful wife of John A. Adkins , who is a citizen, by marriage of the Choctaw Nation; that a male child was born to me on 12th day of August , 1904; that said child has been named Roscoe. Adkins. , and was living March 4, 1905.

Tobitha Adkins

Witnesses To Mark:
{ Wm Symoth
{ Lotin Jones

Subscribed and sworn to before me this 22nd day of April , 1905

8 *(Name Illegible)*
Notary Public.

AFFIDAVIT OF ATTENDING PHYSICIAN OR MID-WIFE.

UNITED STATES OF AMERICA, Okla Territory, }
Cleveland County xxxxxxxx }

I, R. D. Lowther. , a Physician. , on oath state that I attended on Mrs. Tobitha. Adkins. , wife of John A. Adkins. on the 12th day of August , 1904; that there was born to her on said date a male child; that said child was living March 4, 1905, and is said to have been named Roscoe. Adkins.

R.D. Lowther M.D.

Applications for Enrollment of Choctaw Newborn
Act of 1905   Volume XVII

Witnesses To Mark:
{

Subscribed and sworn to before me this 22nd day of April , 1905

(Name Illegible)

Commission Expires April 22, 1908   Notary Public.

BIRTH AFFIDAVIT.

DEPARTMENT OF THE INTERIOR.
COMMISSION TO THE FIVE CIVILIZED TRIBES.

 IN RE APPLICATION FOR ENROLLMENT, as a citizen of the   Choctaw   Nation, of Frank Adkins , born on the ....day of ...., 1........

Name of Father: John A Adkins   Roll ?.W. 623 a citizen of the   Choctaw   Nation.
Name of Mother: Tobitha Adkins   "   384 a citizen of the   Choctaw   Nation.

Postoffice   Norman Okla

AFFIDAVIT OF MOTHER.

UNITED STATES OF AMERICA, Indian Territory, }
.... DISTRICT. }

I, ..., on oath state that I am .... years of age and a citizen by ...., of the .... Nation; that I am the lawful wife of ...., who is a citizen, by .... of the .... Nation; that a .... child was born to me on ......day of ...., 1......., that said child has been named ...., and was living March 4, 1905.

Witnesses To Mark:
{

Subscribed and sworn to before me this ...... day of ...., 1905.

Notary Public.

153

Applications for Enrollment of Choctaw Newborn
Act of 1905 Volume XVII

AFFIDAVIT OF ATTENDING PHYSICIAN OR MID-WIFE.

UNITED STATES OF AMERICA, Okla Territory,
Cleveland County   DISTRICT.

I, RD Lowther , a Physician , on oath state that I attended on Mrs Tobitha Adkins , wife of John A Adkins on the 1st day of December , 1902; that there was born to her on said date a Male child; that said child was living March 4, 1905, and is said to have been named Frank Adkins

R.D. Lowther M.D.

Witnesses To Mark:

Subscribed and sworn to before me this 12th day of June , 1905

(Name Illegible)
Notary Public.

7-188

Muskogee, Indian Territory, April 28, 1905.

John A. Adkins,
    Norman, Oklahoma, Territory.

Dear Sir:

Receipt is hereby acknowledged of the affidavits of Tobitha Adkins and R. D. Lowther to the birth of Frank Adkins and Roscoe Adkins, children of John A. and Tobitha Adkins, December 1, 1902 and August 12, 1904, respectively, and the same have been filed with our records as an application for the enrollment of said children.

Respectfully,

Chairman.

Applications for Enrollment of Choctaw Newborn
Act of 1905   Volume XVII

7--NB--1283

Muskogee, Indian Territory, June 2, 1905.

John A. Adkins,
    Norman, Oklahoma.

Dear Sir:

    There is enclosed you herewith for execution application for the enrollment of your infant child, Frank Adkins.

    In the affidavit of the mother of this applicant dated April 22, 1905, the date of his birth is given as December 1, 1902, while in the affidavit of the physician executed on the same date, this date is given as December 1, 1905. In the enclosed application the date of birth is left blank. Please insert the correct date and when the affidavits are properly executed return them to this office.

    In having these affidavits executed care should be exercised to see that all names are written in full, as they appear in the body of the affidavit, and in the event that either of the persons signing the affidavit are unable to write, signatures by mark must be attested by two witnesses. Each affidavit must be executed before a Notary Public and the notarial seal and signature of the officer must be attached to each separate affidavit.

    This matter should receive your immediate attention as no further action can be taken relative to the enrollment of said [sic] until the Commission has been furnished these affidavits.

                      Respectfully,

Enc-FVK-7   [sic]

---

7 NB 1283

Muskogee, Indian Territory, June 16, 1905.

John A. Adkins,
    Norman, Oklahoma.

Dear Sir:

    Receipt is hereby acknowledged of the affidavit of R. D. Lowther to the birth of Frank Adkins, son of John A. and Tobitha Adkins, December 1, 1902, and the same has been filed with our records in the matter of the enrollment of said child.

                      Respectfully,

                                          Chairman.

Applications for Enrollment of Choctaw Newborn
Act of 1905   Volume XVII

Choc. New Born 1284
    May Middleton
    (Born July 4, 1904)

BIRTH AFFIDAVIT.

DEPARTMENT OF THE INTERIOR.
COMMISSION TO THE FIVE CIVILIZED TRIBES.

IN RE APPLICATION FOR ENROLLMENT, as a citizen of the Choctaw Nation, of May Middleton, born on the 4th day of July, 1904

Name of Father: Charles Middleton   a citizen of the Choctaw Nation.
Name of Mother: Agnes Middleton   a citizen of the Choctaw Nation.

Postoffice   Wade Ind. T

AFFIDAVIT OF MOTHER.

UNITED STATES OF AMERICA, Indian Territory,
    Central   **DISTRICT.**

I, Agnes Middleton, on oath state that I am 30 years of age and a citizen by Blood, of the Choctaw Nation; that I am the lawful wife of Charles Middleton, who is a citizen, by Blood of the Choctaw Nation; that a Female child was born to me on 4th day of July, 1904; that said child has been named May Middleton, and was living March 4, 1905.

                                          Agnes Middleton
Witnesses To Mark:

Subscribed and sworn to before me this 22 day of Apr, 1905

                                          J.M. Reasor
                                              Notary Public.

AFFIDAVIT OF ATTENDING PHYSICIAN OR MID-WIFE.

UNITED STATES OF AMERICA, Indian Territory,
    Central   **DISTRICT.**

I, Margaret Meeks, a Midwife, on oath state that I attended on Mrs. Middleton, wife of Charles Middleton on the 4th day of July,

Applications for Enrollment of Choctaw Newborn
Act of 1905 Volume XVII

1904; that there was born to her on said date a   Female   child; that said child was living March 4, 1905, and is said to have been named   May Middleton

her
Margaret x Meeks
mark

Witnesses To Mark:
   { d french[sic]
    T.J. Hammock Jr.

    Subscribed and sworn to before me this 22 day of   Apr   , 1905

J.M. Reasor
Notary Public.

7-3593

Muskogee, Indian Territory, April 28, 1905.

Charles Middleton,
    Wade, Indian Territory.

Dear Sir:

    Receipt is hereby acknowledged of the affidavits of Agnes Middleton and Margaret Meeks to the birth of Mary Middleton, daughter of Charles and Agnes Middleton, July 4, 1904, and the same have been filed with our records as an application for the enrollment of said child.

Respectfully,

Chairman.

Choc. New Born 1285
    Alice Eva Nail
    (Born Dec. 10, 1904)

Applications for Enrollment of Choctaw Newborn
Act of 1905   Volume XVII

NEW-BORN AFFIDAVIT.

Number..............

Choctaw Enrolling Commission.

IN THE MATTER OF THE APPLICATION FOR ENROLLMENT, as a citizen of the Choctaw   Nation, of   Alice Eva Nail

born on the 10th day of   December   190 4

Name of father   Edward J. Nail   a citizen of   Choctaw
Nation final enrollment No   10071
Name of mother   Beulah M Nail   a citizen of   Choctaw
Nation final enrollment No   139

Postoffice   Durant I.T.

AFFIDAVIT OF MOTHER.

UNITED STATES OF AMERICA,
INDIAN TERRITORY,
Central   DISTRICT

I   Beulah M Nail   on oath state that I am 23 years of age and a citizen by   intermarriage   of the Choctaw   Nation, and as such have been placed upon the final roll of the   Choctaw   Nation, by the Honorable Secretary of the Interior my final enrollment number being   139   ; that I am the lawful wife of   Edward J. Nail   , who is a citizen of the   Choctaw Nation, and as such has been placed upon the final roll of said Nation by the Honorable Secretary of the Interior, his final enrollment number being   10071   and that a   Female child was born to me on the   10th   day of   December   190 4 ; that said child has been named   Alice Eva Nail   , and is now living.

Beulah M Nail

WITNESSETH:
Must be two Witnesses who are Citizens.   *(Name Illegible)*
Green Thompson

Subscribed and sworn to before me this   30th   day of   January   190 5

B.F. Moreman
Notary Public.

My commission expires   Nov 11th 1907

Applications for Enrollment of Choctaw Newborn
Act of 1905 Volume XVII

Affidavit of Attending Physician or Midwife.

UNITED STATES OF AMERICA
INDIAN TERRITORY
  Central   DISTRICT

I, J.J. Stephens   a   Physician on oath state that I attended on Mrs. Beulah M Nail wife of Edward J. Nail on the 10th day of December , 190 4 , that there was born to her on said date a Female child, that said child is now living, and is said to have been named Alice Eva Nail

                            John J Stephens   M.D.

Subscribed and sworn to before me this, the 30th day of January   190 5

                            BF. Moreman
                                  Notary Public.

WITNESSETH:
Must be two witnesses who are citizens and know the child.
    (Name Illegible)
    Green Thompson

We hereby certify that we are well acquainted with J.J. Stephens a Physician and know him to be reputable and of good standing in the community.

    (Name Illegible)
    Green Thompson

BIRTH AFFIDAVIT.

DEPARTMENT OF THE INTERIOR.
COMMISSION TO THE FIVE CIVILIZED TRIBES.

IN RE APPLICATION FOR ENROLLMENT, as a citizen of the Choctaw Nation, of Alice Eva Nail , born on the 10th day of December , 1904

Name of Father: Edward J Nail   a citizen of the Choctaw Nation.
Name of Mother: Beulah M Nail   a citizen of the Choctaw Nation.

                    Postoffice   Durant I.T.

Applications for Enrollment of Choctaw Newborn
Act of 1905   Volume XVII

AFFIDAVIT OF MOTHER.

UNITED STATES OF AMERICA, Indian Territory, }
Central   DISTRICT.

I, Beulah M. Nail, on oath state that I am 23 years of age and a citizen by Marriage, of the Choctaw Nation; that I am the lawful wife of Edward J. Nail, who is a citizen, by blood of the Choctaw Nation; that a female child was born to me on 10th day of December, 1904; that said child has been named Alice Eva Nail, and was living March 4, 1905.

Beulah M. Nail

Witnesses To Mark:
{ (Name Illegible)
  CW Early

Subscribed and sworn to before me this 22nd day of April, 1905

B.F. Moreman
Notary Public.

AFFIDAVIT OF ATTENDING PHYSICIAN OR MID-WIFE.

UNITED STATES OF AMERICA, Indian Territory, }
Central   DISTRICT.

I, J.J. Stephens, a Physician, on oath state that I attended on Mrs. Beulah M Nail, wife of Edward J Nail on the 10th day of December, 1905[sic]; that there was born to her on said date a female child; that said child was living March 4, 1905, and is said to have been named Alice Eva Nail

J.J. Stephens M.D.

Witnesses To Mark:
{ (Name Illegible)
  CW Early

Subscribed and sworn to before me this 22nd day of April, 1905

B.F. Moreman
Notary Public.

Applications for Enrollment of Choctaw Newborn
Act of 1905   Volume XVII

BIRTH AFFIDAVIT.

DEPARTMENT OF THE INTERIOR.
COMMISSION TO THE FIVE CIVILIZED TRIBES.

IN RE APPLICATION FOR ENROLLMENT, as a citizen of the Choctaw Nation, of Alice Eva Nail, born on the _____ day of _____, 1____.

Name of Father: Edward J Nail   Roll 10071   a citizen of the Choctaw Nation.
Name of Mother: Beulah M Nail   " ?.W. 139   a citizen of the Choctaw Nation.

Postoffice   Durant I.T.

AFFIDAVIT OF MOTHER.

UNITED STATES OF AMERICA, Indian Territory, } DISTRICT.

I, _____, on oath state that I am _____ years of age and a citizen by _____, of the _____ Nation; that I am the lawful wife of _____, who is a citizen, by _____ of the _____ Nation; that a child was born to me on _____ day of _____, 1____, that said child has been named _____, and was living March 4, 1905.

Witnesses To Mark:

Subscribed and sworn to before me this _____ day of _____, 1905.

_____
Notary Public.

AFFIDAVIT OF ATTENDING PHYSICIAN OR MID-WIFE.

UNITED STATES OF AMERICA, Indian Territory, } Central   DISTRICT.

I, J.J. Stephens, a Physician, on oath state that I attended on Mrs. Beulah M Nail, wife of Edward J Nail on the 10th day of December, 1904; that there was born to her on said date a female child; that said child was living March 4, 1905, and is said to have been named Alice Eva Nail

J.J. Stephens

Witnesses To Mark:

Applications for Enrollment of Choctaw Newborn
Act of 1905   Volume XVII

Subscribed and sworn to before me this 19th day of June , 1905

B.F. Moreman
Notary Public.

7-3553

Muskogee, Indian Territory, April 28, 1905.

Edward J. Nail,
 Durant, Indian Territory.

Dear Sir:

Receipt is hereby acknowledged of the affidavits of Beulah M. Nail and J. J. Stephens to the birth of Alice Eva Nail, daughter of Edward J. and Beulah M. Nail, December 10, 1904, and the same have been filed with our records as an application for the enrollment of said child.

Respectfully,

Chairman.

7--NB--1285

Muskogee, Indian Territory, June 2, 1905.

Edward J. Nail,
 Durant, Indian Territory.

Dear Sir:

There is enclosed you herewith for execution application for the enrollment of your infant child, Alice Eva Nail.

In the affidavit of the mother of this applicant dated April 22, 1905, the date of her birth is given as December 10, 1904, while in the affidavit of the physician executed on the same date the date of the birth of this applicant is given as December 10, 1905. In the enclosed affidavit the date of birth is left blank. Please insert the correct date and when the affidavit is properly executed return to this office.

In have[sic] the affidavit executed care should be exercised to see that all names are written in full, as they appear in the body of the affidavit, and in the event the person signing the same is unable to write, signature by mark must be attested by two witnesses. The affidavit must be executed before a Notary Public and the notarial seal and signature of the officer must be attached thereto.

Applications for Enrollment of Choctaw Newborn
Act of 1905   Volume XVII

This matter should receive your immediate attention as no further action can be taken relative to the enrollment of this child until the Commission has been furnished this affidavit.

Respectfully,

Enc-FVK-8 [sic]

---

7 NB 1285

Muskogee, Indian Territory, June 21, 1905.

Edward J. Nail,
    Durant, Indian Territory.

Dear Sir:

Receipt is hereby acknowledged of the affidavit of John J. Stephens to the birth of Alice Eva Nail, daughter of Edward J. and Beulah M. Nail, December 10, 1904, and the same has been filed in the matter of the enrollment of said child.

Respectfully,

Chairman.

Choc. New Born 1286
    Lovina Wheeler
    (Born Dec. 31, 1904)

BIRTH AFFIDAVIT.   7-8435

DEPARTMENT OF THE INTERIOR.
COMMISSION TO THE FIVE CIVILIZED TRIBES.

IN RE APPLICATION FOR ENROLLMENT, as a citizen of the Choctaw Nation, of Lovina Wheeler, born on the 31st day of December, 1904

Name of Father: William P. Wheeler   a citizen of the U States Nation.
Name of Mother: Louisa Wheeler   a citizen of the Choctaw Nation.

Postoffice   Heavener I.T.

Applications for Enrollment of Choctaw Newborn
Act of 1905   Volume XVII

AFFIDAVIT OF MOTHER.

UNITED STATES OF AMERICA, Indian Territory, }
Central   DISTRICT.

I, Louisa Wheeler, on oath state that I am 24 years of age and a citizen by blood, of the Choctaw Nation; that I am the lawful wife of William P. Wheeler, who is a citizen, by ——— of the United States Nation; that a female child was born to me on 31st day of December, 1904; that said child has been named Lovina Wheeler, and was living March 4, 1905.

                            her
                     Louisa x Wheeler
Witnesses To Mark: mark
{ Chas T Difendafer
{ OL Johnson

Subscribed and sworn to before me this 18 day of April, 1905

                         OL Johnson
                         Notary Public.

AFFIDAVIT OF ATTENDING PHYSICIAN OR MID-WIFE.

UNITED STATES OF AMERICA, Indian Territory, }
Central   DISTRICT.

I, Lovina Thursten, a midwife, on oath state that I attended on Mrs. Louisa Wheeler, wife of William P Wheeler on the 31 day of December, 1904; that there was born to her on said date a female child; that said child was living March 4, 1905, and is said to have been named Lovina Wheeler

                         Lovina Thursten
Witnesses To Mark:
{

Subscribed and sworn to before me this 25th day of April, 1905

                         R.J. Charles
                         Notary Public.

Applications for Enrollment of Choctaw Newborn
Act of 1905 Volume XVII

7-2867

Muskogee, Indian Territory, April 28, 1905.

William P. Wheeler,
    Heavener, Indian Territory.

Dear Sir:

    Receipt is hereby acknowledged of the affidavits of Louisa Wheeler and Lovina Thursten to the birth of Lovina Wheeler daughter of William P. and Louisa Wheeler, December 31, 1904, and the same have been filed with our records as an application for the enrollment of said child.

                        Respectfully,

                                      Chairman.

Choc. New Born 1287
    Dorsey Edmond Cowen
    (Born Aug. 31, 1904)

BIRTH AFFIDAVIT.

DEPARTMENT OF THE INTERIOR.
COMMISSION TO THE FIVE CIVILIZED TRIBES.

IN RE APPLICATION FOR ENROLLMENT, as a citizen of the Choctaw Nation, of Dorsey Edmond Cowen, born on the 31st day of August, 1904

Name of Father: S. B. Cowen   *not* a citizen of the Choctaw Nation.
Name of Mother: Susan Cowen   a citizen of the Choctaw Nation.

                      Postoffice   Hartshorne, Indian Territory.

AFFIDAVIT OF MOTHER.

UNITED STATES OF AMERICA, Indian Territory, }
    Central   DISTRICT. }

    I, Susan Cowen, on oath state that I am eighteen years of age and a citizen by blood, of the Choctaw Nation; that I am the lawful wife of

Applications for Enrollment of Choctaw Newborn
Act of 1905 Volume XVII

S. B. Cowen, who is *not* a citizen, by Intermarriage of the Choctaw Nation; that a Male child was born to me on 31st day of August, 1904; that said child has been named Dorsey Edmond Cowen, and was living March 4, 1905.

Susan Cowen

Witnesses To Mark:
{

Subscribed and sworn to before me this 25th day of April, 1905

My commission expires
10/8 1906

Geo W Walshe
Notary Public.
Central District, Indian Territory

AFFIDAVIT OF ATTENDING PHYSICIAN OR MID-WIFE.

UNITED STATES OF AMERICA, Indian Territory, }
Central   DISTRICT.

I, Francis Cowen, a Female, on oath state that I attended on Mrs. Susan Cowen, wife of S. B. Cowen on the 31st day of August, 1904; that there was born to her on said date a Male child; that said child was living March 4, 1905, and is said to have been named Dorsey Edmond

Francis Cowen

Witnesses To Mark:
{

Subscribed and sworn to before me this 7th day of April, 1905

My commission expires 12-5-06./

T.M. Hinsley
Central District, I.T.......Notary Public.

Applications for Enrollment of Choctaw Newborn
Act of 1905 Volume XVII

7-3209.

Muskogee, Indian Territory, April 28, 1905.

S. B. Cowen,
    Hartshorne, Indian Territory.

Dear Sir:

    Receipt is hereby acknowledged of the affidavits of Susan Cowen and Francis Cowen to the birth of Dorsey Edmond Cowen, son of S. B. and Susan Cowen, August 31, 1904, and the same have been filed with our records as an application for the enrollment of said child.

                      Respectfully,

                                          Chairman.

Choc. New Born 1288
    Theodore Roosevelt Impson
    (Born Sep. 1, 1903)

NEW BORN AFFIDAVIT

No

CHOCTAW ENROLLING COMMISSION

IN THE MATTER OF THE APPLICATION FOR ENROLLMENT as a citizen of the Choctaw Nation, of   Teddie Impson   born on the 1st day of September 190 3

Name of father   Isaac Impson   a citizen of   Choctaw   Nation, final enrollment No. 659
Name of mother   Lillie Impson   a citizen of   ———   Nation, final enrollment No. ——

                            Caddo I.T.   Postoffice.

Applications for Enrollment of Choctaw Newborn
Act of 1905   Volume XVII

AFFIDAVIT OF MOTHER

UNITED STATES OF AMERICA
    INDIAN TERRITORY
DISTRICT   Central

I   Lillie Impson   , on oath state that I am   21   years of age and a citizen by   ——   of the   ——   Nation, and as such have been placed upon the final roll of the   ——   Nation, by the Honorable Secretary of the Interior my final enrollment number being —— ; that I am the lawful wife of   Isaac Impson   , who is a citizen of the   Choctaw   Nation, and as such has been placed upon the final roll of said Nation by the Honorable Secretary of the Interior, his final enrollment number being   569   and that a   Male   child was born to me on the   1st   day of   September   190 3; that said child has been named   Teddie Impson   , and is now living.

                                Lillie Impson

WITNESSETH:
Must be two witnesses   { J.L. Howell
who are citizens   Theodolia Mugler

Subscribed and sworn to before me this, the   15th   day of   February   , 190 5

                              A.E. Folsom
                                         Notary Public.

My Commission Expires:
Jan 9- 1909

Affidavit of Attending Physician or Midwife

UNITED STATES OF AMERICA,
    INDIAN TERRITORY,
Central   DISTRICT

I,   B.F. Sutherland   a   Practicing Physician on oath state that I attended on Mrs.   Lillie Impson   wife of   Isaac Impson   on the   1st   day of   September   , 190 3, that there was born to her on said date a   male   child, that said child is now living, and is said to have been named   Teddie Impson

                           B.F. Sutherland   M. D.

Subscribed and sworn to before me this the   18   day of   Feb   1905

                           J.E. Grigsley
                                   Notary Public.

WITNESSETH:
Must be two witnesses   { J L Howell
who are citizens and
know the child.   Theodolia Mugler

Applications for Enrollment of Choctaw Newborn
Act of 1905 Volume XVII

We hereby certify that we are well acquainted with B.F. Sutherland a Physician and know him to be reputable and of good standing in the community.

Must be two citizen witnesses. { B.F. Byrd
Mamie E. Byrd

BIRTH AFFIDAVIT.

DEPARTMENT OF THE INTERIOR.
COMMISSION TO THE FIVE CIVILIZED TRIBES.

IN RE APPLICATION FOR ENROLLMENT, as a citizen of the Choctaw Nation, of Theodore Roosevelt Impson , born on the 1st day of September , 1903

Name of Father: Isaac C. Impson a citizen of the Choctaw Nation.
Name of Mother: Lillie Impson a citizen of the Choctaw Nation.

by marriage

Postoffice Ada, Indian Territory

AFFIDAVIT OF MOTHER.

UNITED STATES OF AMERICA, Indian Territory,
Southern DISTRICT.

I, Lillie Impson , on oath state that I am Twenty (20) years of age and a citizen by marriage , of the Choctaw Nation; that I am the lawful wife of Isaac C. Impson , who is a citizen, by blood of the Choctaw Nation; that a male child was born to me on 1st day of September , 1903; that said child has been named Theodore Roosevelt Impson , and was living March 4, 1905.

Lillie Impson

Witnesses To Mark:
{

Subscribed and sworn to before me this 3rd day of April , 1905.

Robt Wimbish
Notary Public.

Applications for Enrollment of Choctaw Newborn
Act of 1905 Volume XVII

AFFIDAVIT OF ATTENDING PHYSICIAN OR MID-WIFE.

UNITED STATES OF AMERICA, Indian Territory, }
Southern DISTRICT.

I, B.F. ~~Sutherland~~ *ullivan*, a Physician, on oath state that I attended on Mrs. Lillie Impson, wife of Isaac C. Impson on the 1st day of September, 1903; that there was born to her on said date a male child; that said child was living March 4, 1905, and is said to have been named Theodore Roosevelt Impson

B.F. Sullivan M.D.

Witnesses To Mark:
{

Subscribed and sworn to before me this 8 day of April, 1905

Minnie Lillard
Notary Public.

(The affidavit below typed as given.)

United States of America
Southern District of the
Indian Territory.

Before me the Undersigned authority on this 28TH day of June 19o5, personally appeared, R C Freeney, who after being duly Sworn to tell the truth, the whole truth and nothing but the truth, deposes and says that he was on the 7th day of Feby, 19o3, was the duly authorized and acting county Judge of Blue County Chocktaw Nation of the Indian Territory; that on the sai 7th day of Feby 19o3, Isaac Impson and Lillie Driver appeared before at my residence at Caddo, said nation and Territory, and requested me to marry them, they each stating to me that the wished to be married Therefore by virtue of the authoity vested in me as such county judge of the county and Territory above mentioned, performed the marriage cermony according to the laws and customs of the Chocktaw Nation of the Indian Territory. That at the time of the said Marriage there was present the following named persons, towit;___Josephine Freeny Mary Freeny   and others whom I cannot now recall

In testimony whereof I hereto set my hand and seal this the 28th day of June 19o5.

Robert C Freeny

Applications for Enrollment of Choctaw Newborn
Act of 1905   Volume XVII

Sworn to and subscribed before me this the 28th Day of June 19o5.

Sol. J. Homer
Notary Public in and for the central District of the Indian Territory.

BIRTH AFFIDAVIT.

DEPARTMENT OF THE INTERIOR.
COMMISSION TO THE FIVE CIVILIZED TRIBES.

IN RE APPLICATION FOR ENROLLMENT, as a citizen of the   Choctaw   Nation, of Theodore Roosevelt Impson   , born on the 1st day of Sept   , 1903

Name of Father: Isaac Impson   a citizen of the   Choctaw   Nation.
Name of Mother: Lillie Impson   a ~~citizen of the~~ non citizen ~~Nation~~.

Postoffice   Ada, Ind Ter

AFFIDAVIT OF MOTHER.

UNITED STATES OF AMERICA, Indian Territory, ⎫
  Southern   DISTRICT. ⎭

I,   Lillie Impson   , on oath state that I am 20   years of age and a citizen by ————, of the   United States   ~~Nation~~; that I am the lawful wife of   Isaac Impson   , who is a citizen, by blood   of the   Choctaw   Nation; that a   male   child was born to me on   1st day of   September   , 1903; that said child has been named Theodore Roosevelt Impson   , and was living March 4, 1905.

Lillie Impson

Witnesses To Mark:
{

Subscribed and sworn to before me this 11th day of   August   , 1905

My Commission   Robt Wimbish
expires Sep 28-1907   Notary Public.

AFFIDAVIT OF ATTENDING PHYSICIAN OR MID-WIFE.

UNITED STATES OF AMERICA, Indian Territory, ⎫
  Southern   DISTRICT. ⎭

I,   B.F. Sullivan   , a   Physician   , on oath state that I attended on Mrs.   Lillie Impson   , wife of   Isaac Impson   on the   1st day of   Sept   ,

Applications for Enrollment of Choctaw Newborn
Act of 1905 Volume XVII

1903; that there was born to her on said date a   male   child; that said child was living March 4, 1905, and is said to have been named Theodore Roosevelt Impson

B.F. Sullivan

Witnesses To Mark:
{

Subscribed and sworn to before me this 10 day of   April   , 1905

N.T. Dykes
Notary Public.

7-NB-1288.

Muskogee, Indian Territory, June 2, 1905.

Isaac C. Impson,
Ada, Indian Territory.

Dear Sir:

Referring to the application for the enrollment of your infant child, Theodore Roosevelt Impson, born Sept 1, 1903, it is noted from the affidavits heretofore filed in this office that the applicant claims through you.

Before this matter can be finally determined it will be necessary that you file in this office either the original or a certified copy of the license and certificate of your marriage to the applicant's mother, Lillie Impson.

Respectfully,

[sic]

7 NB 1288

Muskogee, Indian Territory, June 22, 1905.

Isaac Impson,
Ada, Indian Territory.

Dear Sir:

Receipt is hereby acknowledged of your letter of June 15, 1905, in which you refer to the application for the enrollment of your child Theodore Roosevelt Impson and

Applications for Enrollment of Choctaw Newborn
Act of 1905   Volume XVII

state that you secured no license to marry Lillie Driver, the mother of this child, but were married by a County Judge and will secure from him a certificate to you marriage and forward it to this office.

In reply to your letter you are advised that evidence of your marriage should be forwarded at once in order that disposition may be made of the application for the enrollment of your child Theodore Roosevelt Impson.

Respectfully,

Chairman.

---

7 NB 1288

Muskogee, Indian Territory, July 8, 1905.

Isaac Impson,
 Ada, Indian Territory.

Dear Sir:

Receipt is hereby acknowledged of your letter of July 4, 1905, enclosing affidavit of Robert C. Freeny to the marriage of Isaac Impson and Lillie Driver which you offer in support of the application for the enrollment of your child Theodore Roosevelt Impson and the same has been filed with the record in this case.

Respectfully,

Commissioner.

7-NB-1288   *Substitute*

Muskogee, Indian Territory, August 3, 1905.

Isaac Impson,
 Ada, Indian Territory.

Dear Sir:

There is inclosed you herewith for execution application for the enrollment of your child born September 1, 1903.

Applications for Enrollment of Choctaw Newborn
Act of 1905   Volume XVII

In the affidavits of February 15, 1905, heretofore filed in this office, the name of the applicant is given as "Teddie Impson", while in the affidavits of April 8, 1905, the name is given as "Theodore Roosevelt Impson."

In the inclosed application the name is left blank, and you will please insert therein the correct name under which your child is to be enrolled.

When the affidavits are properly executed, please return immediately to this office, as no further action can be taken relative to the enrollment of your said child until the evidence requested is supplied.

Respectfully,

LM 2/3

Commissioner.

---

7 N B 1288

Muskogee, Indian Territory, August 14, 1905.

Isaac Impson,
Ada, Indian Territory.

Dear Sir:

Receipt is hereby acknowledged of your letter of August 10, inclosing affidavits of Lillie Impson and B. F. Sullivan to the birth of your son, Theodore Roosevelt Impson, September 1, 1903, and the same have been filed with the record in the matter of the enrollment of this child.

Respectfully,

Acting Commissioner.

7-NB-1288

Muskogee, Indian Territory, June 13, 1906.

B. B. Carnes,
Alexa, Indian Territory.

Dear Sir:

Receipt is hereby acknowledged of your letter of May 15, 1906, in which you state that you have been appointed guardian of Theodore Roosevelt Impson, child of Isaac Impson and you ask his roll number and his age.

Applications for Enrollment of Choctaw Newborn
Act of 1905 Volume XVII

In reply to your letter you are advised that Theodore Roosevelt Impson, child of Isaac and Lillie Impson, has been enrolled as a new born citizen of the Choctaw Nation under the act of Congress approved March 3, 1905, and his enrollment approved by the Secretary of the Interior, September 23, 1905, his name appearing upon the approved roll opposite No. 1516.

You are further advised that Theodore Roosevelt Impson was born September 1, 1903, and his age appears upon the approved roll as two years.

Respectfully,

Commissioner.

Choc. New Born 1289
  Joseph Carney
  (Born Feb. 8, 1904)

BIRTH AFFIDAVIT.

Choctaw by Blood
Roll No 8749

DEPARTMENT OF THE INTERIOR.
COMMISSION TO THE FIVE CIVILIZED TRIBES.

IN RE APPLICATION FOR ENROLLMENT, as a citizen of the Choctaw Nation, of Joseph Carney, born on the 8th day of February, 1904

Name of Father: Morton Carney a citizen of the Choctaw Nation.
Name of Mother: Siliway Carney a citizen of the Choctaw Nation.

Postoffice Quinton, Indian Territory.

AFFIDAVIT OF MOTHER.

UNITED STATES OF AMERICA, Indian Territory,
Western District DISTRICT.

I, Siliway Carney, on oath state that I am 34 years of age and a citizen by blood, of the Choctaw Nation; that I am the lawful wife of Morton Carney, who is a citizen, by blood of the Choctaw Nation; that a male child was born to me on 8th day of February, 1904; that said child has been named Joseph Carney, and was living March 4, 1905.

175

Applications for Enrollment of Choctaw Newborn
Act of 1905 Volume XVII

Witnesses To Mark:
{ OA Rabon
  Chas Bascom

her
Siliway x Carney
mark

Subscribed and sworn to before me this 26th day of April, 1905

Guy A Curry
Notary Public.

AFFIDAVIT OF ATTENDING PHYSICIAN OR MID-WIFE.

UNITED STATES OF AMERICA, Indian Territory, }
Western   DISTRICT.   }

I, Jincy Bascom, a mid-wife, on oath state that I attended on Mrs. Siliway Carney, wife of Morton Carney on the 8th day of February, 1904; that there was born to her on said date a Male child; that said child was living March 4, 1905, and is said to have been named Joseph Carney

Jincy Bascom

Witnesses To Mark:
{

Subscribed and sworn to before me this 26th day of April, 1905

Guy A Curry
Notary Public.

7-2984.

Muskogee, Indian Territory, April 29, 1905.

Morton Carney,
    Quinton, Indian Territory.

Dear Sir:

Receipt is hereby acknowledged of the affidavits of Siliway Carney and Jincy Bascom to the birth of Joseph Carney, son of Morton and Siliway Carney, February 8, 1904, and the same have been filed with our records as an application for the enrollment of said child.

Respectfully,

Chairman.

Applications for Enrollment of Choctaw Newborn
Act of 1905 Volume XVII

Choc. New Born 1290
    Rosey Sockey
    (Born Jan. 3, 1903)

Ben Sockey Roll no. 8678
Eliysabeth Sockey Roll No. 8679

BIRTH AFFIDAVIT.

DEPARTMENT OF THE INTERIOR,
COMMISSION TO THE FIVE CIVILIZED TRIBES.

IN RE Application for Enrollment, as a citizen of the Choctaw Nation, of Rosey Sockey, born on the 3 day of Jan, 1903

Name of Father: Ben Sockey   a citizen of the Choctaw Nation.
Name of Mother: Elysabeth Sockey   a citizen of the Choctaw Nation.

Post-Office: Red Oak

AFFIDAVIT OF MOTHER.

UNITED STATES OF AMERICA, }
    INDIAN TERRITORY.
  Central   District.

    I, Elysabeth Sockey, on oath state that I am 35 years of age and a citizen by blood, of the Choctaw Nation; that I am the lawful wife of Ben Sockey, who is a citizen, by blood of the Choctaw Nation; that a girl child was born to me on 3rd day of Jan, 1903, that said child has been named Rosey Sockey, and is now living.

                                her
                         Elysabeth x Sockey
WITNESSES TO MARK: mark
  { Willis Hancock
    Osborne McCurtain

    Subscribed and sworn to before me this 25 *day of* April, 1905.

                         W. W. Ish
                             NOTARY PUBLIC.

Applications for Enrollment of Choctaw Newborn
Act of 1905   Volume XVII

AFFIDAVIT OF ATTENDING PHYSICIAN OR MID-WIFE.

UNITED STATES OF AMERICA, }
INDIAN TERRITORY.
Central   District.

I, Minie Lewis, a Nurse, on oath state that I attended on Mrs. Elysabeth Sockey, wife of Ben Sockey on the 3rd day of Jan, 1903; that there was born to her on said date a girl child; that said child is now living and is said to have been named Rosey Sockey

                her
              Minie x Lewis

WITNESSES TO MARK: mark
{ Willis Hancock
  Osborne McCurtain

Subscribed and sworn to before me this 25 *day of* April, 1905.

            W. W. Ish
               NOTARY PUBLIC.

7-2951.

Muskogee, Indian Territory, April 29, 1905.

Ben Sockey,
    Redoak, Indian Territory.

Dear Sir:

    Receipt is hereby acknowledged of the affidavits of Elysabeth Sockey and Minnie Lewis to the birth of Rosey Sockey, daughter of Ben and Elysabeth Sockey, January 3, 1903, and the same have been filed with our records as an application for the enrollment of said child.

            Respectfully,

                  Chairman.

Applications for Enrollment of Choctaw Newborn
Act of 1905 Volume XVII

Choc. New Born 1291
 James Dewitt Quincy
 (Born Dec. 1, 1904)

NEW BORN AFFIDAVIT

No ....

CHOCTAW ENROLLING COMMISSION

IN THE MATTER OF THE APPLICATION FOR ENROLLMENT as a citizen of the Choctaw Nation, of   James Dewitt Quincy   born on the 1st day of   December   190 4

Name of father   Jerome Ervin Quincy   a citizen of   Choctaw   Nation, final enrollment No. ....
Name of mother   Daisy Bell Quincy   a citizen of   Choctaw   Nation, final enrollment No. 455

Stuart I.T.   Postoffice.

AFFIDAVIT OF MOTHER

UNITED STATES OF AMERICA
 INDIAN TERRITORY
DISTRICT   Central

I   Daisy Bell Quincy   , on oath state that I am 23 years of age and a citizen by   blood   of the   Choctaw   Nation, and as such have been placed upon the final roll of the   Choctaw   Nation, by the Honorable Secretary of the Interior my final enrollment number being 455 ; that I am the lawful wife of   Jerome Ervin Quincy   , who is a citizen of the   Choctaw   Nation, and as such has been placed upon the final roll of said Nation by the Honorable Secretary of the Interior, his final enrollment number being .... and that a   Male   child was born to me on the   1st day of   December   190 4; that said child has been named   James Dewitt Quincy   , and is now living.

Jerome Ervin Quincy

WITNESSETH:
 Must be two witnesses ⎰ Elias Wesley
 who are citizens   ⎱ Samuel L Wooley

Applications for Enrollment of Choctaw Newborn
Act of 1905   Volume XVII

Subscribed and sworn to before me this, the FEB 25 1905 , 190 5

JE Elliott
Notary Public.

My Commission Expires: July 8" 1908

Affidavit of Attending Physician or Midwife

UNITED STATES OF AMERICA,
INDIAN TERRITORY,
.... DISTRICT

I, N. A. Story   a   Mid Wife on oath state that I attended on Mrs. Daisy Bell Quincy   wife of Jerome Ervin Quincy on the 1st day of December , 190 4, that there was born to her on said date a male child, that said child is now living, and is said to have been named James Dewitt Quincy

N. A. Story   *Midwife*

Subscribed and sworn to before me this the   day FEB 25 1905 905

JH Elliott
Notary Public.

WITNESSETH:
Must be two witnesses who are citizens and know the child. { Elias Wesley
Samuel L Wooley

We hereby certify that we are well acquainted with   Mrs M[sic]A Story a   Mid Wife   and know   her   to be reputable and of good standing in the community.

Must be two citizen witnesses. { Elias Wesley
Samuel L Wooley

7-720 7.W.
BIRTH AFFIDAVIT.

DEPARTMENT OF THE INTERIOR.
COMMISSION TO THE FIVE CIVILIZED TRIBES.

IN RE APPLICATION FOR ENROLLMENT, as a citizen of the   Choctaw   Nation, of James Dewitt Quincy   , born on the 1st day of December , 1904

Name of Father: Jerome Ervin Quincy   a citizen of the   Choctaw   Nation.
Name of Mother: Daisy Bell Quincy   a citizen of the   Choctaw   Nation.

Applications for Enrollment of Choctaw Newborn
Act of 1905   Volume XVII

Postoffice   Cabaniss, I.T.

AFFIDAVIT OF MOTHER.

UNITED STATES OF AMERICA, Indian Territory, }
Central   DISTRICT.

I, Daisy Bell Quincy, on oath state that I am 23 years of age and a citizen by Marriage, of the Choctaw Nation; that I am the lawful wife of Jerome Ervin Quincy, who is a citizen, by blood of the Choctaw Nation Nation; that a male child was born to me on 1st day of December, 1904; that said child has been named James Dewitt Quincy, and was living March 4, 1905.

Daisy Bell Quincy

Witnesses To Mark:
{ W L Wooley
  S.L. Wooley

Subscribed and sworn to before me this 26 day of April, 1905

JH Elliott

Com exp July 8 1908   Notary Public.

AFFIDAVIT OF ATTENDING PHYSICIAN OR MID-WIFE.

UNITED STATES OF AMERICA, Indian Territory, }
Central   DISTRICT.

I, Mrs N A Storrie[sic], a Mid Wife, on oath state that I attended on Mrs. Daisy Bell Quincy, wife of J E Quincy on the 1st day of December, 1904; that there was born to her on said date a male child; that said child was living March 4, 1905, and is said to have been named James Dewitt Quincy

N.A. Storie

Witnesses To Mark:
{ W L Wooley
  S.L. Wooley

Subscribed and sworn to before me this 26 day of April, 1905

JH Elliott
Notary Public.

Applications for Enrollment of Choctaw Newborn
Act of 1905 Volume XVII

Choc. New Born 1292
Rena Noel
(Born Apr. 24, 1903)

NEW-BORN AFFIDAVIT.

Number..............

...Choctaw Enrolling Commission...

IN THE MATTER OF THE APPLICATION FOR ENROLLMENT, as a citizen of the Choctaw Nation, of Rena Noah

born on the 24th day of April 1903

not married

Name of father Alfred Worcester   a citizen of Choctaw
Nation final enrollment No..................
Name of mother Georgeana Noah   a citizen of Choctaw
Nation final enrollment No. 14841

Postoffice Blanco IT

AFFIDAVIT OF MOTHER.

UNITED STATES OF AMERICA
INDIAN TERRITORY
  Central   DISTRICT

I Georgeanna[sic] Noah , on oath state that I am 18 years of age and a citizen by blood of the Choctaw Nation, and as such have been placed upon the final roll of the Choctaw Nation, by the Honorable Secretary of the Interior my final enrollment number being 2053 ; that I am the lawful wife of *not married*, Alfred Worcester , who is a citizen of the Choctaw Nation, and as such has been placed upon the final roll of said Nation by the Honorable Secretary of the Interior, his final enrollment number being *do not know* and that a Female child was born to me on the 24th day of April 1903; that said child has been named Rena Noah , and is now living.

Georgianna[sic] Noel

Witnesseth.
Must be two ⎫ Nancy Noel
Witnesses who ⎬
are Citizens. ⎭ Wilson Frazier

182

Applications for Enrollment of Choctaw Newborn
Act of 1905   Volume XVII

Subscribed and sworn to before me this   2nd   day of   March   190 5

A E Folsom
Notary Public.

My commission expires:
Jan 9 - 1909

AFFIDAVIT OF ATTENDING PHYSICIAN OR MIDWIFE

UNITED STATES OF AMERICA
INDIAN TERRITORY
  Central   DISTRICT

I,   Lucy Frazier   a   mid wife   on oath state that I attended on Mrs.   Georgeana Noah   ~~wife of~~ ~~April~~ on the 24th day of April, 190 3, that there was born to her on said date a   Female   child, that said child is now living, and is said to have been named   Rena Noah

her
Lucy x Frazier   *Midwife*
mark

WITNESSETH:

Must be two witnesses who are citizens and know the child.
{ Wilson Frazier
{ Nancy Noel

Subscribed and sworn to before me this, the   2^d   day of   March   190 5

A.E. Folsom   Notary Public.

We hereby certify that we are well acquainted with   Lucy Frazier   a   Mid wife   and know   her   to be reputable and of good standing in the community.

{ Wilson Frazier
{ Nancy Noel

BIRTH AFFIDAVIT.

DEPARTMENT OF THE INTERIOR.
COMMISSION TO THE FIVE CIVILIZED TRIBES.

IN RE APPLICATION FOR ENROLLMENT, as a citizen of the   Choctaw   Nation, of   Rena Noel   , born on the   24 day of April, 1903

Name of Father: Alfred Worcestor   a citizen of the   Choc   Nation.
Name of Mother: Georgie Ann Noel   a citizen of the   Choc   Nation.

Applications for Enrollment of Choctaw Newborn
Act of 1905   Volume XVII

Postoffice   Blanco I T

AFFIDAVIT OF MOTHER.

UNITED STATES OF AMERICA, Indian Territory, }
Central   DISTRICT.

I, Georgie Ann Noel, on oath state that I am 19 years of age and a citizen by blood, of the Choctaw Nation; that I am *not* the lawful wife of Alfred Worcester, who is a citizen, by blood of the Choctaw Nation; that a female child was born to me on 24 day of April, 1903; that said child has been named Rena Noel, and was living March 4, 1905.

                                              her
                                  Georgie Ann x Noel
Witnesses To Mark: mark
  { *(Name Illegible)*
    OL Johnson

Subscribed and sworn to before me this 27 day of April, 1905

                                  OL Johnson
                                  Notary Public.

AFFIDAVIT OF ATTENDING PHYSICIAN OR MID-WIFE.

UNITED STATES OF AMERICA, Indian Territory, }
Central   DISTRICT.

I, Josephine Frazier, a midwife, on oath state that I attended on Mrs. Georgie Ann Noel, wife of Alfred Worcester on the 24 day of April, 1903; that there was born to her on said date a female child; that said child was living March 4, 1905, and is said to have been named Rena Noel

                                              her
                                  Josephine x Frazier
Witnesses To Mark: mark
  { *(Name Illegible)*
    OL Johnson

Subscribed and sworn to before me this 27 day of April, 1905

                                  Notary Public.

Applications for Enrollment of Choctaw Newborn
Act of 1905 Volume XVII

Choc. New Born 1293
    Sallie Byington
    (Born Oct. 17, 1903)

NEW-BORN AFFIDAVIT.

    Number............

…Choctaw Enrolling Commission…

    IN THE MATTER OF THE APPLICATION FOR ENROLLMENT, as a citizen of the Choctaw   Nation, of   Sallie Byington

born on the 17 day of October 190 3

Name of father Simpson Byington   a citizen of Choctaw
Nation final enrollment No. 11292
Name of mother Annie Byington   a citizen of Choctaw
Nation final enrollment No. 11293

    Postoffice Redden I.T.

AFFIDAVIT OF MOTHER.

UNITED STATES OF AMERICA
INDIAN TERRITORY
    Central   DISTRICT

    I Annie Byington , on oath state that I am 38 years of age and a citizen by blood of the Choctaw Nation, and as such have been placed upon the final roll of the Choctaw Nation, by the Honorable Secretary of the Interior my final enrollment number being 11293 ; that I am the lawful wife of Simpson Byington , who is a citizen of the Choctaw Nation, and as such has been placed upon the final roll of said Nation by the Honorable Secretary of the Interior, his final enrollment number being 11292 and that a female child was born to me on the 17 day of October 190 3; that said child has been named Sallie Byington , and is now living.

                                                          her
Witnesseth.   Annie x Byington
                                                            mark
    Must be two   Joe B. Williams
    Witnesses who
    are Citizens.   Juston McIntosh

Applications for Enrollment of Choctaw Newborn
Act of 1905 Volume XVII

Subscribed and sworn to before me this 20th day of Jan 190 5

D.S. Kennedy
Notary Public.

My commission expires:
Nov 1st 1905

AFFIDAVIT OF ATTENDING PHYSICIAN OR MIDWIFE

UNITED STATES OF AMERICA
INDIAN TERRITORY
Central   DISTRICT

I, Simpson Byington a _____
on oath state that I attended on Mrs. Annie Byington wife of Simpson Byington on the 17 day of October , 190 3 , that there was born to her on said date a female child, that said child is now living, and is said to have been named Sallie Byington

his
Simpson x Byington   𝑚. 𝒟.
Subscribed and sworn to before me this, the mark   20th   day of
Jan   190 5

WITNESSETH: D.S. Kennedy   Notary Public.

Must be two witnesses   Joe B. Williams
who are citizens
                        Juston McIntosh

We hereby certify that we are well acquainted with _____
a   Simpson Byington   and know   him   to be reputable and of good standing in the community.

Joe B. Williams

Juston McIntosh

BIRTH AFFIDAVIT.
DEPARTMENT OF THE INTERIOR.
COMMISSION TO THE FIVE CIVILIZED TRIBES.

IN RE APPLICATION FOR ENROLLMENT, as a citizen of the   Choctaw   Nation, of Sallie Byington , born on the 17th day of October , 1903

Name of Father: Simpson Byington   a citizen of the Choctaw Nation.
Name of Mother: Annie Byington   a citizen of the Choctaw Nation.

Applications for Enrollment of Choctaw Newborn
Act of 1905 Volume XVII

Postoffice   Stringtown, I.T.

AFFIDAVIT OF MOTHER.

UNITED STATES OF AMERICA, Indian Territory,
Central   DISTRICT.

I,   Annie Byington   , on oath state that I am   38   years of age and a citizen by   blood   , of the   Choctaw   Nation; that I am the lawful wife of   Simpson Byington   , who is a citizen, by   blood   of the   Choctaw   Nation; that a female   child was born to me on   17th day of   October   , 1903; that said child has been named   Sallie Byington   , and was living March 4, 1905.

her
Annie x Byington
mark

Witnesses To Mark:
{ Arthur O Archer
{ William H. Cunningham

Subscribed and sworn to before me this   27th day of   April   , 1905

W.H. Angell
Notary Public.

AFFIDAVIT OF ATTENDING PHYSICIAN OR MID-WIFE.

UNITED STATES OF AMERICA, Indian Territory,
Central   DISTRICT.

I,   Simpson Byington *a citizen by blood of the Choctaw* on oath state that I attended on Mrs.   Annie Byington   *my*, wife of ——————— on the   17th day of October   , 1903; that there was born to her on said date a   female   child; that said child was living March 4, 1905, and is said to have been named   Sallie Byington *and that no one was present on the date of the birth of said Sallie Byington except myself and said wife*

his
Simpson x Byington
mark

Witnesses To Mark:
{ Arthur O Archer
{ William H. Cunningham

Subscribed and sworn to before me this   27th day of   April   , 1905

W.H. Angell
Notary Public.

Applications for Enrollment of Choctaw Newborn
Act of 1905   Volume XVII

BIRTH AFFIDAVIT.

DEPARTMENT OF THE INTERIOR.
COMMISSION TO THE FIVE CIVILIZED TRIBES.

IN RE APPLICATION FOR ENROLLMENT, as a citizen of the Choctaw Nation, of Sallie Byington, born on the 17th day of October, 1903

Name of Father: Simpson Byington   a citizen of the Choctaw Nation.
Name of Mother: Annie Byington   a citizen of the Choctaw Nation.

Postoffice   Stringtown, I.T.

AFFIDAVIT OF ~~MOTHER~~ *Acquaintance*.

UNITED STATES OF AMERICA, Indian Territory,
Central   DISTRICT.

I, Christopher D. Moore, on oath state that I am 38 years of age and a citizen by blood, of the Choctaw Nation; that I am ~~the lawful wife of~~ *personally acquainted with Annie Byington wife of Simpson Byington*, who is a citizen, by blood of the Choctaw Nation; that a female child was born to me on 17th day of October, 1903; that said child has been named Sallie Byington, and was living March 4, 1905.

Christopher D. Moore

Witnesses To Mark:

Subscribed and sworn to before me this 27th day of April, 1905.

W.H. Angell
Notary Public.

AFFIDAVIT OF ATTENDING PHYSICIAN OR MID-WIFE.

UNITED STATES OF AMERICA, Indian Territory,
Central   DISTRICT.

I, *Elsie James a citizen by blood of the Choctaw Nation*, on oath state that I ~~attended on~~ *am personally acquainted with* Mrs. Annie Byington, wife of Simpson Byington *that* on the 17th day of October, 1903; that there was born to her on said date a female child; that said child was living March 4, 1905, and is said to have been named Sallie Byington

her
Elsie x James
mark

Applications for Enrollment of Choctaw Newborn
Act of 1905 Volume XVII

Witnesses To Mark:
- Arthur O Archer
- William H. Cunningham

Subscribed and sworn to before me this 27th day of April, 1905

W.H. Angell
Notary Public.

Choc. New Born 1294
　　　Guertie Kemp
　　　(Born Apr. 8, 1904)

NEW-BORN AFFIDAVIT.

Number................

...Choctaw Enrolling Commission...

IN THE MATTER OF THE APPLICATION FOR ENROLLMENT, as a citizen of the Choctaw Nation, of Girdie[sic] Kemp

born on the 18th [sic] day of April 190 4

Name of father Stanton Kemp   a citizen of Choctaw
Nation final enrollment No. 13135
Name of mother Jinnie Kemp   a citizen of Choctaw
Nation final enrollment No. 15497

Postoffice Blanco I.T.

AFFIDAVIT OF MOTHER.

UNITED STATES OF AMERICA
INDIAN TERRITORY
　Central DISTRICT

I Jinnie Kemp , on oath state that I am 20 years of age and a citizen by blood of the Choctaw Nation, and as such have been placed upon the final roll of the Choctaw Nation, by the Honorable Secretary of the Interior my final enrollment number being 15497 ; that I am the lawful wife of Stanton Kemp , who is a citizen of the Choctaw Nation, and as such

Applications for Enrollment of Choctaw Newborn
Act of 1905 Volume XVII

has been placed upon the final roll of said Nation by the Honorable Secretary of the Interior, his final enrollment number being 13135 and that a Female child was born to me on the 18th day of April 190 4; that said child has been named Girdie Kemp, and is now living.

Jennie Kemp

Witnesseth.
Must be two Witnesses who are Citizens. } Wilkin Taylor
Aaron Holm

Subscribed and sworn to before me this 2d day of March 190 5

A.E. Folsom
Notary Public.

My commission expires:
Jan 9-1909

AFFIDAVIT OF ATTENDING PHYSICIAN OR MIDWIFE

UNITED STATES OF AMERICA
INDIAN TERRITORY
Central   DISTRICT

I, Stanton Kemp a *The Husband*
on oath state that I attended on Mrs. Jennie Kemp wife of Standley[sic] Kemp *The Father*
on the 18th day of April , 190 4, that there was born to her on said date a Female child, that said child is now living, and is said to have been named Girdie Kemp

Father of child
Stenton[sic] Kemp   ~~M.D.~~

WITNESSETH:
Must be two witnesses who are citizens and know the child. { Wilkin Taylor
Aaron Holm

Subscribed and sworn to before me this, the 2d day of March 190 5

A.E. Folsom   Notary Public.

We hereby certify that we are well acquainted with Standley Kemp a *The Father of Girdie Kemp* and know him to be reputable and of good standing in the community.

{ Wilkin Taylor
Aaron Holm

Applications for Enrollment of Choctaw Newborn
Act of 1905   Volume XVII

DEPARTMENT OF THE INTERIOR,
COMMISSION TO THE FIVE CIVILIZED TRIBES.
SOUTH McALESTER, IND. TER. APRIL 27, 1905.

In the matter of the application for the enrollment of Guertie Kemp as a citizen by blood of the Choctaw Nation.

Stanton Kemp being sworn and examined through interpreter Jake Collins testifies as follows:

EXAMINATION BY THE COMMISSION:

Q What is your name? A Stanton Kemp.
Q How old are you? A Thirty.
Q What is your post office address? A Blanco.
Q You have this date made application for the enrollment of your child, Guertie Kemp, as a citizen by blood of the Choctaw Nation; when was Guertie born? A April 8, 1904.
Q Was Guertie living on March 4, 1905? A Yes, sir.
Q Who attended your wife when Guertie was born in the capacity of Midwife or doctor? A I did.

Witness excused.

Josephine Frazier being duly sworn and examined through interpreter Jake Collins testifies as follows:

EXAMINATION BY THE COMMISSION:

Q What is your name? A Josephine Frazier.
Q How old are you? A Fifty.
Q What is your post office address? A Blanco.
Q Are you a citizen by blood of the Choctaw Nation? A Yes, sir.
Q Are you acquainted with Jennie Kemp and Stanton Kemp who have this day made application for the enrollment of their child Guertie Kemp? A Yes, sir.
Q How far from them do you live? A About a mile and a half.
Q Do you know when Guertie Kemp was born? A Yes, sir.
Q When? A I don't know exactly but it was in April 1904.
Q Was Guertie Kemp living on March 4, 1905? A Yes, sir.

Witness excused.

Chas. T. Difendafer being first duly sworn states that the above and foregoing is a full, true and correct transcript of his stenographic notes taken in said cause on said date.

Chas T. Difendafer

Applications for Enrollment of Choctaw Newborn
Act of 1905 Volume XVII

Subscribed and sworn to before me this 27th day of April 1905.

OL Johnson
Notary Public.

BIRTH AFFIDAVIT.

DEPARTMENT OF THE INTERIOR.
COMMISSION TO THE FIVE CIVILIZED TRIBES.

IN RE APPLICATION FOR ENROLLMENT, as a citizen of the Choctaw Nation, of Guertie Kemp, born on the 8 day of April, 1904

Name of Father: Stanton Kemp   a citizen of the Choc Nation.
Name of Mother: Jennie Kemp nee Noel   a citizen of the Choc Nation.

Postoffice   Blanco I.T.

AFFIDAVIT OF MOTHER.

UNITED STATES OF AMERICA, Indian Territory,
Central DISTRICT.

I, Jennie Kemp nee Noel, on oath state that I am 20 years of age and a citizen by blood, of the Choctaw Nation; that I am the lawful wife of Stanton Kemp, who is a citizen, by blood of the Choctaw Nation; that a female child was born to me on 8 day of April, 1904; that said child has been named Guertie Kemp, and was living March 4, 1905.

Jennie Kemp

Witnesses To Mark:

Subscribed and sworn to before me this 27 day of April, 1905

OL Johnson
Notary Public.

Applications for Enrollment of Choctaw Newborn
Act of 1905   Volume XVII

BIRTH AFFIDAVIT.

DEPARTMENT OF THE INTERIOR.
COMMISSION TO THE FIVE CIVILIZED TRIBES.

IN RE APPLICATION FOR ENROLLMENT, as a citizen of the Choctaw Nation, of Guertie Kemp, born on the 8 day of April, 1904

Name of Father: Stanton Kemp   a citizen of the Choctaw Nation.
Name of Mother: Jennie Kemp   a citizen of the Choctaw Nation.

Postoffice   Blanco Ind. Ter.

~~AFFIDAVIT OF MOTHER.~~

UNITED STATES OF AMERICA, Indian Territory, }
    Central   DISTRICT. }

I, Jimmie Nail, on oath state that I am 22 years of age and ~~a citizen by~~ *that I know*, ~~of the~~ *Jennie Kemp who is* ~~Nation; that I am~~ the lawful wife of Stanton Kemp, who is a citizen, by Blood of the Choctaw Nation; that a female child was born to ~~me~~ *her* on the 8th day of April, 1904; that said child has been named Guertie Kemp, and was living March 4, 1905.

                              Jimmie Nail

Witnesses To Mark:
{

Subscribed and sworn to before me this 17 day of June, 1905

My commission expires   Martin Savage
Feb 28th 1909   Notary Public.

~~AFFIDAVIT OF ATTENDING PHYSICIAN OR MID-WIFE.~~

UNITED STATES OF AMERICA, Indian Territory, }
    Central   DISTRICT. }

am acquainted with
I, Isom Pickens, ~~a~~————, on oath state that I ~~attended on~~ Mrs. Jennie Kemp, wife of Stanton Kemp *that* on the 8th day of April, 1904; that there was born to her on said date a female child; that said child was living March 4, 1905, and is said to have been named Guertie Kemp

                           Isom Pickens

Applications for Enrollment of Choctaw Newborn
Act of 1905   Volume XVII

Witnesses To Mark:

{

Subscribed and sworn to before me this 17 day of June , 1905

My commission expires
Feb 28th 1909

Martin Savage
Notary Public.

7-NB-1294.

Muskogee, Indian Territory, June 3, 1905.

Stanton Kemp,
    Blanco, Indian Territory.

Dear Sir:

    Referring to the application for the enrollment of your infant child, Guertie Kemp, born April 8, 1904, it is noted that you attended upon your wife at the time of birth of the applicant.

    If there was no physician or midwife in attendance at the time of birth of the applicant it will be necessary that the affidavits of two persons, who are disinterested and not related to the applicant, who have actual knowledge of the facts that the child was born, the date of her birth; that she was living on March 4, 1905, and that Jennie Kemp is her mother, be filed in this office.

    This matter should receive your immediate attention, as no further action can be taken until these affidavits are filed in this office.

Respectfully,

[sic]

7-NB- 1294.

Muskogee, Indian Territory, June 13, 1905.

Stanton Kemp,
    Blanco, Indian Territory.

Dear Sir:

    Replying to you letter of June 8, 1905, There is enclosed herewith for execution two blank affidavits in the matter of the enrollment of your infant child, Guertie Kemp,

Applications for Enrollment of Choctaw Newborn
Act of 1905 Volume XVII

born April 8, 1904. You will please have these affidavits executed by two persons who are disinterested and not related to the applicant.

This matter should receive your immediate attention, as no further action can be taken until these affidavits are filed with the Commission.

Respectfully,

Chairman.

DeB--1/13.

---

7 NB 1294

Muskogee, Indian Territory, June 21, 1905.

Stanton Kemp,
    Blanco, Indian Territory.

Dear Sir:

Receipt is hereby acknowledged of the affidavits of Jennie Nail and Isom Pickens to the birth of Guertie Kemp, daughter of Stanton and Jennie Kemp, April 8, 1904, and the same have been filed with our records in the matter of the enrollment of said child.

Respectfully,

Chairman.

Choc. New Born 1295
    Buena Daugherty
    (Born June 16, 1904)
    Beulah Daugherty
    (Born June 16, 1904)

Applications for Enrollment of Choctaw Newborn
Act of 1905 Volume XVII

BIRTH AFFIDAVIT.

DEPARTMENT OF THE INTERIOR.
COMMISSION TO THE FIVE CIVILIZED TRIBES.

IN RE APPLICATION FOR ENROLLMENT, as a citizen of the Choctaw Nation, of Buena Daugherty, born on the 16 day of June, 1904

Name of Father: John F. Daugherty   a citizen of the Choctaw Nation.
Name of Mother: Lillian Daugherty   a citizen of the Choctaw Nation.

Postoffice   Iona I.T.

AFFIDAVIT OF MOTHER.

UNITED STATES OF AMERICA, Indian Territory,
Southern   DISTRICT.

I, Lillian Daugherty, on oath state that I am 28 years of age and a citizen by Int. marriage, of the Choctaw Nation; that I am the lawful wife of John F. Daugherty, who is a citizen, by Blood of the Choctaw Nation; that a Female child was born to me on 16 day of June, 1904; that said child has been named Buena Daugherty, and was living March 4, 1905.

                         Lillian Daugherty

Witnesses To Mark:

Subscribed and sworn to before me this 25th day of Apr, 1905

                         John H Vaughan
                         Notary Public.

AFFIDAVIT OF ATTENDING PHYSICIAN OR MID-WIFE.

UNITED STATES OF AMERICA, Indian Territory,
Southern   DISTRICT.

I, Mattie Stone, a mid wife, on oath state that I attended on Mrs. Lillian Daugherty, wife of John F. Daugherty on the 16 day of June, 1904; that there was born to her on said date a Female child; that said child was living March 4, 1905, and is said to have been named Buena Daugherty

                         Mattie Stone

Witnesses To Mark:

Applications for Enrollment of Choctaw Newborn
Act of 1905   Volume XVII

Subscribed and sworn to before me this 25th day of   Apr   , 1905

John H Vaughan
Notary Public.

BIRTH AFFIDAVIT.

DEPARTMENT OF THE INTERIOR.
COMMISSION TO THE FIVE CIVILIZED TRIBES.

IN RE APPLICATION FOR ENROLLMENT, as a citizen of the   Choctaw   Nation, of Beulah Daugherty   , born on the 16 day of June , 1904

Name of Father: John F. Daugherty   a citizen of the Choctaw   Nation.
Name of Mother: Lillian Daugherty   a citizen of the Choctaw   Nation.

Postoffice   Iona I.T.

AFFIDAVIT OF MOTHER.

UNITED STATES OF AMERICA, Indian Territory,
Southern   DISTRICT.

I,   Lillian Daugherty   , on oath state that I am 28   years of age and a citizen by   Int. marriage   , of the   Choctaw   Nation; that I am the lawful wife of John F. Daugherty   , who is a citizen, by Blood   of the   Choctaw   Nation; that a   Female   child was born to me on   16 day of June   , 1904; that said child has been named   Beulah Daugherty   , and was living March 4, 1905.

Lillian Daugherty

Witnesses To Mark:

Subscribed and sworn to before me this 25th day of   Apr   , 1905

John H Vaughan
Notary Public.

Applications for Enrollment of Choctaw Newborn
Act of 1905   Volume XVII

AFFIDAVIT OF ATTENDING PHYSICIAN OR MID-WIFE.

UNITED STATES OF AMERICA, Indian Territory,　}
　　Southern　　　　　　　　DISTRICT.

　　　　I,　Mattie Stone　, a mid wife　, on oath state that I attended on Mrs.　Lillian Daugherty　, wife of　John F. Daugherty　on the　16　day of June　, 1904; that there was born to her on said date a　Female　child; that said child was living March 4, 1905, and is said to have been named　Beulah Daugherty

　　　　　　　　　　　　　　　　　　　Mattie Stone

Witnesses To Mark:

{ Subscribed and sworn to before me this   25th day of   Apr   , 1905

　　　　　　　　　　　　　　　　　　John H Vaughan
　　　　　　　　　　　　　　　　　　　Notary Public.

　　　　　　　　　　　　　　　　　　　　　　7-2530.

　　　　　　　　　Muskogee, Indian Territory, April 29, 1905.

John F. Daugherty,
　　　Iona, Indian Territory.

Dear Sir:

　　　Receipt is hereby acknowledged of the affidavits of Lillian Daugherty and Mattie Stone to the birth of Buena Daugherty and Beulah Daugherty twin children of John F. and Lillian Daugherty, June 16, 1904, and the same have been filed with our records as applications for the enrollment of said children.

　　　　　　　　　　　　Respectfully,

　　　　　　　　　　　　　　　　Chairman.

Choc. New Born 1296
　　　Oscar Brandy
　　　(Born May 2, 1903)

Applications for Enrollment of Choctaw Newborn
Act of 1905   Volume XVII

BIRTH AFFIDAVIT.

DEPARTMENT OF THE INTERIOR.
COMMISSION TO THE FIVE CIVILIZED TRIBES.

IN RE APPLICATION FOR ENROLLMENT, as a citizen of the Choctaw Nation, of Oscar Brandy, born on the 2nd day of May, 1903, 1

Name of Father: Cornelius Brandy   a citizen of the Choctaw Nation.
Name of Mother: Nettie Brandy Intermarried   a citizen of the Choctaw Nation.

Postoffice   Chant I.T.

AFFIDAVIT OF MOTHER.

UNITED STATES OF AMERICA, Indian Territory,
Central   DISTRICT.

I, Nettie Brandy, on oath state that I am 25 years years of age and a citizen by Intermarriage, of the Choctaw Nation; that I am the lawful wife of Cornelius Brandy, who is a citizen, by Berth[sic] of the Choctaw Nation; that a male child was born to me on 2nd day of May 1903, 1 ; that said child has been named Oscar Brandy, and was living March 4, 1905.

                                     her
                              Nettie Brandy x
Witnesses To Mark: mark
  { John W Wyers
  { Peter Folsom

Subscribed and sworn to before me this April 25 1905. , 190

                              J.F. Hudson
                                 Notary Public.
My com. expires May 5th-1908.

AFFIDAVIT OF ATTENDING PHYSICIAN OR MID-WIFE.

UNITED STATES OF AMERICA, Indian Territory,
Central   DISTRICT.

I, W.H. Holbrook, a midwife, on oath state that I attended on Mrs. Nettie Brandy, wife of Cornelius Brandy on the 2nd day of May 1903, 1 ; that there was born to her on said date a male child; that said child was living March 4, 1905, and is said to have been named Oscar Brandy

                              W.H. Holbrook

Applications for Enrollment of Choctaw Newborn
Act of 1905 Volume XVII

Witnesses To Mark:
- John W. Wyers
- Peter Folsom

Subscribed and sworn to before me this 25th day of April 1905, 190___

J.F. Hudson
Notary Public.

My com. expires May 5th 1908.

BIRTH AFFIDAVIT.

DEPARTMENT OF THE INTERIOR.
COMMISSION TO THE FIVE CIVILIZED TRIBES.

IN RE APPLICATION FOR ENROLLMENT, as a citizen of the Choctaw Nation, of Oscar Brandy, born on the 2nd day of May, 1903

Name of Father: Cornelius Brandy	a citizen of the Choctaw	Nation.
Name of Mother: Nettie Brandy	a citizen of the Choctaw	Nation.

Postoffice   Chant Ind. Ter.

AFFIDAVIT OF MOTHER.

UNITED STATES OF AMERICA, Indian Territory,
Central DISTRICT.

I, Nettie Brandy, on oath state that I am 25 years of age and a citizen by intermarriage, of the Choctaw Nation; that I am the lawful wife of Cornelius Brandy, who is a citizen, by blood of the Choctaw Nation; that a male child was born to me on 2nd day of May, 1903; that said child has been named Oscar Brandy, and was living March 4, 1905.

her
Nettie x Brandy
mark

Witnesses To Mark:
- Floyd Nevins
- D.M. Hopkins

Subscribed and sworn to before me this 29th day of June, 1905

My com. exp
Octob 29th 1908

(Name Illegible)
Notary Public.

Applications for Enrollment of Choctaw Newborn
Act of 1905 Volume XVII

AFFIDAVIT OF ATTENDING PHYSICIAN OR MID-WIFE.

UNITED STATES OF AMERICA, Indian Territory, }
   Central   DISTRICT. }

      I, W.H. Holbrook, a Phisician[sic], on oath state that I attended on Mrs. Nettie Brandy, wife of Cornelius Brandy on the 2nd day of May, 1903; that there was born to her on said date a male child; that said child was living March 4, 1905, and is said to have been named Oscar Brandy

                                      W.H. Holbrook

Witnesses To Mark:
  { Floyd Nevins
    D.M. Hopkins

      Subscribed and sworn to before me this 29th day of June, 1905.

My com. exp   *(Name Illegible)*
Octob 29th 1908   Notary Public.

                                                       7-2424.

                 Muskogee, Indian Territory, April 29, 1905.

Cornelius Brandy,
    Chant, Indian Territory.

Dear Sir:

      Receipt is hereby acknowledged of the affidavits of Nettie Brandy and W. H. Holbrook to the birth of Oscar Brandy, son of Cornelius and Nettie Brandy, May 2, 1903, and the same have been filed with our records as an application for the enrollment of said child.

                              Respectfully,

                                                  Chairman.

Applications for Enrollment of Choctaw Newborn
Act of 1905   Volume XVII

7-NB-1296.

Muskogee, Indian Territory, June 13, 1905.

Cornelius Brandy,   *Nettie Brandy*   6/23/05
    Chant, Indian Territory.

Dear Sir:

    There is enclosed herewith for execution application for the enrollment of your infant child, Oscar Brandy, born May 2, 1903.

    In the affidavit heretofore filed in this office the signature of the Notary Public is typewritten. The Notary Public before whom the enclosed application is executed should sign it in his own hand.

    In having these affidavits executed care should be exercised to see that all names are written in full, as they appear in the body of the affidavit, and in the event either of the persons signing the affidavit are unable to write, signatures by mark must be attested by two witnesses. Each affidavit must be executed before a Notary Public and the notarial seal and signature of the officer must be attached to each separate affidavit.

    Respectfully,

    Chairman.

7-NB-1296

Muskogee, Indian Territory, July 5, 1905.

Nettie Brandy,
    Chant, Indian Territory.

Dear Madam:

    Receipt is hereby acknowledged of the affidavits of Mettie[sic] Brandy and W. H. Holbrook to the birth of Oscar Brandy son of Cornelius and Nettie Brandy, May 2, 1903, and the same have been filed with the records in the matter of the enrollment of said child.

    Respectfully,

    Commissioner.

Applications for Enrollment of Choctaw Newborn
Act of 1905 Volume XVII

Choc. New Born 1297
    Thomas Edward Bell
    (Born March 28, 1903)
    Kinnie May Bell
    (Born June 10, 1904)

BIRTH AFFIDAVIT.

DEPARTMENT OF THE INTERIOR.
COMMISSION TO THE FIVE CIVILIZED TRIBES.

IN RE APPLICATION FOR ENROLLMENT, as a citizen of the Choctaw Nation, of Thomas Edward Bell, born on the 28 day of March, 1903

Name of Father: Thomas W Bell   a citizen of the Choctaw Nation.
Name of Mother: Mary Viola Bell   a citizen of the Choctaw Nation.

Postoffice   Allen Ind. Ter.

AFFIDAVIT OF MOTHER.

UNITED STATES OF AMERICA, Indian Territory,
Central   DISTRICT.

    I, Mary Viola Bell, on oath state that I am 27 years of age and a citizen by Marriage, of the Choctaw Nation; that I am the lawful wife of Thomas W Bell, who is a citizen, by Blood of the Choctaw Nation; that a male child was born to me on 28 day of March, 1903; that said child has been named Thomas Edward Bell, and was living March 4, 1905.

                                    Mary Viola Bell
Witnesses To Mark:

    Subscribed and sworn to before me this 17 day of April, 1905

Commission expires   R E Brians
Jan 20-1909   Notary Public.

Applications for Enrollment of Choctaw Newborn
Act of 1905   Volume XVII

AFFIDAVIT OF ATTENDING PHYSICIAN OR MID-WIFE.

UNITED STATES OF AMERICA, Indian Territory, }
Central   DISTRICT.

I, M[sic].E. Ervin, a mid-wife, on oath state that I attended on Mrs. Mary Viola Bell, wife of Thomas W Bell on the 28 day of March, 1903; that there was born to her on said date a male child; that said child was living March 4, 1905, and is said to have been named Thomas Edward Bell

H.E. Ervin

Witnesses To Mark:
{

Subscribed and sworn to before me this 24 day of April, 1905

Edward D. Sitter
Notary Public.
My commission expires March 20 1907

BIRTH AFFIDAVIT.

DEPARTMENT OF THE INTERIOR.
COMMISSION TO THE FIVE CIVILIZED TRIBES.

IN RE APPLICATION FOR ENROLLMENT, as a citizen of the Choctaw Nation, of Kinnie May Bell, born on the 10 day of June, 1904

Name of Father: Thomas W Bell   a citizen of the Choctaw Nation.
Name of Mother: Mary Viola Bell   a citizen of the Choctaw Nation.

Postoffice   Allen Ind. Ter.

AFFIDAVIT OF MOTHER.

UNITED STATES OF AMERICA, Indian Territory, }
Central   DISTRICT.

I, Mary Viola Bell, on oath state that I am 27 years of age and a citizen by Marriage, of the Choctaw Nation; that I am the lawful wife of Thomas W Bell, who is a citizen, by Blood of the Choctaw Nation; that a Female child was born to me on 10 day of June, 1903; that said child has been named Kinnie May Bell, and was living March 4, 1905.

Mary Viola Bell

Applications for Enrollment of Choctaw Newborn
Act of 1905   Volume XVII

Witnesses To Mark:

{

Subscribed and sworn to before me this 17 day of April , 1905

Commission expires R E Brians
Jan 20-1909 Notary Public.

AFFIDAVIT OF ATTENDING PHYSICIAN OR MID-WIFE.

UNITED STATES OF AMERICA, Indian Territory, }
Central   DISTRICT.

I, J. C. Schlicht M.D. , a Physician , on oath state that I attended on Mrs. Mary Viola Bell , wife of Thomas W Bell on the 10th day of June, 1904; that there was born to her on said date a Female child; that said child was living March 4, 1905, and is said to have been named Kinnie May Bell

J.C. Schlicht M.D.

Witnesses To Mark:

{

Subscribed and sworn to before me this 24 day of April , 1905

Edward D. Sitter
Notary Public.
My commission expires March 20 1907

7-4681.

Muskogee, Indian Territory, April 29, 1905.

Thomas W. Bell,
    Allen, Indian Territory.

Dear Sir:

Receipt is hereby acknowledged of the affidavits of Mary Viola Bell and H. E. Ervin to the birth of Thomas Edward Bell, and also affidavits of Mary Viola Bell and J. C. Schlicht to the birth of Kinnie May Bell, children of Thomas W. and Mary Viola Bell, March 28. 1903 and June 10, 1904, respectively, and the same have been filed with our records as an application for the enrollment of said children.

Respectfully

Chairman.

Applications for Enrollment of Choctaw Newborn
Act of 1905   Volume XVII

Choc. New Born 1298
   McVay Wilson
   (Born Aug. 13, 1903)

NEW-BORN AFFIDAVIT.

Number..................

Choctaw Enrolling Commission.

IN THE MATTER OF THE APPLICATION FOR ENROLLMENT, as a citizen of the Choctaw   Nation, of   McVey [sic] Wilson

born on the 13 day of August   190 3

Name of father   Carlo Wilson   a citizen of   Choctaw
Nation final enrollment No   159
Name of mother   Margrette[sic] Wilson   a citizen of   Choctaw
Nation final enrollment No   159

Postoffice   Alikchi, I.T.

AFFIDAVIT OF MOTHER.

UNITED STATES OF AMERICA,
   INDIAN TERRITORY,
   Central   DISTRICT

   I   Margrette[sic] Wilson   on oath state that I am 27 years of age and a citizen by blood of the Choctaw Nation, and as such have been placed upon the final roll of the   Choctaw   Nation, by the Honorable Secretary of the Interior my final enrollment number being 159 ; that I am the lawful wife of Carlo Wilson   , who is a citizen of the Choctaw   Nation, and as such has been placed upon the final roll of said Nation by the Honorable Secretary of the Interior, his final enrollment number being 159 and that a male child was born to me on the 13 day of August   190 3 ; that said child has been named   McVey Wilson , and is now living.

Margaret Wilson

WITNESSETH:
   Must be two } James Woolery
   Witnesses who }
   are Citizens.   *(Name Illegible)*

Subscribed and sworn to before me this 19 day of January   190 5

William Swink
   Notary Public.

My commission expires   Dec 6th 190

Applications for Enrollment of Choctaw Newborn
Act of 1905   Volume XVII

Affidavit of Attending Physician or Midwife

UNITED STATES OF AMERICA,
INDIAN TERRITORY,
Central   DISTRICT

I, Sissie Homes[sic]   a   midwife on oath state that I attended on Mrs. Margette[sic] Wilson   wife of   Carlo Wilson on the   13   day of   August , 190 3, that there was born to her on said date a   male   child, that said child is now living, and is said to have been named McVey Wilson

Sissie Holmes   M. D.

Subscribed and sworn to before me this the   19   day of   January   1905

William Swink
Notary Public.

WITNESSETH:

Must be two witnesses who are citizens and know the child.
{ James Woolery
(Name Illegible)

We hereby certify that we are well acquainted with   Sissie Holmes   a   midwife   and know   her   to be reputable and of good standing in the community.

Must be two citizen witnesses.
{ Eva Stephens
Alice Leflore

BIRTH AFFIDAVIT.

DEPARTMENT OF THE INTERIOR.
COMMISSION TO THE FIVE CIVILIZED TRIBES.

IN RE APPLICATION FOR ENROLLMENT, as a citizen of the   Choctaw   Nation, of McVay Wilson   , born on the   13 day of   August , 1903

Name of Father: Carlo A Wilson   a citizen of the   Choctaw   Nation.
Name of Mother: Margaret Wilson   a citizen of the   Choctaw   Nation.

Postoffice   Alikchi I.T.

Applications for Enrollment of Choctaw Newborn
Act of 1905   Volume XVII

AFFIDAVIT OF MOTHER.

UNITED STATES OF AMERICA, Indian Territory, }
Central   DISTRICT.

I, Margaret Wilson, on oath state that I am 28 years of age and a citizen by Blood, of the Choctaw Nation; that I am the lawful wife of Carlo A Wilson, who is a citizen, by Blood of the Choctaw Nation; that a Male child was born to me on 13 day of August 1903, 1......; that said child has been named M{c}Vay Wilson, and was living March 4, 1905.

Margaret Wilson

Witnesses To Mark:
{

Subscribed and sworn to before me this 22 day of April, 1905

W.P. Buswell
Notary Public.
Notary Public

AFFIDAVIT OF ATTENDING PHYSICIAN OR MID-WIFE.

UNITED STATES OF AMERICA, Indian Territory, }
Central   DISTRICT.

I, Sissey Holmes, a Mid Wife, on oath state that I attended on Mrs. Margaret Wilson, wife of Carlo A. Wilson on the 13 day of August, 1903; that there was born to her on said date a male child; that said child was living March 4, 1905, and is said to have been named M{c}Vay Wilson

Sissey Holmer

Witnesses To Mark:
{

Subscribed and sworn to before me this 22 day of April, 1905

W.P. Buswell
Notary Public.
Notary Public

Applications for Enrollment of Choctaw Newborn
Act of 1905 Volume XVII

7-NB-1298

Muskogee, Indian Territory, July 24, 1905.

Carlo A. Wilson,
    Alikchi, Indian Territory.

Dear Sir:

    Receipt is hereby acknowledged of your letter of July 17, 1905, asking if your son McVay Wilson has been approved.

    In reply to your letter you are advised that the name of your son McVay Wilson has been placed upon a schedule of citizens by blood of the Choctaw Nation which has been forwarded the Secretary of the Interior, and you will be notified when his enrollment is approved by the Department.

                          Respectfully,

                                                Commissioner.

Choc. New Born 1299
    Rosa Anna Mays
    (Born Jan. 17, 1903)

NEW-BORN AFFIDAVIT.

                Number............

Choctaw Enrolling Commission.

    IN THE MATTER OF THE APPLICATION FOR ENROLLMENT, as a citizen of the Choctaw   Nation, of   Rosana Mays

born on the   17   day of   Jany   190 3

Name of father   Will Mays   a citizen of   Choctaw
Nation final enrollment No ———
Name of mother   Melinda Mays *nee Spring*   a citizen of   Choctaw
Nation final enrollment No   3859

                          Postoffice   Ego I.T.

Applications for Enrollment of Choctaw Newborn
Act of 1905 Volume XVII

AFFIDAVIT OF MOTHER.

UNITED STATES OF AMERICA,
    INDIAN TERRITORY,
Central   DISTRICT

I Melinda Mays, nee Spring   on oath state that I am 22 years of age and a citizen by Blood of the Choctaw Nation, and as such have been placed upon the final roll of the Choctaw Nation, by the Honorable Secretary of the Interior my final enrollment number being 3859 ; that I am the lawful wife of Will Mays , who is a citizen of the Choctaw Nation, and as such has been placed upon the final roll of said Nation by the Honorable Secretary of the Interior, his final enrollment number being ——and that a Female child was born to me on the 17 day of Jany 190 3 ; that said child has been named Rosana Mays , and is now living.

                        Malinda Spring Mays
                        ^now

WITNESSETH:
Must be two Witnesses who are Citizens.
    (Name Illegible)
    W.W. Kendrick

Subscribed and sworn to before me this 19 day of Jany 190 5

                      W.T. Glenn
                      Notary Public.

My commission expires 1907

Affidavit of Attending Physician or Midwife

UNITED STATES OF AMERICA,
    INDIAN TERRITORY,
Central   DISTRICT

I, *Isaac Spring next relative, Pysician*[sic] *being dead* on oath state that I ~~attended on Mrs.~~ *was present when the child was born to the* wife of Will Mays on the 17 day of Jany , 190 3, that there was born to her on said date a Female child, that said child is now living, and is said to have been named Rosana Mays

                    Isaac Spring   M. D.

Subscribed and sworn to before me this the 19 day of Jany 1905

                    W.T. Glenn
                    Notary Public.

WITNESSETH:
Must be two witnesses who are citizens and know the child.
    Thomas W. Everidge
    W.W. Kendrick

Applications for Enrollment of Choctaw Newborn
Act of 1905   Volume XVII

We hereby certify that we are well acquainted with   Isaac Spring   a   citizen   and know   him   to be reputable and of good standing in the community.

Must be two citizen { Thomas W. Everidge
witnesses.   W.W. Kendrick

United States Of America
Indian Territory
Central District
I   Aimie Lee Bills   Of   Hugo Ind. Ter.
On Oath State that I am personally acquainted with   Mrs Malinda Spring Mays wife of   Will Mays
and that there was born to her on   January 17th =1903
a   Female   child, that said child is now living,
and is said to have been named   Rosa Anna Mays

Aimie Lee Bills

Subscribed and sworn to before me this, the 12th day of   July   190 5

J.P. Ward   Notary Public.

(The affidavit below is as given.)

J. T. GARDNER   C. E. RENFROW

GARDNER & RENFROW,
DEALERS IN
GENERAL MERCHANDISE,

| Dry Goods AND Groceries. | Boots and Shoes. | Hardware AND Implements. |

MILBURN, I. T.   *June 17*   190*5*

This is to certify. I am 19 yea of age my Post Office addess is Melbu I.T. I am pearsonally acquainted with Mrs Malinda Springs Mays and ther was bun to her on 17 day of Jan 1903 female child and said child was named Rose Anna Mays and is now Living and I am not interested in any way in this matter.

wtn to mark.   his
S.G. Moore   *George x Chotau*
John Craig   mark

Applications for Enrollment of Choctaw Newborn
Act of 1905   Volume XVII

Subscribed and sworn to before me this 17 day of Jun 1905
JT Gardner
nPS.D. I.T.

BIRTH AFFIDAVIT.

DEPARTMENT OF THE INTERIOR.
COMMISSION TO THE FIVE CIVILIZED TRIBES.

IN RE APPLICATION FOR ENROLLMENT, as a citizen of the   Choctaw   Nation, of Rosa Anna Mays   , born on the   17th   day of   Jan   , 1903

Name of Father: Will Mays   a citizen of the   U.S.   ~~Nation~~.
Name of Mother: Molinda[sic] Spring (Mays)   a citizen of the   Choctaw   Nation.

Postoffice   Milburn Ind Ter

AFFIDAVIT OF MOTHER.

UNITED STATES OF AMERICA, Indian Territory, ⎱
     Central   DISTRICT.   ⎰

I,   Molinda Spring (Mays)   , on oath state that I am   22   years of age and a citizen by   Blood   , of the   Choctaw   Nation; that I am the lawful wife of   Will Mays   , who is a citizen, by   Blood   of the   U S———   Nation; that a Female   child was born to me on   17th   day of   January   , 1903; that said child has been named   Rosa Anna Mays   , and was living March 4, 1905.

Malinda Spring (Mays)

Witnesses To Mark:
{

Subscribed and sworn to before me this   25th day of   April   , 1905

J. T. Hoover
Notary Public.

Applications for Enrollment of Choctaw Newborn
Act of 1905   Volume XVII

United States of America }
Central Dist. Ind Ter }

I Isaac Spring state on oath that Mrs Mary Benson a midwife attended on Mrs Molinda Spring (Mays) on the 17th day of January 1903 and that the said Mary Benson is now dead.

And being a brother to Mrs Molinda Spring (Mays) I was there and that there was a female child born to Mrs Molinda Spring (Mays) on the 17th day of January 1903 and that said child has bin named Rosa Anna Mays and was living March 4th 1905.

                                       Isaac Spring

Sworn and subscribed to before me this the 25th day of April 1905

                                     J.T. Hoover Notary Public

My commission expires Feb 26-1906

                                                           7-1399.

                           Muskogee, Indian Territory, April 29, 1905.

Will Mays,
        Milburn, Indian Territory.

Dear Sir:

        Receipt is hereby acknowledged of the affidavits of Melinda (Spring) Mays and Isaac Spring to the birth of Rose Anna Mays, daughter of Will and Melinda (Spring) Mays, January 17, 1903, and the same have been filed with our records as an application for the enrollment of said child.

                         Respectfully,

                                       Chairman.

Applications for Enrollment of Choctaw Newborn
Act of 1905   Volume XVII

Sub -

7-NB-1299.

Muskogee, Indian Territory, June 13, 1905.

Will Mays,
    Milburn, Indian Territory.

Dear Sir:

    Referring to the application for the enrollment of your infant child, Rosa Anna Mays, born January 17, 1903, it is noted in the affidavits heretofore filed in this office that the midwife who attended upon your wife at the time of the birth of the applicant is dead.

    In this event it will be necessary for you to file in this office the affidavits of two persons who are disinterested and not related to the applicant, who have actual knowledge of the facts: that the child was born, the date of her birth, that she was living on March 4, 1905 and that Molinda[sic] Spring Mays is her mother.

    This matter should receive your immediate attention as no further action can be taken until these affidavits have been furnished the Commission.

    Respectfully,

    Chairman.

7-NB-1299

Muskogee, Indian Territory, July 21, 1905.

Will Mays,
    Hugo, Indian Territory.

Dear Sir:

    Receipt is hereby acknowledged of your letter of July 12, 1905, enclosing affidavits of George Chotau and Annie Lee Bills to the birth of Rose Anna Mays daughter of Malinda Spring Mays and Will Mays, January 17, 1903, and the same have been filed with the records of this office in the matter of the enrollment of said child.

    Respectfully,

    Commissioner.

Applications for Enrollment of Choctaw Newborn
Act of 1905 Volume XVII

Choc. New Born 1300
    Samuel C. Tigert
    (Born Feb. 8, 1903)
    Bertha M. Tigert
    (Born March 3, 1904)

NEW-BORN AFFIDAVIT.

Number

...Choctaw Enrolling Commission...

IN THE MATTER OF THE APPLICATION FOR ENROLLMENT, as a citizen of the Choctaw Nation, of Samuel C. Tigert

born on the 8th day of February 190 3

Name of father Samuel Tigert   a citizen of ———
Nation final enrollment No. ———
Name of mother Julia A Tigert   a citizen of Choctaw
Nation final enrollment No. 10676

                                               Postoffice   Matoy I.T.

AFFIDAVIT OF MOTHER.

UNITED STATES OF AMERICA
INDIAN TERRITORY
  Central   DISTRICT

        I   Julia A Tigert   , on oath state that I am 25 years of age and a citizen by blood of the Choctaw Nation, and as such have been placed upon the final roll of the Choctaw Nation, by the Honorable Secretary of the Interior my final enrollment number being 10676 ; that I am the lawful wife of Samuel Tigert , who is a citizen of the ——— Nation, and as such has been placed upon the final roll of said Nation by the Honorable Secretary of the Interior, his final enrollment number being ——— and that a Male child was born to me on the 8th day of February 190 3; that said child has been named Samuel C. Tigert , and is now living.

                                               Julia A Tigert

Witnesseth.
  Must be two ⎫ Inez Reid
  Witnesses who ⎬
  are Citizens. ⎭ Fannie Wilson

Applications for Enrollment of Choctaw Newborn
Act of 1905   Volume XVII

Subscribed and sworn to before me this 23ᵈ day of February 190 5

A.E. Folsom
Notary Public.

My commission expires:
Jan 9-1909

AFFIDAVIT OF ATTENDING PHYSICIAN OR MIDWIFE

UNITED STATES OF AMERICA
INDIAN TERRITORY
Central   DISTRICT

I, Caroline Folsom   a   mid wife on oath state that I attended on Mrs. Julia A Tigert   wife of Samuel Tigert on the 8ᵗʰ day of February, 190 3, that there was born to her on said date a   male child, that said child is now living, and is said to have been named   Samuel C. Tigert

R. T. Largen
Dan Smith

her
Caroline x Folsom
mark

mid wife
~~M.D.~~

WITNESSETH:
Must be two witnesses who are citizens and know the child. { Inez Reid
Fannie Wilson

Subscribed and sworn to before me this, the   25   day of Feb A.D. 190 5

J.H.P. Smith   Notary Public.

We hereby certify that we are well acquainted with   Caroline Folsom   a   mid wife   and know   her   to be reputable and of good standing in the community.

{ Inez Reid
Fannie Wilson

216

Applications for Enrollment of Choctaw Newborn
Act of 1905 Volume XVII

NEW-BORN AFFIDAVIT.

Number..............

...Choctaw Enrolling Commission...

IN THE MATTER OF THE APPLICATION FOR ENROLLMENT, as a citizen of the Choctaw Nation, of Bertha May Tigert

born on the 3 day of March 190 4

Name of father Samuel Tigert   a citizen of ————
Nation final enrollment No. ——
Name of mother Julia A Tigert   a citizen of   Choctaw
Nation final enrollment No. 10676

Postoffice   Matoy I.T.

AFFIDAVIT OF MOTHER.

UNITED STATES OF AMERICA
INDIAN TERRITORY
Central   DISTRICT

I   Julia A Tigert   , on oath state that I am 25 years of age and a citizen by blood of the Choctaw Nation, and as such have been placed upon the final roll of the Choctaw Nation, by the Honorable Secretary of the Interior my final enrollment number being 10676 ; that I am the lawful wife of Samuel Tigert , who is a citizen of the —— Nation, and as such has been placed upon the final roll of said Nation by the Honorable Secretary of the Interior, his final enrollment number being —— and that a Female child was born to me on the 3^d day of March 190 4; that said child has been named Bertha May Tigert , and is now living.

Julia A Tigert

Witnesseth.
Must be two ⎫ Theodore Benton
Witnesses who ⎬
are Citizens. ⎭ Inez Reid

Subscribed and sworn to before me this 23^d day of February 190 5

A.E. Folsom
Notary Public.

My commission expires:
Jan 9-1909

Applications for Enrollment of Choctaw Newborn
Act of 1905 Volume XVII

AFFIDAVIT OF ATTENDING PHYSICIAN OR MIDWIFE

UNITED STATES OF AMERICA
INDIAN TERRITORY
Central DISTRICT

I, Caroline Folsom a mid wife on oath state that I attended on Mrs. Julia A Tigert wife of Samuel Tigert on the 3^d day of March, 190 4, that there was born to her on said date a Female child, that said child is now living, and is said to have been named Bertha May Tigert

R.T. Largen her *mid wife*
Dan Smith Caroline x Folsom ~~M.D.~~
WITNESSETH: mark

Must be two witnesses who are citizens and know the child.
{ Theodore Benton
Inez Reid }

Subscribed and sworn to before me this, the 25 day of Feb A.D. 190 5

J.H.P. Smith Notary Public.

We hereby certify that we are well acquainted with Caroline Folsom a mid wife and know her to be reputable and of good standing in the community.

{ Theodore Benton
Inez Reid }

BIRTH AFFIDAVIT.

DEPARTMENT OF THE INTERIOR.
COMMISSION TO THE FIVE CIVILIZED TRIBES.

IN RE APPLICATION FOR ENROLLMENT, as a citizen of the Choctaw Nation, of Samuel C Tigert, born on the 8 day of Feb, 1903

Name of Father: Samuel Tigert   a citizen of the Choctaw Nation.
Name of Mother: Julia A Tigert   a citizen of the Choctaw Nation.

Postoffice Matoy I.T.

Applications for Enrollment of Choctaw Newborn
Act of 1905 Volume XVII

AFFIDAVIT OF MOTHER.

UNITED STATES OF AMERICA, Indian Territory,
Central DISTRICT.

I, Julia A. Tigert, on oath state that I am 25 years of age and a citizen by Blood, of the Choctaw Nation; that I am the lawful wife of Samuel Tigert, who is a citizen, by U.S. of the ——— Nation; that a male child was born to me on 8th day of February, 1903; that said child has been named Samuel C. Tigert, and was living March 4, 1905.

Julia A. Tigert

Witnesses To Mark:
{

Subscribed and sworn to before me this 24 day of Apr, 1905

J.H.P. Smith
Notary Public.

AFFIDAVIT OF ATTENDING PHYSICIAN OR MID-WIFE.

UNITED STATES OF AMERICA, Indian Territory,
DISTRICT.

I, Catherine Folsom, a midwife, on oath state that I attended on Mrs. Julia A Tigert, wife of Samuel Tigert on the 8 day of Feb, 1903; that there was born to her on said date a male child; that said child was living March 4, 1905, and is said to have been named Samuel C Tigert

her
Catherine x Folsom
mark

Witnesses To Mark:
{ L L Robertson
{ J.H.P. Smith

Subscribed and sworn to before me this 25 day of April, 1905

JHP Smith
Notary Public.

Applications for Enrollment of Choctaw Newborn
Act of 1905   Volume XVII

BIRTH AFFIDAVIT.

DEPARTMENT OF THE INTERIOR.
COMMISSION TO THE FIVE CIVILIZED TRIBES.

IN RE APPLICATION FOR ENROLLMENT, as a citizen of the   Choctaw   Nation, of Bertha M Tigert   , born on the   3   day of   Mch   , 1904

Name of Father: Samuel Tigert   a citizen of the   U.S.   Nation.
Name of Mother: Julia A Tigert   a citizen of the   Choctaw   Nation.

Postoffice   Matoy I.T.

AFFIDAVIT OF MOTHER.

UNITED STATES OF AMERICA, Indian Territory,
Central   DISTRICT.

I,   Julia A. Tigert   , on oath state that I am   25   years of age and a citizen by   Blood   , of the   Choctaw   Nation; that I am the lawful wife of   Samuel Tigert   , who is a citizen, by   U.S.   of the   ———   Nation; that a   Female   child was born to me on   3rd day of   Mch   , 1904; that said child has been named Bertha M. Tigert   , and was living March 4, 1905.

Julia A. Tigert

Witnesses To Mark:
{

Subscribed and sworn to before me this   24   day of   April   , 1905

J.H.P. Smith
Notary Public.

AFFIDAVIT OF ATTENDING PHYSICIAN OR MID-WIFE.

UNITED STATES OF AMERICA, Indian Territory,
....DISTRICT.

I,   Catherine Folsom   , a   midwife   , on oath state that I attended on Mrs.   Julia A Tigert   , wife of   Samuel Tigert   on the   3rd day of   Mch   , 1904; that there was born to her on said date a .... child; that said child was living March 4, 1905, and is said to have been named   Bertha M Tigert

her
Catherine x Folsom
mark

Applications for Enrollment of Choctaw Newborn
Act of 1905 Volume XVII

Witnesses To Mark:
 { L L Robertson
   J.H.P. Smith

    Subscribed and sworn to before me this 25 day of April , 1905

                              J.H.P. Smith
                                    Notary Public.

                                                        7-3782.

                        Muskogee, Indian Territory, April 29, 1905.

Samuel Tigert,
    Matoy, Indian Territory.

Dear Sir:

    Receipt is hereby acknowledged of the affidavits of Julia A. Tigert and Catherine Folsom to the birth of Samuel C. Tigert and Bertha M. Tigert, children of Samuel and Julia A. Tigert February 8, 1903, and March 3, 1904, respectively, and the same have been filed with our records as an application for the enrollment of said children.

                        Respectfully,

                                          Chairman.

Choc. New Born 1301
    Ester James
    (Born Oct. 11, 1904)

Applications for Enrollment of Choctaw Newborn
Act of 1905   Volume XVII

NEW-BORN AFFIDAVIT.

Number..............

...Choctaw Enrolling Commission...

IN THE MATTER OF THE APPLICATION FOR ENROLLMENT, as a citizen of the Choctaw Nation, of Ester James born on the 11th day of October 190 4

Name of father W.C. James   a citizen of Choctaw Nation final enrollment No. 13597
Name of mother Rhoda N Vinson *now James*   a citizen of Choctaw Nation final enrollment No. 11403

Postoffice Lehigh I.T.

AFFIDAVIT OF MOTHER.

UNITED STATES OF AMERICA
INDIAN TERRITORY
Central   DISTRICT

I Rhoda N Vinson, *now James*, on oath state that I am 20 years of age and a citizen by blood of the Choctaw Nation, and as such have been placed upon the final roll of the Choctaw Nation, by the Honorable Secretary of the Interior my final enrollment number being 11403 ; that I am the lawful wife of W. C. James, who is a citizen of the Choctaw Nation, and as such has been placed upon the final roll of said Nation by the Honorable Secretary of the Interior, his final enrollment number being 13597 and that a female child was born to me on the 11th day of October 190 4; that said child has been named Ester James, and is now living.

Rhoda N Vinson *now James*

Witnesseth.
Must be two Witnesses who are Citizens.   W.H. Marshall
                                          Ben Moses

Subscribed and sworn to before me this 12th day of Jan 190 5

W A Shoney
Notary Public.

My commission expires:
Jan 11th 1909

Applications for Enrollment of Choctaw Newborn
Act of 1905   Volume XVII

Affidavit of Attending Physician or Midwife.

UNITED STATES OF AMERICA
INDIAN TERRITORY
Central   DISTRICT

I, T. W. Hensel a practicing physician on oath state that I attended on Mrs. Rhoda James wife of W.C. James on the 11th day of October , 190 4 , that there was born to her on said date a female child, that said child is now living, and is said to have been named Ester James

Thos. W. Hensel   M.D.

Subscribed and sworn to before me this, the 13 day of January 190 5

Dwight Brown
Notary Public.

WITNESSETH:
Must be two witnesses who are citizens and know the child.
C C Rose
M.A. Vinson

We hereby certify that we are well acquainted with T.W. Hensel a practicing physician and know him to be reputable and of good standing in the community.

M.A. Vinson
N C James

BIRTH AFFIDAVIT.

DEPARTMENT OF THE INTERIOR.
COMMISSION TO THE FIVE CIVILIZED TRIBES.

IN RE APPLICATION FOR ENROLLMENT, as a citizen of the Choctaw Nation, of Ester James , born on the 11th day of October , 1904

Name of Father: Willie C. James   a citizen of the Choctaw Nation.
Name of Mother: Rhoda James (nee Vinson)   a citizen of the Choctaw Nation.

Postoffice   Lehigh, Ind. Terr.

Applications for Enrollment of Choctaw Newborn
Act of 1905 Volume XVII

AFFIDAVIT OF MOTHER.

UNITED STATES OF AMERICA, Indian Territory, }
Central DISTRICT. }

I, Rhoda James, on oath state that I am 20 years of age and a citizen by blood, of the Choctaw Nation; that I am the lawful wife of Willie C. James, who is a citizen, by blood of the Choctaw Nation; that a female child was born to me on 11th day of October, 1905[sic]; that said child has been named Ester James, and was living March 4, 1905.

Rhoda James

Witnesses To Mark:
{

Subscribed and sworn to before me this 26th day of April, 1905

Dwight Brown
Notary Public.

AFFIDAVIT OF ATTENDING PHYSICIAN OR MID-WIFE.

UNITED STATES OF AMERICA, Indian Territory, }
Central DISTRICT. }

I, T.W. Hensal, a physician, on oath state that I attended on Mrs. Rhoda James, wife of Willie C James on the 11th day of October, 1904; that there was born to her on said date a female child; that said child was living March 4, 1905, and is said to have been named Ester James

Thos. W. Hensal M.D.

Witnesses To Mark:
{

Subscribed and sworn to before me this 25 day of April, 1905

Dwight Brown
Notary Public.

Applications for Enrollment of Choctaw Newborn
Act of 1905   Volume XVII

BIRTH AFFIDAVIT.

DEPARTMENT OF THE INTERIOR.
COMMISSION TO THE FIVE CIVILIZED TRIBES.

IN RE APPLICATION FOR ENROLLMENT, as a citizen of the Choctaw Nation, of Ester James, born on the 11th day of Oct, 1904

Name of Father: Willie C. James   Roll 13597   a citizen of the Choctaw Nation.
Name of Mother: Rhoda James   " 11403   a citizen of the Choctaw Nation.

Postoffice   Lehigh, I.T.

AFFIDAVIT OF MOTHER.

UNITED STATES OF AMERICA, Indian Territory,
Central   DISTRICT.

I, Rhoda James, on oath state that I am 20 years of age and a citizen by blood, of the Choctaw Nation; that I am the lawful wife of Willie C. James, who is a citizen, by blood of the Choctaw Nation; that a female child was born to me on 11th day of October, 1904; that said child has been named Ester James, and was living March 4, 1905.

Rhoda James

Witnesses To Mark:

Subscribed and sworn to before me this 19 day of June, 1905.

Dwight Brown
Notary Public.

7-4077.

Muskogee, Indian Territory, April 29, 1905.

Willie C. James,
   Lehigh, Indian Territory.

Dear Sir:

Receipt is hereby acknowledged of the affidavits of Rhoda James and Thos. W. Hensal to the birth of Ester James daughter of Willie C. and Rhoda James, October 11,

Applications for Enrollment of Choctaw Newborn
Act of 1905 Volume XVII

1904, and the same have been filed with our records as an application for the enrollment of said child.

Respectfully,

Chairman.

7--NB--1302[sic]

Muskogee, Indian Territory, June 2, 1905.

Willie C. James,
    Lehigh, Indian Territory.

Dear Sir:

There is enclosed you herewith for execution in support of the application for the enrollment of your infant child, Ester James.

In the affidavit of the mother of the applicant dated April 26, 1905, the date of birth is given as October 11, 1905, while in the affidavit of the attending physician this date is given as October 11, 1904. In the enclosed affidavit the date of birth is left blank. Please insert the correct date and when the affidavit is properly executed return to this office.

In having the affidavit executed care should be exercised to see that all names are written in full, as they appear in the body of the affidavit, and in the event the person signing the affidavit is unable to write, signature by mark must be attested by two witnesses. The affidavit must be executed before a Notary Public and the notarial seal and signature of the officer must be attached thereto.

This matter should receive your immediate attention as no further action can be taken relative to the enrollment of said child until the Commission has been furnished this affidavit.

Respectfully,

Commissioner in Charge.

Enc-FVK-14

Applications for Enrollment of Choctaw Newborn
Act of 1905   Volume XVII

7 NB 1301

Muskogee, Indian Territory, June 21, 1905.

Willie C. James,
    Lehigh, Indian Territory.

Dear Sir:

    Receipt is hereby acknowledged of the affidavit of Rhoda James to the birth of Ester James, daughter of Willie C. and Rhoda James, October 11, 1904, and the same has been filed in the matter of the enrollment of said child.

    Respectfully,

    Chairman.

Choc. New Born 1302
    Eddie Luttrel
    (Born Feb. 23, 1904)

BIRTH AFFIDAVIT.

DEPARTMENT OF THE INTERIOR.
COMMISSION TO THE FIVE CIVILIZED TRIBES.

IN RE APPLICATION FOR ENROLLMENT, as a citizen of the Choctaw Nation, of Eddie Luttrel, born on the 23rd day of February, 1904

Name of Father: Elzy Luttrel   a citizen of the United States ~~Nation~~.
Name of Mother: Ida Luttrel   a citizen of the Choctaw Nation.

Postoffice   Atoka, IT

AFFIDAVIT OF MOTHER.

UNITED STATES OF AMERICA, Indian Territory, }
    Central   DISTRICT.

    I, Ida Luttrel, on oath state that I am 25 years of age and a citizen by blood, of the Choctaw Nation; that I am the lawful wife of Elzy Luttrel, who is a citizen, ~~by~~ of the United States ~~Nation~~; that a female child was

Applications for Enrollment of Choctaw Newborn
Act of 1905   Volume XVII

born to me on   23rd   day of   February   , 1904; that said child has been named Eddie Luttrel   , and was living March 4, 1905.

                                  her
                              Ida x Luttrel

Witnesses To Mark: mark
{ Arthur O. Archer
{ V. Hicks

    Subscribed and sworn to before me this   27th   day of   April   , 1905

                                  W.H. Angell
                                     Notary Public.

AFFIDAVIT OF ATTENDING PHYSICIAN OR MID-WIFE.

UNITED STATES OF AMERICA, Indian Territory, }
   Central   DISTRICT. }

    I,   Ada Shepperd[sic]   , a   midwife   , on oath state that I attended on Mrs.   Ida Luttrel   , wife of   Elzy Luttrel   on the   23rd   day of   February   , 1904; that there was born to her on said date a   female   child; that said child was living March 4, 1905, and is said to have been named   Eddie Luttrel

                              her
                         Ada x Shepperd
Witnesses To Mark: mark
{ Arthur O. Archer
{ V. Hicks

    Subscribed and sworn to before me this   27th   day of   April   , 1905

                                  W.H. Angell
                                   Notary Public.

Choc. New Born 1303
    Lily Wade
    (Born Sept. 2, 1903)
    Eli Wade
    (Born Feb. 1, 1905)

Applications for Enrollment of Choctaw Newborn
Act of 1905   Volume XVII

7 - 13359

BIRTH AFFIDAVIT.

DEPARTMENT OF THE INTERIOR.
COMMISSION TO THE FIVE CIVILIZED TRIBES.

IN RE APPLICATION FOR ENROLLMENT, as a citizen of the Choctaw Nation, of Eli Wade, born on the 1st day of February, 1905

Name of Father: Willis Wade   a citizen of the Choctaw Nation.
Name of Mother: Emma Wade   a citizen of the Choctaw Nation.

Postoffice   Shady Point, I. T.

AFFIDAVIT OF MOTHER.

UNITED STATES OF AMERICA, Indian Territory,
Central   DISTRICT.

I, Emma Wade, on oath state that I am 23 years of age and a citizen by blood, of the Choctaw Nation; that I am the lawful wife of Willis Wade, who is a citizen, by blood of the Choctaw Nation; that a male child was born to me on 1st day of February, 1905; that said child has been named Eli Wade, and was living March 4, 1905.

　　　　　　　　　　　　　　　　　her
　　　　　　　　　　　　　Emma x Wade
Witnesses To Mark:　　　　　　mark
　{ Chas T Difendafer
　 OL Johnson

Subscribed and sworn to before me this 6 day of April, 1905

　　　　　　　　　　　　OL Johnson
　　　　　　　　　　　　　Notary Public.

AFFIDAVIT OF ATTENDING PHYSICIAN OR MID-WIFE.

UNITED STATES OF AMERICA, Indian Territory,
　　　　　　　　　　　DISTRICT.

I, Sadie Jim, a midwife, on oath state that I attended on Mrs. Emma Wade, wife of Willis Wade on the 1st day of February, 1905; that there was born to her on said date a male child; that said child was living March 4, 1905, and is said to have been named Eli Wade

Applications for Enrollment of Choctaw Newborn
Act of 1905 Volume XVII

Witnesses To Mark:
{ Chas T Difendafer
{ OL Johnson

Sadie x Jim
(her mark)

Subscribed and sworn to before me this 6 day of April, 1905

OL Johnson
Notary Public.

7- 13359
BIRTH AFFIDAVIT.

DEPARTMENT OF THE INTERIOR.
COMMISSION TO THE FIVE CIVILIZED TRIBES.

IN RE APPLICATION FOR ENROLLMENT, as a citizen of the Choctaw Nation, of Lily Wade, born on the 2 day of September, 1903

Name of Father: Willis Wade   a citizen of the Choctaw Nation.
Name of Mother: Emma Wade   a citizen of the Choctaw Nation.

Postoffice   Shady Point, I.T.

AFFIDAVIT OF MOTHER.

UNITED STATES OF AMERICA, Indian Territory,
Central DISTRICT.

I, Emma Wade, on oath state that I am 23 years of age and a citizen by blood, of the Choctaw Nation; that I am the lawful wife of Willis Wade, who is a citizen, by blood of the Choctaw Nation; that a female child was born to me on 2 day of September, 1903; that said child has been named Lily Wade, and was living March 4, 1905.

Emma x Wade
(her mark)

Witnesses To Mark:
{ Chas T Difendafer
{ OL Johnson

Subscribed and sworn to before me this 6 day of April, 1905

OL Johnson
Notary Public.

Applications for Enrollment of Choctaw Newborn
Act of 1905   Volume XVII

AFFIDAVIT OF ATTENDING PHYSICIAN OR MID-WIFE.

UNITED STATES OF AMERICA, Indian Territory, }
.... DISTRICT. }

    I, Louvicy Barnett, a midwife, on oath state that I attended on Mrs. Emma Wade, wife of Willis Wade on the 2 day of September, 1903; that there was born to her on said date a female child; that said child was living March 4, 1905, and is said to have been named Lily Wade

                                              her
                                    Louvicy x Barnett
Witnesses To Mark: mark
  { Chas T Difendafer
  { OL Johnson

    Subscribed and sworn to before me this 6 day of April, 1905

                                  OL Johnson
                                        Notary Public.

                            Muskogee, Indian Territory, April 12, 1905.

Willis Wade,
    Shadypoint, Indian Territory.

Dear Sir:

    Receipt is hereby acknowledged of the affidavits of Emma Wade and Louvicy Barnett to the birth of Lily Wade, daughter of Willis and Emma Wade, September 2nd, 1903; also the affidavits of Emma Wade and Sadie Jim to the birth of Eli Wade, son of Willis and Emma Wade, February 1st, 1905. These affidavits have been filed with our records as an application for the enrollment of said children.

    It appears from the affidavits of the mother that she is a citizen by blood of the Chickasaw Nation, and if this is correct, you are requested to state the name under which she was enrolled, the names of her parents, and if she has selected an allotment of the lands of the Choctaw and Chickasaw Nations please give her roll number as it appears upon her allotment certificate.

                            Respectfully,

                                      Commissioner in Charge.

Applications for Enrollment of Choctaw Newborn
Act of 1905   Volume XVII

(The letter below typed as given.)

Shadypoint, I. T. April 25, 1905/

The Commission,

Dear Sir:

In reply to your of 12th inst will say that my wife enrolled name is Emma Thomas Her enroll No. is 1244 or at least that is the number on her certificate.

Yours Resp.
Willis Wade.

Choc. New Born 1304
    Jewel Edward Atkins
    (Born March 8, 1904)

NEW-BORN AFFIDAVIT.

Number............

Choctaw Enrolling Commission.

IN THE MATTER OF THE APPLICATION FOR ENROLLMENT, as a citizen of the Choctaw   Nation, of   Jewel Edward Atkins

born on the   8   day of   March   190 4

Name of father   John E Atkins   a citizen of   Choctaw
Nation final enrollment No   9758
Name of mother   Ethel Atkins   a citizen of   white
Nation final enrollment No ——

Postoffice   Wade I.T.

Applications for Enrollment of Choctaw Newborn
Act of 1905   Volume XVII

AFFIDAVIT OF MOTHER.

UNITED STATES OF AMERICA,
INDIAN TERRITORY,
Central   DISTRICT

I   Ethel Atkins   on oath state that I am 25 years of ~~age and a citizen~~ by   white   of the —— Nation, and as such have been placed upon the final roll of the   ————   Nation, by the Honorable Secretary of the Interior my final enrollment number being —— ; that I am the lawful wife of   John E. Atkins, who is a citizen of the   Choctaw *(blood)*   Nation, and as such has been placed upon the final roll of said Nation by the Honorable Secretary of the Interior, his final enrollment number being 9758 and that a   male   child was born to me on the 8 day of   March   190 4 ; that said child has been named   Jewel Edward Atkins   , and is now living.

Ethel Atkins

WITNESSETH:
Must be two Witnesses who are Citizens.   E E Dyer
Frances Durr

Subscribed and sworn to before me this   16   day of   January   190 5

James Bower
Notary Public.

My commission expires Sept 23-1908

AFFIDAVIT OF ATTENDING PHYSICIAN OR MIDWIFE

UNITED STATES OF AMERICA
INDIAN TERRITORY
Central   DISTRICT

I,   Mrs Edna Todd   a   midwife on oath state that I attended on Mrs.   Ethel Atkins   wife of   John E Atkins on the 8 day of   March , 190 4 , that there was born to her on said date a   Male child, that said child is now living, and is said to have been named   Jewel Edward Atkins

Edna Todd   *Midwife* M.D.

Subscribed and sworn to before me this, the .... day of .... 190......

L.D. Horton
Notary Public.

WITNESSETH:
Must be two witnesses who are citizens and know the child.   E.E. Dyer
Frances Durr

Applications for Enrollment of Choctaw Newborn
Act of 1905   Volume XVII

We hereby certify that we are well acquainted with ....
a .... and know .... to be reputable and of good standing in the community.

{ E.E. Dyer

Frances Durr

BIRTH AFFIDAVIT.

DEPARTMENT OF THE INTERIOR.
COMMISSION TO THE FIVE CIVILIZED TRIBES.

IN RE APPLICATION FOR ENROLLMENT, as a citizen of the   Choctaw   Nation, of Jewel Edward Atkins   , born on the 8th day of March , 1904

Name of Father: John E. Atkins   a citizen of the Choctaw   Nation.
Name of Mother: Ethel Atkins   a citizen of the Choctaw   Nation.

Postoffice   Wade Ind Ter

AFFIDAVIT OF MOTHER.

UNITED STATES OF AMERICA, Indian Territory, }
Central   DISTRICT.

I, Ethel Atkins , on oath state that I am 25 years of age and a citizen by Intermarriage , of the Choctaw Nation; that I am the lawful wife of John E Atkins , who is a citizen, by Blood of the Choctaw Nation; that a Male child was born to me on 8th day of March , 1904; that said child has been named Jewel Edward Atkins , and was living March 4, 1905.

Ethel Atkins

Witnesses To Mark:

Subscribed and sworn to before me this 20 day of April , 1905

Chas.P.Smith
Notary Public.

Applications for Enrollment of Choctaw Newborn
Act of 1905   Volume XVII

AFFIDAVIT OF ATTENDING PHYSICIAN OR MID-WIFE.

UNITED STATES OF AMERICA, Indian Territory,　⎫
　Central　　　　　　　　DISTRICT.　⎭

　　　I,　W.E. Howard　　, a　Physician　　, on oath state that I attended on Mrs.　Ethel Atkins　, wife of　John E Atkins　　on the 8th　day of　March　, 1904; that there was born to her on said date a　male　child; that said child was living March 4, 1905, and is said to have been named　Jewel Edward Atkins

　　　　　　　　　　　　　　　　　　Dr. W.E. Howard

Witnesses To Mark:
{

　　　Subscribed and sworn to before me this 20th　day of　April　　, 1905

　　　　　　　　　　　　　　　　　Chas.P.Smith
　　　　　　　　　　　　　　　　　　　Notary Public.

　　　　　　　　　　　　　　　　　　　　　7-3421

　　　　　　　　　Muskogee, Indian Territory, May 1, 1905.

John E. Atkins,
　　　Wade, Indian Territory.

Dear Sir:

　　　Receipt is hereby acknowledged of the affidavits of Ethel Atkins and Dr. W. E. Howard to the birth of Jewel Edward Atkins son of John E. and Ethel Atkins, March 8, 1904, and the same have been filed with our records as an application for the enrollment of said child.

　　　　　　　　　　　　Respectfully,

　　　　　　　　　　　　　　　　　　　　Chairman.

Applications for Enrollment of Choctaw Newborn
Act of 1905 Volume XVII

Choc. New Born 1305
   Cora Bell Beames
   (Born July 12, 1904)

NEW-BORN AFFIDAVIT.

Number..............

...Choctaw Enrolling Commission...

IN THE MATTER OF THE APPLICATION FOR ENROLLMENT, as a citizen of the Choctaw Nation, of Cora Bell Beams[sic]

born on the 12th day of ___July___ 190 4

Name of father William T Beams   a citizen of Choctaw Nation final enrollment No. 15512
Name of mother Lavina Victoria Beams   a citizen of Choctaw Nation final enrollment No. Pending

Postoffice Indianola I.T.

AFFIDAVIT OF MOTHER.

UNITED STATES OF AMERICA
INDIAN TERRITORY
   Western   DISTRICT

I Lavina Victoria Beams , on oath state that I am 31 years of age and a citizen by Intermarriage of the Choctaw Nation, and as such have been placed upon the final roll of the Choctaw Nation, (by the Honorable Secretary of the Interior) *Dawes Commission Feb 7th 1905* my final enrollment number being Pending ; that I am the lawful wife of William T Beams , who is a citizen of the Choctaw Nation, and as such has been placed upon the final roll of said Nation by the Honorable Secretary of the Interior, his final enrollment number being 15512 and that a Female child was born to me on the 12th day of July 190 4; that said child has been named Cora Bell Beams , and is now living.

                                                                  her
Witnesseth.   Lavina Victoria x Beams
   Must be two   } L H Perkins   mark
   Witnesses who }
   are Citizens.   Robert T Pearson

Applications for Enrollment of Choctaw Newborn
Act of 1905 Volume XVII

Subscribed and sworn to before me this 22^d day of Feb 190 5

SM Gold
Notary Public.

My commission expires: 2/19-1905

AFFIDAVIT OF ATTENDING PHYSICIAN OR MIDWIFE

UNITED STATES OF AMERICA
INDIAN TERRITORY
Western DISTRICT

I, Phoeby C Staton a Midwife on oath state that I attended on Mrs. Lavina Victoria Beams wife of William T Beams on the 12th day of July , 190 4 , that there was born to her on said date a Female child, that said child is now living, and is said to have been named Cora Bell Beams

her
Phoeby C x Staton 𝑚.𝒟.
mark

Subscribed and sworn to before me this, the 22^d day of February 190 5

WITNESSETH: S.M. Gold Notary Public.

Must be two witnesses who are citizens { L H Perkins
Robert T. Pearson

We hereby certify that we are well acquainted with Phoeby C Staton a Midwife and know her to be reputable and of good standing in the community.

_____ L.H. Perkins

_____ Robert T. Pearson

BIRTH AFFIDAVIT.

DEPARTMENT OF THE INTERIOR,
COMMISSION TO THE FIVE CIVILIZED TRIBES.

IN RE *Application for Enrollment,* as a citizen of the Choctaw Nation, of Cora Bell Beames , born on the 12 day of July , 1904

Name of Father: William T. Beames a citizen of the Choctaw Nation.
Name of Mother: Lavina Victory[sic] Beames a citizen of the United States Nation.

Post-Office: Indianola I.T.

Applications for Enrollment of Choctaw Newborn
Act of 1905 Volume XVII

AFFIDAVIT OF MOTHER.

UNITED STATES OF AMERICA, }
INDIAN TERRITORY.
Western District.

I, Lavina Victory Beames, on oath state that I am 30 years of age and a citizen by intermarriage, of the Choctaw Nation; that I am the lawful wife of William T. Beames, who is a citizen, by Blood of the Choctaw Nation; that a Female child was born to me on 12 day of July, 1904, that said child has been named Cora Bell Beames, and is now living.

                                            her
                                Lavina x Victory Beames

WITNESSES TO MARK: mark
{ E.L. Reed
  L.H. Perkins

Subscribed and sworn to before me this 22 *day of* April, 1905.

                              T.J. Rice
                              NOTARY PUBLIC.

AFFIDAVIT OF ATTENDING PHYSICIAN OR MID-WIFE.

UNITED STATES OF AMERICA, }
INDIAN TERRITORY.
                 District.

I, Pheby[sic] C Staton, a midwife, on oath state that I attended on Mrs. Lavina Victory Beames, wife of William T. Beames on the 12 day of July, 1904; that there was born to her on said date a Female child; that said child is now living and is said to have been named Cora Bell Beames

                              Pheby C Saton[sic]

WITNESSES TO MARK:
{

Subscribed and sworn to before me this 22 *day of* April, 1905.

                              T.J. Rice
                              NOTARY PUBLIC.

Applications for Enrollment of Choctaw Newborn
Act of 1905   Volume XVII

7-5710

Muskogee, Indian Territory, May 2, 1905.

William T. Beames,
    Indianola, Indian Territory.

Dear Sir:

    Receipt is hereby acknowledged of the affidavits of Lavina Victory Beames and Pheby C. Saton[sic] to the birth of Cora Bell Beames daughter of William T. and Lavina Victory Beames, July 12, 1904, and the same have been filed with our records as an application for the enrollment of said child.

               Respectfully,

                        Chairman.

<u>Choc. New Born 1306</u>
    Wyle E. Devenport
    (Born April 3, 1903)

NEW-BORN AFFIDAVIT.

        Number..................

Choctaw Enrolling Commission.

    IN THE MATTER OF THE APPLICATION FOR ENROLLMENT, as a citizen of the Choctaw   Nation, of   Wyley[sic] Edmond Devenport

born on the   3   day of   April   190 3

Name of father   George A Devenport   a citizen of   Choctaw *by intern*
Nation final enrollment No   181
Name of mother   Narcissa S Devenport   a citizen of   Choctaw
Nation final enrollment No   4973

              Postoffice   Soper I.T.

Applications for Enrollment of Choctaw Newborn
Act of 1905   Volume XVII

AFFIDAVIT OF MOTHER.

UNITED STATES OF AMERICA,
　INDIAN TERRITORY,
Central　　DISTRICT

I　　Narcissa S Devenport　　on oath state that I am 27 years of age and a citizen by Blood of the Choctaw Nation, and as such have been placed upon the final roll of the Choctaw Nation, by the Honorable Secretary of the Interior my final enrollment number being 4973 ; that I am the lawful wife of George A Devenport , who is a citizen of the Choctaw *by interm* Nation, and as such has been placed upon the final roll of said Nation by the Honorable Secretary of the Interior, his final enrollment number being 181 and that a male child was born to me on the 3 day of April 190 3 ; that said child has been named Wyley Edmond Devenport , and is now living.

　　　　　　　　　　　　　　　　　　her
　　　　　　　　　　　　　　Narcissa x Devenport
WITNESSETH:　　　　　　　　　　　　mark
Must be two Witnesses who are Citizens.　Robert Smallwood
　　　　　　　　　　　　　　Henry Williams

Subscribed and sworn to before me this 25 day of January 190 5

　　　　　　　　　　　　WE Larecy
　　　　　　　　　　　　　　Notary Public.

My commission expires ....

Affidavit of Attending Physician or Midwife

UNITED STATES OF AMERICA,
　INDIAN TERRITORY,
Central　　DISTRICT

I,　J.R.W. Kerr　　a　　Practicing Physician on oath state that I attended on Mrs. Narcissa S Devenport wife of George A Devenport on the 3 day of April , 190 3, that there was born to her on said date a male child, that said child is now living, and is said to have been named Wyley E Devenport

　　　　　　　　　　　James R.W. Kerr　　M. D.

Subscribed and sworn to before me this the 25 day of Jan 1905

　　　　　　　　　　　　WE Larecy
　　　　　　　　　　　　　　Notary Public.

WITNESSETH:
Must be two witnesses who are citizens and know the child.　Henry Williams
　　　　　　　　Robert Smallwood

Applications for Enrollment of Choctaw Newborn
Act of 1905 Volume XVII

We hereby certify that we are well acquainted with J.R.W. Kerr a Practicing Physician and know him to be reputable and of good standing in the community.

Must be two citizen witnesses. { R.C. Bills
Willy Griggs

BIRTH AFFIDAVIT.

DEPARTMENT OF THE INTERIOR.
COMMISSION TO THE FIVE CIVILIZED TRIBES.

IN RE APPLICATION FOR ENROLLMENT, as a citizen of the Choctaw Nation, of Wyle E. Devenport, born on the 3rd day of April, 1903

Name of Father: George A. Devenport   a citizen of the Choctaw Nation.
Name of Mother: Narcissa Devenport   a citizen of the Choctaw Nation.

Postoffice   Soper I.T.

AFFIDAVIT OF MOTHER.

UNITED STATES OF AMERICA, Indian Territory,
Central   DISTRICT.

I, Narcissa Devenport, on oath state that I am 27 years of age and a citizen by Blood, of the Choctaw Nation; that I am the lawful wife of George Devenport, who is a citizen, by Intm of the Choctaw Nation; that a male child was born to me on 3rd day of April, 1903; that said child has been named Wyle E Devenport, and was living March 4, 1905.

           her
Narcissa x Davenport[sic]
Witnesses To Mark: mark
{ *(Name Illegible)*
   Ellis Jones

Subscribed and sworn to before me this 22nd day of April, 1905

My commission expires
July 9th, 1908.   W.E. Larecy
           Notary Public.

Applications for Enrollment of Choctaw Newborn
Act of 1905   Volume XVII

AFFIDAVIT OF ATTENDING PHYSICIAN OR MID-WIFE.

UNITED STATES OF AMERICA, Indian Territory, }
Central   DISTRICT.

I, J.R.W. Kerr, a Physician, on oath state that I attended on Mrs. Narcissa Devenport, wife of George A Devenport on the 3rd day of April, 1903; that there was born to her on said date a _____ child; that said child was living March 4, 1905, and is said to have been named Wyle E. Devenport

James R.W. Kerr M.D.

Witnesses To Mark:
{

Subscribed and sworn to before me this 22nd day of April, 1905

My commission expires
July 9th, 1908.

W.E. Larecy
Notary Public.

7-1755

Muskogee, Indian Territory, May 2, 1905.

George A. Davenport[sic],
  Soper, Indian Territory.

Dear Sir:

Receipt is hereby acknowledged of the affidavits of Narcissa Davenport and James R. W. Kerr to the birth of Wyle E. Davenport son of George A. and Narcissa Davenport, April 3, 1903, and the same have been filed with our records as an application for the enrollment of said child.

Respectfully,

Chairman.

Applications for Enrollment of Choctaw Newborn
Act of 1905 Volume XVII

Choc. New Born 1307
    Viola Bell Goldston
    (Born March 20, 1903)

BIRTH AFFIDAVIT.

DEPARTMENT OF THE INTERIOR.
COMMISSION TO THE FIVE CIVILIZED TRIBES.

IN RE APPLICATION FOR ENROLLMENT, as a citizen of the Choctaw Nation, of Viola Bell Goldston, born on the 20 day of March, 1903

Name of Father: James William Goldston   a citizen of the Choctaw Nation.
Name of Mother: Estelle Goldston   a citizen of the Choctaw Nation.

        Postoffice   Allen, Indian Territory

AFFIDAVIT OF MOTHER.

UNITED STATES OF AMERICA, Indian Territory, }
    Central   DISTRICT. }

    I, Estelle Goldston, on oath state that I am twenty two years of age and a citizen by Blood, of the Choctaw Nation; that I am the lawful wife of James William Goldston, who is a citizen, by inter-marriage of the Choctaw Nation; that a Female child was born to me on 20 day of March, 1903; that said child has been named Viola Bell Goldston, and was living March 4, 1905.

                                    Estelle Goldston

Witnesses To Mark:
{

    Subscribed and sworn to before me this 17 day of April, 1905

                                      Richard E. Kemp
                                      Notary Public.

AFFIDAVIT OF ATTENDING PHYSICIAN OR MID-WIFE.

UNITED STATES OF AMERICA, Indian Territory, }
    Central   DISTRICT. }

    I, C. L. Goldston, a physician, on oath state that I attended on Mrs. Estelle Goldston, wife of James William Goldston on the 20 day of

Applications for Enrollment of Choctaw Newborn
Act of 1905   Volume XVII

March   , 1903; that there was born to her on said date a   Female   child; that said child was living March 4, 1905, and is said to have been named Viola Bell Goldston

                                              C. L. Goldston

Witnesses To Mark:
{

    Subscribed and sworn to before me this 17 day of   April   , 1905

                                                Richard E. Kemp
                                                Notary Public.

                                                7-339

                        Muskogee, Indian Territory, May 1, 1905.

James William Goldston,
    Allen, Indian Territory.

Dear Sir:

    Receipt is hereby acknowledged of your letter of April 22, 1905 enclosing the affidavits of Estelle Goldston and C. L. Goldston to the birth of Viola Bell Goldston daughter of James William Goldston and Estelle Goldston, March 20, 1903, and the same have been filed with our records as an application for the enrollment of said child.

                                Respectfully,

                                                Chairman.

Choc. New Born 1308
    Gracie Marie Bowlin
    (Born June 18, 1903)
    Dora Maud Laughlin
    (Born Oct. 24, 1904)

Applications for Enrollment of Choctaw Newborn
Act of 1905   Volume XVII

BIRTH AFFIDAVIT.

DEPARTMENT OF THE INTERIOR.
COMMISSION TO THE FIVE CIVILIZED TRIBES.

IN RE APPLICATION FOR ENROLLMENT, as a citizen of the Choctaw Nation, of Gracie Marie Bowlin, born on the 18 day of June, 1903

Name of Father: R M Bowlin   a citizen of the Choctaw Nation.
Name of Mother: Susie Bowlin   a citizen of the Choctaw Nation.

Postoffice   Conway, IT

AFFIDAVIT OF MOTHER.

UNITED STATES OF AMERICA, Indian Territory,
Southern   DISTRICT.

I, Susie Bowlin, on oath state that I am 19 years of age and a citizen by blood, of the Choctaw Nation; that I am the lawful wife of RM Bowlin *(now dead)*, who ~~is~~ *was* a citizen, by marriage of the Choctaw Nation; that a female child was born to me on the 18 day of June, 1903; that said child has been named Gracie Marie Bowlin, and was living March 4, 1905.

                        her
                Susie x Laughlin
Witnesses To Mark: mark
  JE Williams
  J.A. Laughlin

Subscribed and sworn to before me this 26 day of April, 1905

                JE Williams
                Notary Public.

BIRTH AFFIDAVIT.

DEPARTMENT OF THE INTERIOR.
COMMISSION TO THE FIVE CIVILIZED TRIBES.

IN RE APPLICATION FOR ENROLLMENT, as a citizen of the Choctaw Nation, of Dora Maud Laughlin, born on the 24 day of October, 1904

Name of Father: JA Laughlin   a citizen of the US ~~Nation~~.
Name of Mother: Susie Laughlin   a citizen of the Choctaw Nation.
                (Nee Bowlin)

Applications for Enrollment of Choctaw Newborn
Act of 1905 Volume XVII

Postoffice   Conway, I.T.

AFFIDAVIT OF MOTHER.

UNITED STATES OF AMERICA, Indian Territory, }
Southern   DISTRICT.

I, Susie Laughlin , on oath state that I am 19 years of age and a citizen by blood , of the Choctaw Nation; that I am the lawful wife of JA Laughlin , who is a citizen, by marriage of the Choctaw Nation; that a female child was born to me on the 24 day of October , 1904; that said child has been named Dora Maud Laughlin , and was living March 4, 1905.

                                    her
                             Susie x Laughlin
Witnesses To Mark: mark
{ JE Williams
{ J.A. Laughlin

Subscribed and sworn to before me this 26 day of April , 1905

                            JE Williams
                                Notary Public.

AFFIDAVIT OF ATTENDING PHYSICIAN OR MID-WIFE.

UNITED STATES OF AMERICA, Indian Territory, }
Southern   DISTRICT.

I, Dr O.F. Coffey , a Physician , on oath state that I attended on Mrs. Susie Bowlin , wife of R.M. Bowlin on the 18th day of June , 1903; that there was born to her on said date a Female child; that said child was living March 4, 1905, and is said to have been named Gracie Marie Bowlin

                              Dr O.F. Coffey
Witnesses To Mark:
{ ~~O.F. Coffey~~

Subscribed and sworn to before me this 28 day of April , 1905

                            J.W. Fulker
                               Notary Public.

Applications for Enrollment of Choctaw Newborn
Act of 1905   Volume XVII

AFFIDAVIT OF ATTENDING PHYSICIAN OR MID-WIFE.

UNITED STATES OF AMERICA, Indian Territory,
Southern   DISTRICT.

I, S D Rowe Midwife   , a................, on oath state that I attended on Mrs. Susie Laughlin , wife of J A Laughlin on the 24 day of October , 1904; that there was born to her on said date a   Female   child; that said child was living March 4, 1905, and is said to have been named Dora Maud Laughlin

S D Rowe

Witnesses To Mark:
{

Subscribed and sworn to before me this 29 day of April , 1905

J D Price
Notary Public.
My Time expires April 4 1905[sic]

BIRTH AFFIDAVIT.

DEPARTMENT OF THE INTERIOR.
COMMISSION TO THE FIVE CIVILIZED TRIBES.

IN RE APPLICATION FOR ENROLLMENT, as a citizen of the   Choctaw   Nation, of Gracie May[sic] Bowlin , born on the 18th day of June , 1903

Name of Father: R M Bowlin, deceased   a citizen of the   U.S.   ~~Nation~~.
Name of Mother: Susie Laughlin *formerly Bowlin* a citizen of the   Choctaw   Nation.
Roll 9429
Postoffice   Conway I.T

AFFIDAVIT OF MOTHER.

UNITED STATES OF AMERICA, Indian Territory,
.... DISTRICT.

I, Susie Laughlin *(Bowlin)*   , on oath state that I am 19 years of age and a citizen by   blood   , of the   Choctaw   Nation; that I ~~am~~ *was* the lawful wife of R M Bowlin, deceased , who ~~is~~ *was* a citizen, ~~by~~ ——— of the   United States   Nation; that a   female   child was born to me on 18th   day of June , 1903; that said child has been named   Gracie Marie Bowlin   , and was living March 4, 1905.

247

Applications for Enrollment of Choctaw Newborn
Act of 1905 Volume XVII

                                                      her
                                           Susie x Laughlin *(Bowlin)*
Witnesses To Mark: mark
{ OB Price
{ ? T Price

Subscribed and sworn to before me this 9 day of June, 1905

                                   J.D. Price
                                          Notary Public.

AFFIDAVIT OF ATTENDING PHYSICIAN OR MID-WIFE.

UNITED STATES OF AMERICA, Indian Territory, }
Southern Dist 16   DISTRICT.

    I, O.F. Coffey, a Physician, on oath state that I attended on Mrs. Susie Laughlin *formerly Bowlin*, ~~wife of~~ who was the wife of R M Bowlin *dec^d* on the 18 day of June, 1903; that there was born to her on said date a female child; that said child was living March 4, 1905, and is said to have been named Gracie Marie Bowlin

                                       O.F. Coffey
Witnesses To Mark:

{

Subscribed and sworn to before me this 9th day of June, 1905

                                   Jno. W. Fulker
                                       Notary Public.

BIRTH AFFIDAVIT.

DEPARTMENT OF THE INTERIOR.
COMMISSION TO THE FIVE CIVILIZED TRIBES.

      IN RE APPLICATION FOR ENROLLMENT, as a citizen of the Choctaw Nation, of Dora Maud Laughlin, born on the 24th day of October, 1904

Name of Father: J.A. Laughlin   a citizen of the U.S. ~~Nation~~.
Name of Mother: Susie Laughlin *nee Bowlin*   a citizen of the Choctaw Nation.

                            Postoffice   Conway I.T.

Applications for Enrollment of Choctaw Newborn
Act of 1905 Volume XVII

AFFIDAVIT OF MOTHER.

UNITED STATES OF AMERICA, Indian Territory, }
.... DISTRICT. }

I, ... on oath state that I am .... years of age and a citizen by ...., of the .... Nation; that I am the lawful wife of ...., who is a citizen, by .... of the .... Nation; that a .... child was born to me on .... day of ...., 1......., that said child has been named .... and was living March 4, 1905.

Witnesses To Mark:
{
....

Subscribed and sworn to before me this ...... day of ...., 1905.

....
Notary Public.

AFFIDAVIT OF ATTENDING PHYSICIAN OR MID-WIFE.

UNITED STATES OF AMERICA, Indian Territory, }
Southern Dist 16   DISTRICT. }

I,   S.D. Rowe , a   Midwife , on oath state that I attended on Mrs.   Susie Laughlin , wife of   J A Laughlin   on the 24th day of October , 1904; that there was born to her on said date a   female   child; that said child was living March 4, 1905, and is said to have been named   Dora Maud Laughlin

                                           S.D. Rowe

Witnesses To Mark:
{
....

Subscribed and sworn to before me this   9   day of   June , 1905

                                       Jno. W. Fulker
                                          Notary Public.

Applications for Enrollment of Choctaw Newborn
Act of 1905 Volume XVII

7-3267

Muskogee, Indian Territory, May 2, 1905.

J. A. Laughlin,
Conway, Indian Territory.

Dear Sir:

    Receipt is hereby acknowledged of the affidavit of Susie Laughlin to the birth of Dora Maud Laughlin daughter of J. A. and Susie Laughlin, October 24, 1904, also the affidavit of Susie Laughlin to the birth of Gracie Marie Bowlin daughter of R. M. Bowlin and Susie Laughlin, June 18, 1903, and the same have been filed with our records as applications for the enrollment of said children.

Respectfully,

Chairman.

7-NB-1308.

Muskogee, Indian Territory, June 5, 1905.

Susie Laughlin,
Conway, Indian Territory.

Dear Madam:

    There are enclosed herewith application for the enrollment of your infant child, Gracie May[sic] Bowlin, and a blank affidavit to be executed by the attending physician or midwife in the matter of the application for the enrollment of your infant child, Dora Maud Laughlin.

    In the affidavits heretofore filed, in the matter of the application for the enrollment of your infant child, Gracie Marie Bowlin, you give your name as Susie Bowlin, stating that your[sic] are the wife of R. M. Bowlin and then sign your name as "Susie Laughlin." It also appears that R. M. Bowlin, the father of the applicant, is now dead. The enclosed affidavit is to who that you were the wife of R. M. Bowlin which you will please sign as Susie Laughlin (Bowlin.) In the application above referred to the affidavit of the attending physician or midwife has been omitted. It will be necessary that you supply this affidavit.

    In the matter of the application for the enrollment of Dora Maud Laughlin it is noted that the affidavit of the attending physician or midwife was omitted from the application heretofore file in this office, which you will please supply.

Applications for Enrollment of Choctaw Newborn
Act of 1905   Volume XVII

In having these affidavits executed care should be exercised to see that all names are written in full, as they appear in the body of the affidavit, and in the event that either of the persons signing the affidavit are unable to write, signatures by mark must be attested by two witnesses. Each affidavit must be executed before a Notary Public and the notarial seal and signature of the officer must be attached to each separate affidavit.

This matter should receive your immediate attention, as no further action can be taken until these affidavits are filed with the Commission.

Respectfully,

VR 5-3. [sic]

7-NB 1308

Muskogee, Indian Territory, June 13, 1905.

J. A. Laughlin,
   Conway, Indian Territory.

Dear Sir:

Receipt is hereby acknowledged of the affidavits of Susie Laughlin and O. F. Coffey to the birth of Gracie May[sic] Bowlin, daughter of R. M. and Susie Laughlin (Bowlin), and also the affidavit of S. D. Rowe to the birth of Dora Maud Laughlin, daughter of J. A. and Susie Laughlin, June 18, 1903 and October 24, 1904, respectively, and the same have been filed in the matter of the enrollment of said children.

Respectfully,

Chairman.

7-NB-1308

Muskogee, Indian Territory, August 19, 1905.

J. A. Laughlin,
   Conway, Indian Territory.

Dear Sir:

Receipt is hereby acknowledged of your letter of August 13, 1905, asking if Gracie Marie Bowlin and Dora Maud Laughlin, children of Susie Laughlin, have been approved.

In reply to your letter you are advised that the names of Gracie Marie Bowlin and Dora Maud Laughlin, have been placed upon a schedule of citizens by blood of the

Applications for Enrollment of Choctaw Newborn
Act of 1905   Volume XVII

Choctaw Nation, prepared for forwarding to the Secretary of the Interior. You will be notified when their enrollment is approved by the Department.

Respectfully,

Acting Commissioner.

Choc. New Born 1309
    Jim Joel
    (Born Dec. 26, 1904)

BIRTH AFFIDAVIT.

DEPARTMENT OF THE INTERIOR.
COMMISSION TO THE FIVE CIVILIZED TRIBES.

IN RE APPLICATION FOR ENROLLMENT, as a citizen of the Choctaw Nation, of Jim Joel, born on the 26th day of December, 1904

Name of Father: Hampton Joel   a citizen of the Choctaw Nation.
Name of Mother: Sallie Joel   a citizen of the Choctaw Nation.

Postoffice   Alikchi, Ind. Ter.

AFFIDAVIT OF MOTHER.

UNITED STATES OF AMERICA, Indian Territory,
    Central   DISTRICT.

I, Sallie Joel, on oath state that I am 20 years of age and a citizen by blood, of the Choctaw Nation; that I am the lawful wife of Hampton Joel, who is a citizen, by blood of the Choctaw Nation; that a male child was born to me on 26th day of December, 1904; that said child has been named Jim Joel, and was living March 4, 1905.

                her
            Sallie x Joel
                mark

Witnesses To Mark:
    { Robert Anderson
    { Vester W Rose

Applications for Enrollment of Choctaw Newborn
Act of 1905   Volume XVII

Subscribed and sworn to before me this 29th day of April, 1905

Wirt Franklin
Notary Public.

AFFIDAVIT OF ATTENDING PHYSICIAN OR MID-WIFE.

UNITED STATES OF AMERICA, Indian Territory,
Central   DISTRICT.

I, Lizzie Carney, a mid-wife, on oath state that I attended on Mrs. Sallie Joel, wife of Hampton Joel on the 26th day of December, 1904; that there was born to her on said date a male child; that said child was living March 4, 1905, and is said to have been named Jim Joel

Lizzie Carney

Witnesses To Mark:

Subscribed and sworn to before me this 29th day of April, 1905

Wirt Franklin
Notary Public.

(The letter below typed as given.)

Alikchi, I. T. May 25, 05

Commission to the Five Civilized Tribes,
    Muskogee, Ind. Ter.

Dear Sirs.

Replying to your letter of reason date will say my wife Silen Willis father name Rayson Willis her mother name Betsy Willis Choctaw by Blood, Silen Willis Roll No 2247 my child name is Jim Joel. Hoping this will be satisfactory, I remain

Yours truly,
Hampton Joel.

Applications for Enrollment of Choctaw Newborn
Act of 1905 Volume XVII

Muskogee, Indian Territory, May 10, 1905.

Hampton Joel,
 Alikchi, Indian Territory.

Dear Sir:

Receipt is hereby acknowledged of the affidavits of Sallie Joel and Lizzie Carney to the birth of Jim Joel, son of Hampton and Sallie Joel, December 26, 1904.

It is stated in the affidavit of the mother that she is a citizen by blood of the Choctaw Nation. If this is correct you are requested to state the name under which she was enrolled, the names of her parents, and if she has selected an allotment of the lands of the Choctaw or Chickasaw Nation, please give her roll number as it appears upon her allotment certificate.

Respectfully,

Chairman.

7-861

Muskogee, Indian Territory, June 6, 1905.

Hampton Joel,
 Alikchi, Indian Territory.

Dear Sir:

Receipt is hereby acknowledged of your letter of May 25, 1905, giving the names of the parents of your wife Cillin[sic] Willis and stating that her roll number is 2247 upon the approved roll of citizens by blood of the Choctaw Nation.

In reply to your letter you are advised that this information has enabled the Commission to identify Cillin Willis upon our records as an enrolled citizen by blood of the Choctaw Nation and the affidavits heretofore forwarded to the birth of your child Jim Joel have been filed as an application for the enrollment of said child.

Respectfully,

Chairman.

Applications for Enrollment of Choctaw Newborn
Act of 1905   Volume XVII

Choc. New Born 1310
    Valley May Duer
    (Born Jan. 1, 1903)

BIRTH AFFIDAVIT.

DEPARTMENT OF THE INTERIOR.
COMMISSION TO THE FIVE CIVILIZED TRIBES.

    IN RE APPLICATION FOR ENROLLMENT, as a citizen of the   Chocktaw[sic]   Nation, of   Valley May Duer   , born on the   1st day of   January   , 1903

Name of Father: Isaac Duer   a citizen of the   Chocktaw   Nation.
Name of Mother: Martha Duer   a citizen of the   Chocktaw   Nation.

                 Postoffice   Durant I.T.

AFFIDAVIT OF MOTHER.

UNITED STATES OF AMERICA, Indian Territory,
    Central   DISTRICT.

    I,   Martha Duer   , on oath state that I am   28   years of age and a citizen by Intermarriage   , of the   Chocktaw   Nation; that I am the lawful wife of   Isaac Duer   , who is a citizen, by Blood   of the   Chocktaw   Nation; that a female   child was born to me on   1st day of   January   , 1903; that said child has been named   Valley May Duer   , and was living March 4, 1905.

                               Martha Duer

Witnesses To Mark:
{

    Subscribed and sworn to before me this 26th   day of   April   , 1905

Com Ex
Feb 8th 1908
                               Charles A Phillips
                               Notary Public.

AFFIDAVIT OF ATTENDING PHYSICIAN OR MID-WIFE.

UNITED STATES OF AMERICA, Indian Territory,
    Central   DISTRICT.

    I,   Jane Pate   , a   Mid Wife   , on oath state that I attended on Mrs.   Martha Duer   , wife of   Isaac Duer   on the 1st   day of   January   ,

Applications for Enrollment of Choctaw Newborn
Act of 1905   Volume XVII

1903; that there was born to her on said date a   female   child; that said child was living March 4, 1905, and is said to have been named Valley May Duer

Jane Pate

Witnesses To Mark:
{

    Subscribed and sworn to before me this 26th day of April   , 1905

Com. Ex Feb 8th 1908   Charles A Phillips
Notary Public.

7-3561

Muskogee, Indian Territory, May 2, 1905.

Isaac Duer,
    Durant, Indian Territory.

Dear Sir:

    Receipt is hereby acknowledged of the affidavits of Martha Duer and Jane Pate to the birth of Valley May Duer daughter of Isaac and Martha Duer, January 1, 1903, and the same have been filed with our records as an application for the enrollment of said child.

Respectfully,

Chairman.

Choc. New Born 1311
    Christanie Bell Carter
    (Born July 23, 1903)
    Minnie Elsie Carter
    (Born Jan. 13, 1905)

Applications for Enrollment of Choctaw Newborn
Act of 1905   Volume XVII

NEW BORN AFFIDAVIT

No ....

CHOCTAW ENROLLING COMMISSION

IN THE MATTER OF THE APPLICATION FOR ENROLLMENT as a citizen of the Choctaw Nation, of   Crissannie Belle[sic] Carter   born on the 23^d day of   July   190 3

    Name of father   T. L. Carter   a citizen of   U. States   Nation, final enrollment No. ~~158~~
    Name of mother   Ella Carter *(Nee Woods)* a citizen of   Choctaw   Nation, final enrollment No.   158

Tupelo I.T.   Postoffice.

AFFIDAVIT OF MOTHER

UNITED STATES OF AMERICA
    INDIAN TERRITORY
District   Central

    I   Ella Carter   , on oath state that I am   25   years of age and a citizen by   Blood   of the   Choctaw   Nation, and as such have been placed upon the final roll of the   Choctaw   Nation, by the Honorable Secretary of the Interior my final enrollment number being 158 ; that I am the lawful wife of   T.L. Carter , who is a citizen of the   U.S.   Nation, and as such has been placed upon the final roll of said Nation by the Honorable Secretary of the Interior, his final enrollment number being —— and that a   Female   child was born to me on the   23^d day of   July   190 3; that said child has been named   Crissannie Belle Carter   , and is now living.

WITNESSETH: Ella Carter
  Must be two witnesses   { Wesley Benton
  who are citizens   { Minnie Willis

    Subscribed and sworn to before me this, the 4   day of   Mch   , 190 5

                           R.T. Breedlove
                               Notary Public.

My Commission Expires: Oct 5th 1907

Applications for Enrollment of Choctaw Newborn
Act of 1905   Volume XVII

Affidavit of Attending Physician or Midwife

UNITED STATES OF AMERICA,
INDIAN TERRITORY,
Central   DISTRICT

I, Isibel[sic] Whitlock   a   Midwife
on oath state that I attended on Mrs. Ella Carter   wife of T.L. Carter
on the 23ᵈ day of July   , 190 5[sic], that there was born to her on said date a   Female
child, that said child is now living, and is said to have been named Crissannie Belle Carter
witness) J.B. Anglin   her
witness) E.C. Breedlove   Isibel x Whitlock   M. W.
                                                         mark
        Subscribed and sworn to before me this the   4   day of   Mch   1905

                                        R.T. Breedlove
                                              Notary Public.

WITNESSETH:
Must be two witnesses { Wesley Benton
who are citizens and
know the child. { Minnie Willis

We hereby certify that we are well acquainted with   Isibel Whitlock
a   Midwife   and know   Her   to be reputable and of good standing in the
community.

                        Must be two citizen { Wesley Benton
                        witnesses.   { Minnie Willis

NEW BORN AFFIDAVIT

No

CHOCTAW ENROLLING COMMISSION

IN THE MATTER OF THE APPLICATION FOR ENROLLMENT as a citizen of the Choctaw
Nation, of   Minnie Elsie Carter   born on the 13ᵗʰ   day
of   Jan   190 5

    Name of father   T. L. Carter   a citizen of   U. States   Nation,
final enrollment No. ———
    Name of mother   Ella Carter (nee Woods) a citizen of   Choctaw   Nation,
final enrollment No. 158

Applications for Enrollment of Choctaw Newborn
Act of 1905   Volume XVII

Tupelo I.T.　　　　　　　　　　Postoffice.

AFFIDAVIT OF MOTHER

UNITED STATES OF AMERICA
INDIAN TERRITORY
DISTRICT   Central

I   Ella Carter   , on oath state that I am   25   years of age and a citizen by   Blood   of the   Choctaw   Nation, and as such have been placed upon the final roll of the   Choctaw   Nation, by the Honorable Secretary of the Interior my final enrollment number being   158 ; that I am the lawful wife of   T.L. Carter , who is a citizen of the   U.S.   Nation, and as such has been placed upon the final roll of said Nation by the Honorable Secretary of the Interior, his final enrollment number being ——— and that a   Female   child was born to me on the   13   day of   Jan   190 5; that said child has been named   Minnie Elsie Carter   , and is now living.

WITNESSETH:　　　　　　　　　　　　Ella Carter

Must be two witnesses ｛ Wesley Benton
who are citizens 　　　Minnie Willis

Subscribed and sworn to before me this, the   4   day of   Mch   , 190 5

R.T. Breedlove
Notary Public.

My Commission Expires: Oct 5th 1907

Affidavit of Attending Physician or Midwife

UNITED STATES OF AMERICA,
INDIAN TERRITORY,
Central   DISTRICT

I,   Isibel[sic] Whitlock   a   Midwife   on oath state that I attended on Mrs. Ella Carter   wife of T.L. Carter on the   13th day of Jan   , 190 5, that there was born to her on said date a   Female child, that said child is now living, and is said to have been named   Minnie Elsie Carter

witness) J.B. Anglin
witness) E.C. Breedlove

　　　　　　　　　　　　　　　her
　　　　　　　　　　　Isibel x Whitlock　　M.W.
　　　　　　　　　　　　　　　mark

Subscribed and sworn to before me this the   4   day of   Mch   1905

R.T. Breedlove
Notary Public.

Applications for Enrollment of Choctaw Newborn
Act of 1905 Volume XVII

WITNESSETH:

Must be two witnesses who are citizens and know the child. { Wesley Benton
Minnie Willis

We hereby certify that we are well acquainted with **Isibel Whitlock** a Midwife and know Her to be reputable and of good standing in the community.

Must be two citizen witnesses. { Wesley Benton
Minnie Willis

BIRTH AFFIDAVIT.

DEPARTMENT OF THE INTERIOR.
COMMISSION TO THE FIVE CIVILIZED TRIBES.

IN RE APPLICATION FOR ENROLLMENT, as a citizen of the Choctaw Nation, of Christanie Bell Carter, born on the 23 day of July, 1903

Name of Father: Thomas L. Carter a ~~citizen~~ Non of the Choctaw Nation.
Name of Mother: Ella Carter a citizen of the Choctaw Nation.

Postoffice Tupelo I.T.

AFFIDAVIT OF MOTHER.

UNITED STATES OF AMERICA, Indian Territory,
Central DISTRICT.

I, Ella Carter, on oath state that I am 25 years of age and a citizen by Blood, of the Choctaw Nation; that I am the lawful wife of Thomas L Carter, who is a ~~citizen~~ Non, by Blood of the Choctaw Nation; that a Girl child was born to me on 23 day of July, 1903; that said child has been named Christanie Bell Carter, and was living March 4, 1905.

Ella Carter

Witnesses To Mark:
R.F. Anderson
O H Mathews

Subscribed and sworn to before me this 19 day of Apr, 1905

W.S. Partain
Notary Public.

Applications for Enrollment of Choctaw Newborn
Act of 1905 Volume XVII

AFFIDAVIT OF ATTENDING PHYSICIAN OR MID-WIFE.

UNITED STATES OF AMERICA, Indian Territory, }
Central   DISTRICT.

I, Mrs Isabelle Whitlock, a midwife, on oath state that I attended on Mrs. Mrs Ella Carter, wife of Thomas L Carter on the 23 day of July, 1903; that there was born to her on said date a Girl child; that said child was living March 4, 1905, and is said to have been named Christanie Bell Carter

Witnesses To Mark:
{ R.F. Anderson
  O.H. Mathews

Isabelle Whitlock x
O H Mathews
R.F. Anderson

Subscribed and sworn to before me this 19 day of Apr, 1905

W.S. Partain
Notary Public.

BIRTH AFFIDAVIT.

DEPARTMENT OF THE INTERIOR.
COMMISSION TO THE FIVE CIVILIZED TRIBES.

IN RE APPLICATION FOR ENROLLMENT, as a citizen of the Choctaw Nation, of Minnie Elsie Carter, born on the 13 day of Jan, 1905

Name of Father: Thomas L. Carter   a ~~citizen~~ Non of the Choctaw Nation.
Name of Mother: Ella Carter   a citizen of the Choctaw Nation.

Postoffice   Tupelo I.T.

AFFIDAVIT OF MOTHER.

UNITED STATES OF AMERICA, Indian Territory, }
Central   DISTRICT.

I, Ella Carter, on oath state that I am 25 years of age and a citizen by Blood, of the Choctaw Nation; that I am the lawful wife of Thomas L Carter, who is a ~~citizen~~ Non, by Blood of the Choctaw Nation; that a Girl child was born to me on 13 day of Jan, 1905; that said child has been named Minnie Elsie Carter, and was living March 4, 1905.

Applications for Enrollment of Choctaw Newborn
Act of 1905   Volume XVII

Ella Carter

Witnesses To Mark:
{ R.F. Anderson
  O H Mathews

Subscribed and sworn to before me this 19   day of   Apr   , 1905

W.S. Partain
Notary Public.

AFFIDAVIT OF ATTENDING PHYSICIAN OR MID-WIFE.

UNITED STATES OF AMERICA, Indian Territory, }
    Central   DISTRICT. }

I,   Mrs Isabelle Whitlock   , a   Midwife   , on oath state that I attended on Mrs.   Ella Carter   , wife of Thomas L Carter   on the 13 day of Jan , 1905; that there was born to her on said date a   Girl   child; that said child was living March 4, 1905, and is said to have been named Minnie Elsie Carter

Isabelle Whitlock x
Witnesses To Mark: O H Mathews
{ R.F. Anderson   R.F. Anderson
  O.H. Mathews

Subscribed and sworn to before me this 19   day of   Apr   , 1905

W.S. Partain
Notary Public.

Muskogee, Indian Territory, April 24, 1905.

Thomas L. Carter,
    Tupelo, Indian Territory.

Dear Sir:

Receipt is hereby acknowledged of the affidavits of Ella Carter and joint affidavit of Isabella Whitlock, O. H. Mathews and R. F. Anderson to the birth of Minnie Elsie Carter, and Christanie Bele[sic] Carter, children of Thomas L. and Ella Carter January 13, 1905, and July 23, 1903.

It is stated in the affidavit of the mother that she is a citizen by blood of the Choctaw Nation. If this is correct you are requested to state the name under which she was enrolled, the names of her parents, and if she has selected an allotment of the lands

Applications for Enrollment of Choctaw Newborn
Act of 1905   Volume XVII

of the Choctaw and Chickasaw Nation[sic] please give her roll number as it appears upon her allotment certificate.

Respectfully,

Chairman.

(COPY)

Tupelo, I. T.

May 8, 1905.

Commission to the Five Civilized Tribes,
Muskogee, Indian Territory.

Dear Sir:

Your letter of May 1 just received in regards to the enrollment of my wife, Ella Carter, formerly the wife of Harrisson[sic] Wood, her father and mother's name was Gipson and Isabelle Fillmore, but her mother now is the wife of W P. Whitlock, and I beg to state that the roll number given 158 was an error of mine. I have examined her allotment Certificate and find that her enrollment number is 11956 as states in your letter.

Yours truly,

Thomas L. Carter.

7-N.B. 1311

Thomas L. Carter,
Tupelo, Indian Territory.

Dear Sir:

Receipt is hereby acknowledged of your letter of May 8, giving information relative to the enrollment of your wife, Ella Carter, and this information has enabled us to identify her upon our records as an enrolled citizen by blood of the Choctaw Nation and the affidavits heretofore forwarded to the birth of your children, Christanie Belle and Minnie Elsie Carter, have been filed with our records as applications for the enrollment of said children.

Respectfully,

Chairman.

Applications for Enrollment of Choctaw Newborn
Act of 1905   Volume XVII

7-NB-1311.

Muskogee, Indian Territory, June 1, 1905.

Thomas L. Carter,
    Tupelo, Indian Territory.

Dear Sir:

    There is enclosed herewith application for the enrollment of your infant child, Minnie Elsie Carter, born January 13, 1905, in which the Notary Public failed to sign the affidavit executed by the applicant's mother.

    Please have this affidavit signed and then return the application to this office.

Respectfully,

Chairman.

VR 1-5.

7-NB-1311

Muskogee, Indian Territory, July 8, 1905.

Thomas L. Carter,
    Tupelo, Indian Territory.

Dear Sir:

    Receipt is hereby acknowledged of the application for the enrollment of your child Minnie Elsie Carter corrected by having the Notary Public sign the affidavit of the mother and the same has now been filed in the matter of the enrollment of said child.

Respectfully,

Chairman.

Applications for Enrollment of Choctaw Newborn
Act of 1905   Volume XVII

Choc. New Born 1312
    Emoline Lewis
    (Born Dec. 10, 1903)
    Dorothy Lewis
    (Born April 23, 1905)

1312

NEW BORN
CHOCTAW
ENROLLMENT

EMOLINE LEWIS
(BORN DEC. 10, 1903)
DOROTHY LEWIS
(BORN APRIL 22, 1905) born
subsequent to march[sic] 4, 1905.
Dorothy Lewis transferred to N. B. 679 under Act of April 26, 1906.
    Decision rendered June 30, 1905
    Decline to receive or consider
    Copy of decision forwarded June 30 1905
    attorneys for Choctaw and Chickasaw
    nations.   June 30, 1905
        COPY OF DECISION FORWARDED
        APPLICANT'S FATHER   JUNE 30, 1905

As Citizen of the
CHOCTAW NATION
Act of Congress
Approved March 3, 1905

RECORD FORWARDED DEPARTMENT
June 30, 1905
Action approved by Secretary of
Interior.   Oct. 20, 1905

Notice of departmental action forwarded attorneys for Choctaw and Chickawas[sic] nations.   Nov. 1-1905
Notice of departmental action mailed applicant's Father   Nov. 1-1905.

1312

Applications for Enrollment of Choctaw Newborn
Act of 1905 Volume XVII

No. 1710

Certificate of Record of Marriages.

UNITED STATES OF AMERICA,
INDIAN TERRITORY, } SCT:
Central DISTRICT.

I, E.J. Fannin , Clerk of the United States Court in the Indian Territory and District aforesaid, do hereby CERTIFY, that the License for and Certificate of the Marriage of

Mr. Anderson Lewis and

Miss Beulah Cordlish was

filed in my office in said Territory and District the 20 day of Jany A.D., 190 3 and duly recorded in Book 2 of Marriage Record, Page 237

WITNESS my hand and seal of said Court, at Atoka , this 20 day of Jany , A.D. 190 3

E.J. Fannin
Clerk.

By JD Carter *Deputy.*

DEPARTMENT OF THE INTERIOR,
Commission to the Five Civilized Tribes.

FILED

APR 27 1905
Tams Bixby CHAIRMAN.

Applications for Enrollment of Choctaw Newborn
Act of 1905 Volume XVII

No. 1710

FORM NO. 598.

MARRIAGE LICENSE.

UNITES STATES OF AMERICA,
THE INDIAN TERRITORY, } ss:
Central   DISTRICT.

To any Person Authorized by Law to Solemnize Marriage—Greeting:

You are hereby commanded to solemnize the Rite and publish the Banns of Matrimony *between* Mr. Anderson Lewis *of* Ti *in the Indian Territory, aged* 25 *years, and M*iss Beulah Cordlish *of* Paris *in the Indian Territory,* State of Texas *aged* 19 *years, according to law, and do you officially sign and return this License to the parties therein named.*

WITNESS my hand and official seal, this 19 day of Jany   A. D. 190 3

E.J. Fannin
Clerk of the United States Court.

JD Carter   Deputy

CERTIFICATE OF MARRIAGE.

UNITES STATES OF AMERICA,
THE INDIAN TERRITORY, } ss:
_____ DISTRICT.

I, *(Name Illegible)*
a Minister of Gospel

do hereby CERTIFY, that on the   19   day of   Jan   A, D. 190 3 ; I did duly and according to law, as commanded in the foregoing License, solemnize the Rite and publish the BANNS OF MATRIMONY between the parties therein named.

Witness my hand this 19 day of   Jan , A. D. 190 3

My credentials are recorded in the office of the Clerk of the United States Court in the Indian Territory, Central District, Book   B   Page   69

Rev *(Name Illegible)*
a Minister of Gospel

Applications for Enrollment of Choctaw Newborn
Act of 1905 Volume XVII

NEW-BORN AFFIDAVIT.

Number..................

...Choctaw Enrolling Commission...

IN THE MATTER OF THE APPLICATION FOR ENROLLMENT, as a citizen of the Choctaw Nation, of Emoline Lewis

born on the 10th day of __Dec.__ 190 3

Name of father Anderson Lewis	a citizen of Choctaw
Nation final enrollment No. 9189	~~non~~
Name of mother Bulah[sic] Lewis	a^citizen of Choctaw
Nation final enrollment No. ———	
	Postoffice Ti, Ind. Ter.

AFFIDAVIT OF MOTHER.

UNITED STATES OF AMERICA
INDIAN TERRITORY
Central   DISTRICT

I   Bulah Lewis   , on oath state that I am 27 years of age and a ~~non~~ citizen by marriage of the Choctaw Nation, and as such have ~~not~~ been placed upon the final roll of the Choctaw Nation, by the Honorable Secretary of the Interior my final enrollment number being —; that I am the lawful wife of   Anderson Lewis   , who is a citizen of the Choctaw Nation, and as such has been placed upon the final roll of said Nation by the Honorable Secretary of the Interior, his final enrollment number being   9189   and that a   female   child was born to me on the   10th   day of   December   190 3; that said child has been named   Emoline Lewis   , and is now living.

Bulah Lewis

Witnesseth.

Must be two Witnesses who are Citizens. } Robert Gardner

JD Chastain

Subscribed and sworn to before me this   16th   day of   Jan   190 5

Wm J Hulsey
Notary Public.

My commission expires: 1908

Applications for Enrollment of Choctaw Newborn
Act of 1905   Volume XVII

AFFIDAVIT OF ATTENDING PHYSICIAN OR MIDWIFE

UNITED STATES OF AMERICA
INDIAN TERRITORY
    Central   DISTRICT

    I,   Cynthia Lewis   a   midwife   on oath state that I attended on Mrs. Bulah Lewis   wife of Anderson Lewis on the   10th   day of   December , 190 3 , that there was born to her on said date a female child, that said child is now living, and is said to have been named   Emoline Lewis

                                Cynthia Lewis   *m.w*
        Subscribed and sworn to before me this, the   28th   day of
                Jan   190 5

WITNESSETH: Wm J Hulsey   Notary Public.
    Must be two witnesses ⎧ JD Chastain
    who are citizens   ⎨
                           ⎩ Joseph B McMurtrey

    We hereby certify that we are well acquainted with   Cynthia Lewis   a   midwife   and know   her   to be reputable and of good standing in the community.

        JD Chastain   _____X_____

        Joseph B McMurtrey   _____X_____

BIRTH AFFIDAVIT.
                    DEPARTMENT OF THE INTERIOR.
            COMMISSION TO THE FIVE CIVILIZED TRIBES.

    IN RE APPLICATION FOR ENROLLMENT, as a citizen of the   Choctaw Nation Nation, of Emoline Lewis   , born on the 10th   day of December , 1903

Name of Father: Anderson Lewis   a citizen of the   Choctaw   Nation.
                                            non
Name of Mother: Bulah Lewis   a citizen of the   Choctaw   Nation.

                    Postoffice   Ti, Indian Territory

Applications for Enrollment of Choctaw Newborn
Act of 1905   Volume XVII

AFFIDAVIT OF MOTHER.

UNITED STATES OF AMERICA, Indian Territory, }
Central   DISTRICT.

I, Bulah Lewis, on oath state that I am 27 years of age and a citizen by _____, of the _____ Nation; that I am the lawful wife of Anderson Lewis, who is a citizen, by Blood of the Choctaw Nation; that a Female child was born to me on 10th day of December, 1903; that said child has been named Emoline Lewis, and was living March 4, 1905.

Bulah Lewis

Witnesses To Mark:
{

Subscribed and sworn to before me this 25th day of April, 1905

WR Patterson
Notary Public.

AFFIDAVIT OF ATTENDING PHYSICIAN OR MID-WIFE.

UNITED STATES OF AMERICA, Indian Territory, }
Central   DISTRICT.

I, Cyntha Lewis, a Midwife, on oath state that I attended on Mrs. Bulah Lewis, wife of Anderson Lewis on the 10th day of December, 1903; that there was born to her on said date a Female child; that said child was living March 4, 1905, and is said to have been named Emoline Lewis

Cyntha Lewis

Witnesses To Mark:
{

Subscribed and sworn to before me this 25th day of April, 1905

WR Patterson
Notary Public.

Applications for Enrollment of Choctaw Newborn
Act of 1905   Volume XVII

7--3176.
7 N.B. 1312.

Muskogee, Indian Territory, May 25, 1905.

Anderson Lewis,
    Ti, Indian Territory.

Dear Sir:

    Receipt is hereby acknowledged of your letter of May 17, stating that you made application for the enrollment of your two children, Emoline and Dorothy Lewis, and as you have not heard from them, you desire to know if the children have been placed on the rolls.

    In reply to your letter you are advised that the affidavits heretofore forwarded to the birth of Emeline[sic] Lewis, have been filed with our records as an application for the enrollment of said child, but her name has not yet been placed upon a schedule of citizens by blood of the Choctaw Nation prepared for forwarding to the Secretary of the Interior.

    You are further advised with reference to the affidavits to the birth of your child, Dorothy Lewis, that it appears this child was born April 3, 1905, and under the provisions of the act of Congress approved March 3, 1905, the Commission was authorized for a period of sixty days from that date to receive applications for the enrollment of children born to citizens by blood of the Choctaw and Chickasaw Nations between September 25, 1902 and March 4, 1905, and living on the latter date.

    You will therefore see that the commission is without authority to enroll your child, Dorothy Lewis.

    You are also advised that the affidavits to the birth of your two children were received with a letter from Hulsey & Patterson, attorneys at Law, Hartshorne, Indian Territory, and receipt thereof was acknowledged to them on May 1, 1905.

Respectfully,

Chairman.

Applications for Enrollment of Choctaw Newborn
Act of 1905   Volume XVII

Choc. New Born 1313
       Henry Lee Pebworth
       (Born Apr. 21, 1903)

NEW BORN AFFIDAVIT

No

CHOCTAW ENROLLING COMMISSION

IN THE MATTER OF THE APPLICATION FOR ENROLLMENT as a citizen of the Choctaw Nation, of   Henry Lee Pebworth   born on the 21st day of   April   190 3

Name of father   Henry Pebworth   a citizen of   Choctaw   Nation, final enrollment No.   9258
Name of mother   Dora E. Pebworth   a citizen of   Choctaw   Nation, final enrollment No.   9259

Coalgate, I.T.   Postoffice.

AFFIDAVIT OF MOTHER

UNITED STATES OF AMERICA
    INDIAN TERRITORY
DISTRICT   Central

I   Dora E. Pebworth   , on oath state that I am 29   years of age and a citizen by   birth   of the   Choctaw   Nation, and as such have been placed upon the final roll of the   Choctaw   Nation, by the Honorable Secretary of the Interior my final enrollment number being   9259   ; that I am the lawful wife of   Henry Pebworth   , who is a citizen of the   Choctaw   Nation, and as such has been placed upon the final roll of said Nation by the Honorable Secretary of the Interior, his final enrollment number being   9258   and that a   male   child was born to me on the   21st day of   April   190 3; that said child has been named   Henry Lee Pebworth   , and is now living.

Dora E. Pebworth

WITNESSETH:
   Must be two witnesses { Nancy C. Hampton
   who are citizens   Lillie E. Carter

Applications for Enrollment of Choctaw Newborn
Act of 1905   Volume XVII

Subscribed and sworn to before me this, the 21st day of Feb. , 190 5

                Theo von Keller
                       Notary Public.

My Commission Expires:
Feb 8th 1906

Affidavit of Attending Physician or Midwife

UNITED STATES OF AMERICA, }
   INDIAN TERRITORY,
 Central   DISTRICT

I, Waverly M Hume a Physician on oath state that I attended on Mrs. Dora E Pebworth wife of Henry Pebworth on the 21st day of April , 190 3, that there was born to her on said date a male child, that said child is now living, and is said to have been named Henry Lee Pebworth

              W.M. Hume   M. D.

Subscribed and sworn to before me this the 11th day of Feb 1905

            Theo von Keller
                 Notary Public.

WITNESSETH:

Must be two witnesses who are citizens and know the child.
{ Cyrus R Thompson
     his
 Johnson x Ott
     mark

We hereby certify that we are well acquainted with W. M. Hume a Physician and know him to be reputable and of good standing in the community.

        Must be two citizen witnesses. { Samuel A*his* Ott
    Johnson x Ott
      mark

Applications for Enrollment of Choctaw Newborn
Act of 1905   Volume XVII

BIRTH AFFIDAVIT.

DEPARTMENT OF THE INTERIOR.
COMMISSION TO THE FIVE CIVILIZED TRIBES.

IN RE APPLICATION FOR ENROLLMENT, as a citizen of the   Choctaw   Nation, of Henry Lee Pebworth   , born on the   21st day of   April   , 1903

Name of Father: Henry Pebworth   a citizen of the   Choctaw   Nation.
Name of Mother: Dora Ella Pebworth   a citizen of the   Choctaw   Nation.

Postoffice   Coalgate, Ind. Ter

AFFIDAVIT OF MOTHER.

UNITED STATES OF AMERICA, Indian Territory, }
Central   DISTRICT. }

I,   Dora Ella Pebworth   , on oath state that I am   29   years of age and a citizen by   blood   , of the   Choctaw   Nation; that I am the lawful wife of Henry Pebworth   , who is a citizen, by   blood   of the   Choctaw   Nation; that a   male   child was born to me on   21st day of   April   , 1903; that said child has been named   Henry Lee Pebworth   , and was living March 4, 1905.

Dora Ella Pebworth

Witnesses To Mark:
{ Nancy C. Hampton

Subscribed and sworn to before me this   25th day of   April   , 1905

Theo von Keller
Notary Public.

AFFIDAVIT OF ATTENDING PHYSICIAN OR MID-WIFE.

UNITED STATES OF AMERICA, Indian Territory, }
Central   DISTRICT. }

I,   Waverly M. Hume   , a   Physician   , on oath state that I attended on Mrs.   Dora Ella Pebworth   , wife of   Henry Pebworth   on the   21st day of April   , 1903; that there was born to her on said date a   male   child; that said child was living March 4, 1905, and is said to have been named   Henry Lee Pebworth

Waverly M. Hume, M.D.

Applications for Enrollment of Choctaw Newborn
Act of 1905   Volume XVII

Witnesses To Mark:
  { Nancy C. Hampton

      Subscribed and sworn to before me this 25th day of April , 1905

                              Theo von Keller
                                  Notary Public.

                                  7-3201

              Muskogee, Indian Territory, May 1, 1905.

Henry Pebworth,
    Coalgate, Indian Territory.

Dear Sir:

      Receipt is hereby acknowledged of the affidavits of Dora Ella Pebworth and Waverly M. Hume to the birth of Henry Lee Pebworth son of Henry Pebworth and Dora Ella Pebworth, April 21, 1903, and the same have been filed with our records as an application for the enrollment of said child.

                        Respectfully,

                                              Chairman.

Blank 731.

Choctaw Roll Citizens By Blood

New Born

Act of Congress Approved March 3rd, 1905. (Public No. 212)

No.	Name	Age	Sex	Blood	Card No.
1163	Pebworth. Henry Lee	2	M	1/2	1313

Applications for Enrollment of Choctaw Newborn
Act of 1905   Volume XVII

DEPARTMENT OF THE INTERIOR,
United States Indian Service
Five Civilized Tribes
Muskogee, Oklahoma.

This is to certify that I am the officer having the custody of the records pertaining to the enrollment of the members of the Choctaw, Chickasaw, Cherokee, Creek and Seminole tribes of Indians, and the disposition of the land of said tribes, and the following described papers, attached hereto, are true and correct copies of the entire enrollment record on file in this office in connection with the application of Henry Lee Pebworth

Roll No. __1163__, for enrollment as a citizen by blood of the __Choctaw__ Nation: Choctaw New Born Census Card No. 1313; Three (3) Birth Affidavits; Letter dated 5-1-05; and copy of Approved Choctaw New Born Roll No. 1163

C. L. ELLIS
Dist. Supt. in Charge.

BY E.C. Funk   CLERK
IN CHARGE Choctaw   RECORDS
DATE 3-26-29

Choc. New Born 1314
  Agnes Noel
  (Born March 29, 1903)

BIRTH AFFIDAVIT.

DEPARTMENT OF THE INTERIOR.
COMMISSION TO THE FIVE CIVILIZED TRIBES.

IN RE APPLICATION FOR ENROLLMENT, as a citizen of the   Choctaw   Nation, of Agnes Noel   , born on the 29 day of March , 1903

Name of Father: Joe Moore   a citizen of the Choc Nation.
Name of Mother: Nancy Noel   a citizen of the Choc Nation.

Postoffice   Blanco I.T

Applications for Enrollment of Choctaw Newborn
Act of 1905   Volume XVII

AFFIDAVIT OF MOTHER.

UNITED STATES OF AMERICA, Indian Territory, ⎱
   Central   DISTRICT.   ⎰

   I,   Nancy Noel   , on oath state that I am   24   years of age and a citizen by blood   , of the   Choctaw   Nation; that I am *not* the lawful wife of   Joe Moore   , who is a citizen, by blood   of the   Choctaw   Nation; that a   female   child was born to me on   29   day of   March   , 1903; that said child has been named   Agnes Noel   , and was living March 4, 1905.

                                        Nancy Noel
Witnesses To Mark:
   ⎰
   ⎱

   Subscribed and sworn to before me this   27   day of   April   , 1905

                                        OL Johnson
                                           Notary Public.

AFFIDAVIT OF ATTENDING PHYSICIAN OR MID-WIFE.

UNITED STATES OF AMERICA, Indian Territory, ⎱
   Central   DISTRICT.   ⎰

   I,   Josephine Frazier   , a   midwife   , on oath state that I attended on Mrs.   Nancy Noel   , wife of   Joe Moore   on the   29   day of   March   , 1903; that there was born to her on said date a   female   child; that said child was living March 4, 1905, and is said to have been named   Agnes Noel

                                              her
                                   Josephine x Frazier
Witnesses To Mark: mark
   ⎰ Jake Collins
   ⎱ OL Johnson

   Subscribed and sworn to before me this   27   day of   April   , 1905

                                        OL Johnson
                                           Notary Public.

Applications for Enrollment of Choctaw Newborn
Act of 1905 Volume XVII

Wm O.B.

COMMISSIONERS:
TAMS BIXBY,
THOMAS B. NEEDLES,
C.R. BRECKINBRIDGE.

WM. O. BEALL
Secretary

DEPARTMENT OF THE INTERIOR,
COMMISSIONER TO THE FIVE CIVILIZED TRIBES.

REFER IN REPLY TO THE FOLLOWING:

ADDRESS ONLY THE
COMMISSION TO THE FIVE CIVILIZED TRIBES.

Muskogee, Indian Territory, May 1, 1905.

Nancy Noel,
    Blanco, Indian Territory.

Dear Madam:

    Receipt is hereby acknowledged of the affidavits of Nancy Noel and Josephine Frazier to the birth of Agnes Noel daughter of Joe Moore and Nancy Noel, March 29, 1903.

    It is stated in your affidavit that you are a citizen by blood of the Choctaw Nation. If this is correct you are requested to state the name under which you were enrolled, the names of your parents, and if you have selected an allotment of the lands of the Choctaw or Chickasaw Nation please give your roll number as it appears upon your allotment certificate.

                      Respectfully
                            Tams Bixby
                                  Chairman.

(The letter below typed as given.)

                            May 23th 1905
                    Blanco

I will write you scet you want the roll number I give you

      lynes Noel 29 March 1905

      agnes Noel 2 year old

      Ella Noel 5 year old June 28

      rolls number No. 1690

      rolls number No. 1749

            Natsy[sic] Noel

Applications for Enrollment of Choctaw Newborn
Act of 1905   Volume XVII

7-N.B. 1314.

Muskogee, Indian Territory, May 29, 1905.

Natsy Noel,
    Blanco, Indian Territory.

Dear Sir:

    Receipt is hereby acknowledged of your letter of May 23, giving information as to your identification in the matter of the enrollment of your child, Agnes Noel.

    You have now been identified as an enrolled citizen by blood of the Choctaw Nation and the affidavits heretofore forwarded to the birth of your child, Agnes Noel, have been filed with our records as an application for the enrollment of said child.

                Respectfully,

                                  Chairman.

Choc. New Born 1315
    Edith M. Drake
    (Born Nov. 19, 1904)

BIRTH AFFIDAVIT.

DEPARTMENT OF THE INTERIOR.
COMMISSION TO THE FIVE CIVILIZED TRIBES.

IN RE APPLICATION FOR ENROLLMENT, as a citizen of the Choctaw Nation, of Edith M. Drake, born on the 19 day of ~~December~~ November, 1904

Name of Father: George Drake   a citizen of the Choc Nation.
Name of Mother: Bula[sic] Drake   a citizen of the United States Nation.

                Postoffice   Haileyville I.T.

Applications for Enrollment of Choctaw Newborn
Act of 1905   Volume XVII

AFFIDAVIT OF MOTHER.

UNITED STATES OF AMERICA, Indian Territory, }
Central   DISTRICT. }

I, Bula Drake , on oath state that I am 17 years of age and a citizen by ———— , of the   United States   Nation; that I am the lawful wife of George Drake, who is a citizen, by blood of the   Choctaw   Nation; that a   female child was born to me on 19 day of ~~December~~ November ,1904; that said child has been named Edith M. drake , and was living March 4, 1905.

Witnesses To Mark:
{ Beulah Drake
{ Ann J Williams

Subscribed and sworn to before me this ……. day of ………, 1905.

Notary Public.

AFFIDAVIT OF ATTENDING PHYSICIAN OR MID-WIFE.

UNITED STATES OF AMERICA, Indian Territory, }
Central   DISTRICT. }

I, Edward D. James , a physician , on oath state that I attended on Mrs. Bula Drake , wife of George Drake   on the 19 day of ~~December~~ November , 1904; that there was born to her on said date a   female   child; that said child was living March 4, 1905, and is said to have been named Edith M Drake

Ed D James M.D.

Witnesses To Mark:
{

Subscribed and sworn to before me this 27th day of April , 1905

Edward R Jolly
Notary Public.

Applications for Enrollment of Choctaw Newborn
Act of 1905 Volume XVII

BIRTH AFFIDAVIT.

DEPARTMENT OF THE INTERIOR.
COMMISSION TO THE FIVE CIVILIZED TRIBES.

IN RE APPLICATION FOR ENROLLMENT, as a citizen of the Choctaw Nation, of Edith M. Drake, born on the 19th day of November, 1904

Name of Father: George Drake *Roll 15483* a citizen of the Choctaw Nation.
Name of Mother: Beulah Drake a citizen of the non citizen Nation.

Postoffice Haileyville Ind. Ter.

AFFIDAVIT OF MOTHER.

UNITED STATES OF AMERICA, Indian Territory,}
Central DISTRICT.}

I, Beulah Drake, on oath state that I am 17 years of age and a citizen by ———, of the United States Nation; that I am the lawful wife of George Drake, who is a citizen, by blood of the Choctaw Nation; that a female child was born to me on 19th day of November, 1904; that said child has been named Edith M. drake, and was living March 4, 1905.

Beulah Drake

Witnesses To Mark:
{

Subscribed and sworn to before me this 8th day of August, 1905

(Name Illegible)
Notary Public.

7-4516

Muskogee, Indian Territory, May 1, 1905.

George Drake,
 Haileyville, Indian Territory.

Dear Sir:

Receipt is hereby acknowledged of the affidavit of Ed D. James to the birth of Edith M. Drake, daughter of George and Bula[sic] Drake, November 19, 1904, and the same has been filed with our records as an application for the enrollment of said child.

Applications for Enrollment of Choctaw Newborn
Act of 1905   Volume XVII

Respectfully,

Chairman.

7-NB-1315.

Muskogee, Indian Territory, June 3, 1905.

George Drake,
    Haileyville, Indian Territory.

Dear Sir:

    There is enclosed herewith for execution the mother's affidavit, in the matter of the enrollment of your infant child, Edith M. Drake, born November 19, 1904.

    It appears from the application heretofore filed in this office that the applicant claims through you. If this is correct it will be necessary that you file in this office either the original or a certified copy of the license and certificate of your marriage to the applicant's mother, Beulah Drake.

    In the above mentioned application the affidavit of the mother was not executed. It will, therefore, be necessary that you have the enclosed application executed and return to this office.

    In having the affidavit executed care should be exercised to see that all names are written in full, as they appear in the body of the affidavit. Signature by mark must be attested by two witnesses. Each affidavit must be executed before a Notary Public and the notarial seal and signature of the officer must be attached to each separate affidavit.

Respectfully,

VR 2-5.   [sic]

7-NB-1315

Muskogee, Indian Territory, July 25, 1905.

George Drake,
    Haileyville, Indian Territory.

Dear Sir:

    Your attention is called to a communication addressed to you by the Commission to the Five Civilized Tribes, under date of June 3, 1905, with which there was inclosed,

Applications for Enrollment of Choctaw Newborn
Act of 1905   Volume XVII

for execution, the mother's affidavit, in the matter of the enrollment of your infant child, Edith M. Drake, born November 19, 1904.

In said letter you were advised that in the application heretofore filed with the Commission to the Five Civilized Tribes, for the enrollment of said child, the mother's affidavit was not executed. You were requested to supply same together with either the original or a certified copy of the license and certificate of your marriage to Beulah Drake, the applicant's mother. No reply to this letter has been received.

You are requested to give this matter your immediate attention as no further action can be taken relative to the enrollment of said child, until the evidence heretofore requested has been supplied.

Respectfully,

Commissioner.

Substitute

7-NB-1315

Muskogee, Indian Territory, August 15, 1905.

George W. Drake,
Haileyville, Indian Territory.

Dear Sir:

Receipt is hereby acknowledged of your letter of August 11, 1905, transmitting the affidavit of Beulah Drake to the birth of Edith M. Drake, November 19, 1904, and the same has been filed in the matter of the enrollment of said child.

It is noted that you state you left your marriage license at Tishomingo when you selected your allotment, and it will not be necessary for you to introduce further evidence of your marriage.

Respectfully,

Acting Commissioner.

Applications for Enrollment of Choctaw Newborn
Act of 1905 Volume XVII

Choc. New Born 1316
    Hester May Rail
    (Born Feb. 9, 1905)

7- 6430

BIRTH AFFIDAVIT.

DEPARTMENT OF THE INTERIOR.
COMMISSION TO THE FIVE CIVILIZED TRIBES.

IN RE APPLICATION FOR ENROLLMENT, as a citizen of the Choctaw Nation, of Hester May Rail, born on the 8 day of February, 1905

Name of Father: William Rail   a citizen of the United States Nation.
Name of Mother: Mary Rail   a citizen of the _____ Nation.

Postoffice   Guertie I.T.

AFFIDAVIT OF MOTHER.

UNITED STATES OF AMERICA, Indian Territory,
    Central   DISTRICT.

    I, Mary Rail, on oath state that I am 24 years of age and a citizen by blood, of the Choctaw Nation; that I am the lawful wife of William Rail, who is a citizen, by —— of the United States Nation; that a female child was born to me on 8 day of February, 1905; that said child has been named Hester May Rail, and was living March 4, 1905.

                                      Mary Rail

Witnesses To Mark:
   {

    Subscribed and sworn to before me this 24 day of April, 1905

                            OL Johnson
                                 Notary Public.

Applications for Enrollment of Choctaw Newborn
Act of 1905   Volume XVII

AFFIDAVIT OF ATTENDING PHYSICIAN OR MID-WIFE.

UNITED STATES OF AMERICA, Indian Territory, }
  Central   DISTRICT.

    I, Rhoda Noles[sic], a midwife, on oath state that I attended on Mrs. Mary Rail, wife of William Rail on the 8 day of February, 1905; that there was born to her on said date a female child; that said child was living March 4, 1905, and is said to have been named Hester May Rail

                                        her
                              Rhoda x Nolan

Witnesses To Mark: mark
   { E.F. Hunter
   { E.W. Moore

    Subscribed and sworn to before me this 26" day of April, 1905

                        J.M. Young
                              Notary Public.

My com exp Mch 9-1909

                                              7-2221

                Muskogee, Indian Territory, May 1, 1905.

William Rail,
    Guertie, Indian Territory.

Dear Sir:

    Receipt is hereby acknowledged of the affidavits of Mary Rail and Rhoda Nolan to the birth of Hester May Rail, daughter of William and Mary Rail, February 8, 1905, and the same have been filed with our records as an application for the enrollment of said child.

                      Respectfully,

                                            Chairman.

Applications for Enrollment of Choctaw Newborn
Act of 1905 Volume XVII

Choc. New Born 1317
Verna Austin McDonald
(Born Jan. 10, 1905)

BIRTH AFFIDAVIT.

No. 71

DEPARTMENT OF THE INTERIOR.
COMMISSION TO THE FIVE CIVILIZED TRIBES.

IN RE APPLICATION FOR ENROLLMENT, as a citizen of the Choctaw Nation, of Verna Austin McDonald, born on the 10th day of January, 1905

Name of Father: Joseph Richard McDonald   a citizen of the United States Nation.
Name of Mother: Lucy E. McDonald   a citizen of the Choctaw Nation.

Postoffice   Ada, Indian Territory.

AFFIDAVIT OF MOTHER.

UNITED STATES OF AMERICA, Indian Territory,
Southern DISTRICT.

22

I, Lucy E McDonald, on oath state that I am ~~24~~ years of age and a citizen by Blood, of the Choctaw Nation; that I am the lawful wife of Joseph Richard McDonald, who is a citizen, by birth of the United States ~~Nation~~; that a male child was born to me on 10th day of January, 1905, that said child has been named Verna Austin McDonald, and is now living.

Lucy E McDonald

Witnesses To Mark:

Subscribed and sworn to before me this 27 day of Jan, 1905.

R.C. Jeter
Notary Public.
My commition[sic] expires 2-4-07

Applications for Enrollment of Choctaw Newborn
Act of 1905   Volume XVII

AFFIDAVIT OF ATTENDING PHYSICIAN OR MID-WIFE.

UNITED STATES OF AMERICA, Indian Territory, }
    Southern   DISTRICT.

I, ... , a   mid-wife   , on oath state that I attended on Mrs. Lucy E McDonald   , wife of   Joseph Richard McDonald   on the   10th day of January , 1905; that there was born to her on said date a   male   child; that said child is now living and is said to have been named   Verna Austin McDonald

J A Lukwell

Witnesses To Mark:
{

Subscribed and sworn to before me this   27 day of   Jan   , 1905.

R.C. Jeter
Notary Public.
My commition[sic] expires 2-4-07

BIRTH AFFIDAVIT.

DEPARTMENT OF THE INTERIOR.
COMMISSION TO THE FIVE CIVILIZED TRIBES.

IN RE APPLICATION FOR ENROLLMENT, as a citizen of the   Choctaw   Nation, of Verna Austin McDonald   , born on the   10th day of   January , 1905

Name of Father: Joseph R McDonald   a citizen of the   US   Nation.
Name of Mother: Lucy E McDonald   a citizen of the   Choctaw   Nation.

Postoffice   Ada, I.T.

AFFIDAVIT OF MOTHER.

UNITED STATES OF AMERICA, Indian Territory, }
    Southern   DISTRICT.

I,   Lucy E McDonald   , on oath state that I am   22   years of age and a citizen by   blood   , of the   Choctaw   Nation; that I am the lawful wife of Joseph R McDonald   , who is a citizen, by birth   of the   United States ~~Nation~~; that a   male   child was born to me on   the 10th day of   January   , 1905; that said child has been named   Verna Austin McDonald   , and was living March 4, 1905.

Lucy E McDonald

Applications for Enrollment of Choctaw Newborn
Act of 1905   Volume XVII

Witnesses To Mark:
{

    Subscribed and sworn to before me this 27 day of   April   , 1905

                              JE Williams
                              Notary Public.

AFFIDAVIT OF ATTENDING PHYSICIAN OR MID-WIFE.

UNITED STATES OF AMERICA, Indian Territory, }
   Southern   DISTRICT.

    I,   Jane A Lukwell   , a mid-wife , on oath state that I attended on Mrs. Lucy E. McDonald   , wife of   Joseph R McDonald   on the 10th day of January , 1905; that there was born to her on said date a   male   child; that said child was living March 4, 1905, and is said to have been named Verna Austin McDonald

                              J.A. Lukwell
Witnesses To Mark:
{

    Subscribed and sworn to before me this 27 day of   April   , 1905

                              JE Williams
                              Notary Public.

                                    7-346

              Muskogee, Indian Territory, May 1, 1905.

Joseph R. McDonald,
    Ada, Indian Territory.

Dear Sir:

    Receipt is hereby acknowledged of the affidavits of Lucy E. McDonald and J. A. Lukwell to the birth of Verna Austin McDonald, son of Joseph R. and Lucy E. McDonald, January 10, 1905, and the same have been filed with our records as an application for the enrollment of said child.

                    Respectfully,

                              Chairman.

Applications for Enrollment of Choctaw Newborn
Act of 1905   Volume XVII

7-NB-1317

Muskogee, Indian Territory, July 24, 1905.

Lucy E. McDonald,
    Ada, Indian Territory.

Dear Madam:

    Receipt is hereby acknowledged of your letters of July 6 and 18, 1905, relative to the status of the application for the enrollment of your child Verna Austin McDonald; you also ask if you can improve a part of the public domain and hold the same for your child until his enrollment is approved.

    In reply to your letter you are advised that the name of your child Verna Austin McDonald has been placed upon a schedule of citizens by blood of the Choctaw Nation which has been forwarded the Secretary of the Interior, and you will be notified when his enrollment is approved.

    You are further advised that no reservation of land can be made for children enrolled under the provisions of the act of Congress approved March 3, 1905, but it is believed that if you placed improvements on land subsequent to March 4, 1905, you would have a right to hold the same against any other citizen until the enrollment of your child is approved.

                  Respectfully,

                                    Commissioner.

Choc. New Born 1318
    Lula Jones
    (Born Aug. 6, 1903)
    Luella Jones
    (Born Aug. 6, 1903)

Applications for Enrollment of Choctaw Newborn
Act of 1905   Volume XVII

BIRTH AFFIDAVIT.

DEPARTMENT OF THE INTERIOR.
COMMISSION TO THE FIVE CIVILIZED TRIBES.

IN RE APPLICATION FOR ENROLLMENT, as a citizen of the   Choctaw   Nation, of Lula Jones , born on the 6th day of August , 1903

Name of Father: Osborn Jones   a citizen of the   Choctaw   Nation.
Name of Mother: Virginia Jones   a citizen of the   Choctaw   Nation.

Postoffice   Bennington, Ind. Ter.

AFFIDAVIT OF MOTHER.

UNITED STATES OF AMERICA, Indian Territory, }
    Central   DISTRICT.   }

I, Virginia Jones , on oath state that I am 20 years of age and a citizen by Blood , of the Choctaw Nation; that I am the lawful wife of Osborn Jones , who is a citizen, by Blood of the Choctaw Nation; that a Female child was born to me on 6th day of August , 1903; that said child has been named Lula Jones , and was living March 4, 1905.

Virginia Jones

Witnesses To Mark:
{

Subscribed and sworn to before me this 1st day of April , 1905

C.C. McClard
Notary Public.

AFFIDAVIT OF ATTENDING PHYSICIAN OR MID-WIFE.

UNITED STATES OF AMERICA, Indian Territory, }
    Central   DISTRICT.   }

I, Ellen Jones , a midwife , on oath state that I attended on Mrs. Virginia Jones , wife of Osborn Jones on the 6th day of August , 1903; that there was born to her on said date a female child; that said child was living March 4, 1905, and is said to have been named Lula Jones

her
Ellen x Jones
mark

Applications for Enrollment of Choctaw Newborn
Act of 1905   Volume XVII

Witnesses To Mark:
- Kibbie Anderson
- J H Caruthers

Subscribed and sworn to before me this 1st day of April , 1905

C.C. McClard
Notary Public.

BIRTH AFFIDAVIT.

DEPARTMENT OF THE INTERIOR.
COMMISSION TO THE FIVE CIVILIZED TRIBES.

IN RE APPLICATION FOR ENROLLMENT, as a citizen of the   Choctaw   Nation, of   Luella Jones   , born on the 6th   day of   August   , 1903

Name of Father: Osborn Jones   a citizen of the   Choctaw   Nation.
Name of Mother: Virginia Jones   a citizen of the   Choctaw   Nation.

Postoffice   Bennington, Ind. Ter.

AFFIDAVIT OF MOTHER.

UNITED STATES OF AMERICA, Indian Territory,
Central   DISTRICT.

I,   Virginia Jones   , on oath state that I am   20   years of age and a citizen by   Blood   , of the   Choctaw   Nation; that I am the lawful wife of   Osborn Jones   , who is a citizen, by Blood   of the   Choctaw   Nation; that a   Female   child was born to me on   6th   day of   August   , 1903; that said child has been named   Luella Jones   , and was living March 4, 1905.

Virginia Jones

Witnesses To Mark:

Subscribed and sworn to before me this 1st day of April , 1905

C.C. McClard
Notary Public.

Applications for Enrollment of Choctaw Newborn
Act of 1905   Volume XVII

AFFIDAVIT OF ATTENDING PHYSICIAN OR MID-WIFE.

UNITED STATES OF AMERICA, Indian Territory, }
Central   DISTRICT.

I,   Ellen Jones   , a midwife   , on oath state that I attended on Mrs. Virginia Jones , wife of Osborn Jones   on the 6th day of August , 1903; that there was born to her on said date a   Female   child; that said child was living March 4, 1905, and is said to have been named   Luella Jones

her
Ellen x Jones
mark

Witnesses To Mark:
 { Kibbie Anderson
 { J H Caruthers

Subscribed and sworn to before me this 1st day of   April   , 1905

C.C. McClard
Notary Public.

Muskogee, Indian Territory, April 8, 1905.

Osborn Jones,
 Bennington, Indian Territory.

Dear Sir:

Receipt is hereby acknowledged of the affidavits of Virginia Jones and Ellen Jones to the birth of Lula and Luella Jones, twin children of Osborn and Virginia Jones, august[sic] 6, 1903.

It is stated in the affidavit of the mother that she is a citizen by blood of the Choctaw Nation. If this is correct, you are requested to state her maiden name, the names of her parents and, if she has taken her allotment, her roll number as it appears on her allotment certificate.

This matter should receive immediate attention in order that proper disposition may be made of the applications for the enrollment of the above named children.

Respectfully,

Commissioner in Charge.

Applications for Enrollment of Choctaw Newborn
Act of 1905   Volume XVII

Choctaw 3859.

Muskogee, Indian Territory, May 2, 1905.

Osgorn[sic] Jones,
    Bennington, Indian Territory.

Dear Sir:

    Receipt is hereby acknowledged of your letter of April 24, stating the names of your wife's parents in the matter of the application for the enrollment of your children, Lula and Luella Jones, and the affidavits heretofore forwarded have been filed with our records as applications for the enrollment of said children.

        Respectfully,

                Chairman.

7-NB-1318

Muskogee, Indian Territory, July 24, 1905.

Osborn N. Jones,
    Cade, Indian Territory.

Dear Sir:

    Receipt is hereby acknowledged of your letter of July 1905, asking if your two children have been enrolled so that you can now select their allotments.

    In reply to your letter you are advised that the names of your children Lula and Luella Jones have been placed upon a schedule of citizens by blood of the Choctaw Nation which has been forwarded the Secretary of the Interior and you will be notified when their enrollment is approved by the department.

    Pending the approval of their enrollment, however, no selection of allotment could be made in behalf of said children.

        Respectfully,

                Commissioner.

Applications for Enrollment of Choctaw Newborn
Act of 1905 Volume XVII

Choc. New Born 1319
    Brady Efflet Fields
    (Born Apr. 15, 1904)

BIRTH AFFIDAVIT.

DEPARTMENT OF THE INTERIOR,
COMMISSION TO THE FIVE CIVILIZED TRIBES.

IN RE *Application for Enrollment*, as a citizen of the Choctaw Nation, of Brady Efflet Fields , born on the 15 day of April , 1904

Name of Father: William Efflet Fields   a citizen of the United States Nation.
Name of Mother: Cora Bell Fields   a citizen of the Choctaw Nation.

           Post-Office: Checotah Ind Tery

AFFIDAVIT OF MOTHER.

UNITED STATES OF AMERICA, }
    INDIAN TERRITORY.
Western   District.

    I, Cora Bell Fields , on oath state that I am 19 years of age and a citizen by Blood , of the Choctaw Nation; that I am the lawful wife of William Efflet Fields , who is a citizen, by intermarriage of the Choctaw Nation; that a male child was born to me on 15 day of April , 1904 , that said child has been named Brady Efflet Fields , and is now living.

                                     Cora Bell Fields

WITNESSES TO MARK:

    Subscribed and sworn to before me this 20th *day of* April , 1905.

                                      T.J. Rice
                                         NOTARY PUBLIC.

Applications for Enrollment of Choctaw Newborn
Act of 1905 Volume XVII

AFFIDAVIT OF ATTENDING PHYSICIAN OR MID-WIFE.

UNITED STATES OF AMERICA,
    INDIAN TERRITORY.
  Western   District.

I, P S Johnston , a Physician , on oath state that I attended on Mrs. Cora Bell Fields , wife of William Efflet Fields on the 15th day of April , 1904 ; that there was born to her on said date a male child; that said child is now living and is said to have been named Brady Efflet Fields

P.S. Johnston M.D.

WITNESSES TO MARK:

Subscribed and sworn to before me this 20th day of April , 1905.

T.J. Rice
NOTARY PUBLIC.

NEW-BORN AFFIDAVIT.

Number..................

...Choctaw Enrolling Commission...

IN THE MATTER OF THE APPLICATION FOR ENROLLMENT, as a citizen of the Choctaw Nation, of Brady Effelet[sic] Fields

born on the 15 day of April 190 4

Name of father W.E. Fields	a citizen of Choctaw
Nation final enrollment No. 12702	
Name of mother Cora Fields	a citizen of Choctaw
Nation final enrollment No.	

Postoffice Indianola, I.T.

AFFIDAVIT OF MOTHER.

UNITED STATES OF AMERICA
INDIAN TERRITORY
United States of America
Indian Territory Western District

I Cora Fields , on oath state that I am 18 years of age and a citizen by Birth of the Choctaw Nation, and as such have been placed upon the final roll of the Choctaw Nation, by the Honorable

Applications for Enrollment of Choctaw Newborn
Act of 1905 Volume XVII

Secretary of the Interior my final enrollment number being   12702 ; that I am the lawful wife of   W.E. Fields , who is a citizen of the   Choctaw   Nation, and as such has been placed upon the final roll of said Nation by the Honorable Secretary of the Interior, his final enrollment number being   Intermarried   and that a   Male   child was born to me on the   15th day of   April   190 4; that said child has been named   Brady Effelet Fields , and is now living.

Cora Fields

Witnesseth.

Must be two Witnesses who are Citizens. } John F. Bolling
Robert T Pearson

Subscribed and sworn to before me this   12   day of   Jan   190 5

DM Crawford
Notary Public.

My commission expires:
Sept 19 1907

AFFIDAVIT OF ATTENDING PHYSICIAN OR MIDWIFE

UNITED STATES OF AMERICA
INDIAN TERRITORY
United States of America
Indian Territory Western District

I,   P.S. Johnston   a   Physician   on oath state that I attended on Mrs.   Cora Fields   wife of   W.E. Fields   on the   15th day of   April , 190 4 , that there was born to her on said date a   male   child, that said child is now living, and is said to have been named   Brady Effelet Fields

P.S. Johnston   M.D.

Subscribed and sworn to before me this, the   12   day of   Jan   190 5

DM Crawford   Notary Public.

WITNESSETH:
Must be two witnesses who are citizens { John F Bolling
Sept 19, 1907   Robert T. Pearson

We hereby certify that we are well acquainted with_____
a _____ and know _____ to be reputable and of good standing in the community.

Applications for Enrollment of Choctaw Newborn
Act of 1905   Volume XVII

Muskogee, Indian Territory, April 24, 1905.

William Efflet Fields,
    Checotah, Indian Territory.

Dear Sir:

    Receipt is hereby acknowledged of the affidavits of Cora Belle Fields and P. S. Johnson[sic] to the birth of Brady Efflet Fields, son of William Efflet Fields and Cora Belle Fields, April 15, 1904.

    It is stated in the affidavit of the mother that she is a citizen by blood of the Choctaw Nation of the Choctaw Nation. If this is correct you are requested to state the name under which she was enrolled, the names of her parents, and if she has selected an allotment of the lands of the Choctaw and Chickasaw Nations please give her roll number as it appears upon her allotment certificate.

    Respectfully,

    Chairman.

(COPY)

Checotah, I. T. April 26, 1905.

Com. to the Five Civilized Tribes,
    Muskogee, I. T.

Gents,

    I herewith hand you Mrs. Cora Belle Fields Roll Number and also names of parents.

    She was enrolled as Cora Belle Perkins her Roll Number is 12702, Choctaw by Blood. her parents are Lyman Humes Perkins and Hattie Adaline Perkins.

    Respty Yours

    William Efflet Fields.

Applications for Enrollment of Choctaw Newborn
Act of 1905   Volume XVII

Choctaw 4591.

Muskogee, Indian Territory, May 2, 1905.

William Efflet Fields,
    Checotah, Indian Territory.

Dear Sir:

    Receipt is hereby acknowledged of your letter of April 26, in which you state that your wife was enrolled as Cora Belle Perkins and her roll number is 12702, Choctaw by blood.

    This information has enables[sic] us to identify her upon our records as an enrolled citizen by blood of the Choctaw Nation, and the affidavits heretofore forwarded of Cora Belle Fields and P. S. Johnston to the birth of Brady Efflet Fields, April 15, 1904, have been filed with our records as an application for the enrollment of said child.

                         Respectfully,

                                    Chairman.

Choc. New Born 1320
    Everidge Austin
    (Born Oct. 3, 1904)

NEW-BORN AFFIDAVIT.

                Number............

...Choctaw Enrolling Commission...

    IN THE MATTER OF THE APPLICATION FOR ENROLLMENT, as a citizen of the Choctaw Nation, of Everidge Austin

born on the 3rd day of October 190 4

Name of father Louie Austin   a citizen of Choctaw
Nation final enrollment No. 3277
Name of mother Pauline Austin   a citizen of Choctaw
Nation final enrollment No. 3278

Applications for Enrollment of Choctaw Newborn
Act of 1905 Volume XVII

Postoffice   Valliant I.T.

AFFIDAVIT OF MOTHER.

UNITED STATES OF AMERICA
INDIAN TERRITORY
Central   DISTRICT

I   Pauline Austin   , on oath state that I am 24   years of age and a citizen by blood   of the   Choctaw   Nation, and as such have been placed upon the final roll of the   Choctaw   Nation, by the Honorable Secretary of the Interior my final enrollment number being   3278   ; that I am the lawful wife of   Louie Austin   , who is a citizen of the   Choctaw   Nation, and as such has been placed upon the final roll of said Nation by the Honorable Secretary of the Interior, his final enrollment number being   3278[sic]   and that a   Male   child was born to me on the   3rd day of   October   190 4; that said child has been named   Everidge Austin , and is now living.

her
Pauline x Austin
mark

Witnesseth.

Must be two Witnesses who are Citizens.   Willis Austin
H B Jacob

Subscribed and sworn to before me this   23rd day of   Feb   190 5

W A Shoney
Notary Public.

My commission expires: Jan 10, 1909

AFFIDAVIT OF ATTENDING PHYSICIAN OR MIDWIFE

UNITED STATES OF AMERICA
INDIAN TERRITORY
Central   DISTRICT

I,   Annie Chika   a   midwife on oath state that I attended on Mrs.   Pauline Austin   wife of   Louie Austin on the 3rd day of   October , 190 4, that there was born to her on said date a   male   child, that said child is now living, and is said to have been named   Everidge Austin

her
Annie x Chika   M.D.
mark

WITNESSETH:

Must be two witnesses who are citizens and know the child.   Willis Austin
H B Jacob

Applications for Enrollment of Choctaw Newborn
Act of 1905 Volume XVII

Subscribed and sworn to before me this, the 22nd day of Feb 190 5

W A Shoney Notary Public.

We hereby certify that we are well acquainted with Annie Chika a midwife and know her to be reputable and of good standing in the community.

{ Willis Austin
H B Jacob

BIRTH AFFIDAVIT.

DEPARTMENT OF THE INTERIOR.
COMMISSION TO THE FIVE CIVILIZED TRIBES.

IN RE APPLICATION FOR ENROLLMENT, as a citizen of the Choctaw Nation, of Everidge Austin , born on the 3 day of Oct , 1904

Name of Father: Louie Austin a citizen of the Choctaw Nation.
Name of Mother: Pauline Austin a citizen of the Choctaw Nation.

Postoffice Valliant

AFFIDAVIT OF MOTHER.

UNITED STATES OF AMERICA, Indian Territory,
Central DISTRICT.

I, Pauline Austin , on oath state that I am 25 years of age and a citizen by Blood , of the Choctaw Nation; that I am the lawful wife of Louie Austin , who is a citizen, by Blood of the Choctaw Nation; that a mail[sic] child was born to me on 3 day of Oct , 1904; that said child has been named Everidge Austin , and was living March 4, 1905.

Pauline Austin

Witnesses To Mark:
{ W M Stanley
Sims Alsabrook

Subscribed and sworn to before me this 1 day of May , 1905

H L Fowler
Notary Public.

Applications for Enrollment of Choctaw Newborn
Act of 1905 Volume XVII

AFFIDAVIT OF ATTENDING PHYSICIAN OR MID-WIFE.

UNITED STATES OF AMERICA, Indian Territory, }
.... DISTRICT. }

    I,   Annie Chika   , a ...., on oath state that I attended on Mrs. Pauline Austin , wife of Louie Austin on the 3 day of Oct , 1904; that there was born to her on said date a   male   child; that said child was living March 4, 1905, and is said to have been named Everidge Austin

                                                            her
                                                   Annie x Chika
Witnesses To Mark: mark
   { W M Stanley
   { Sims Alsabrook

    Subscribed and sworn to before me this 1 day of May   , 1905

                                            H L Fowler
                                            Notary Public.

Choc. New Born 1321
    Charley Bench
    (Born Jan. 8, 1903)

NEW-BORN AFFIDAVIT.

        Number........................

...Choctaw Enrolling Commission...

    IN THE MATTER OF THE APPLICATION FOR ENROLLMENT, as a citizen of the Choctaw   Nation, of   Charley Bench

born on the 8th day of __January__   190 3

Name of father Sam Bench   a citizen of   White
Nation final enrollment No. ———
Name of mother Matilda Bench   a citizen of   Choctaw
Nation final enrollment No. 8860

                                        Postoffice   Quinton IT

Applications for Enrollment of Choctaw Newborn
Act of 1905 Volume XVII

AFFIDAVIT OF MOTHER.

UNITED STATES OF AMERICA
INDIAN TERRITORY
Western   DISTRICT

I   Matilda Bench   , on oath state that I am 30 years of age and a citizen by blood of the Choctaw Nation, and as such have been placed upon the final roll of the Choctaw Nation, by the Honorable Secretary of the Interior my final enrollment number being 8860 ; that I am the lawful wife of Sam Bench , who is a citizen of the Choctaw Nation, and as such has been placed upon the final roll of said Nation by the Honorable Secretary of the Interior, his final enrollment number being .... and that a Male child was born to me on the 8th day of January 190 3; that said child has been named Charley Bench , and is now living.

                                                her
                                  Matilda Bench x
Witnesseth.   mark

Must be two Witnesses who are Citizens. } T.J. Walls
                      Jess Walls

Subscribed and sworn to before me this 4 day of Jan 190 5

                                    John M Lentz
                                          Notary Public.

My commission expires: Nov 27-1907

AFFIDAVIT OF ATTENDING PHYSICIAN OR MIDWIFE

UNITED STATES OF AMERICA
INDIAN TERRITORY
Western   DISTRICT

I, Elizabeth Quinton a midwife on oath state that I attended on Mrs. Matilda Bench wife of Sam Bench on the 8th day of January , 190 3 , that there was born to her on said date a male child, that said child is now living, and is said to have been named Charley Bench

                                  Elizabeth Quinton

Subscribed and sworn to before me this, the 4 day of January 190 5

WITNESSETH: John M Lentz   Notary Public.
Must be two witnesses who are citizens { Katie Quinton
                         her
                 Sallie Quinton
                    mark

Applications for Enrollment of Choctaw Newborn
Act of 1905   Volume XVII

We hereby certify that we are well acquainted with   Elizabeth Quinton   a   midwife   and know   her   to be reputable and of good standing in the community.

Jess Walls   _____

Katie Quinton   _____

BIRTH AFFIDAVIT.

DEPARTMENT OF THE INTERIOR.
COMMISSION TO THE FIVE CIVILIZED TRIBES.

IN RE APPLICATION FOR ENROLLMENT, as a citizen of the   Choctaw   Nation, of   Charley Bench   , born on the 8th   day of   January   , 1903

Name of Father: Sam Bench   a citizen of the .... Nation.
Name of Mother: Matilda Bench   a citizen of the   Choctaw   Nation.

Postoffice   Quinton, Indian Territory.

AFFIDAVIT OF MOTHER.

UNITED STATES OF AMERICA, Indian Territory, }
    Western   DISTRICT.

I,   Matilda Bench   , on oath state that I am   30   years of age and a citizen by   blood   , of the   Choctaw   Nation; that I am the lawful wife of   Sam Bench   , who is a citizen, by   ---------   of the   --------------------   Nation; that a   Male   child was born to me on   8th   day of   January   , 1903; that said child has been named   Charley Bench   , and was living March 4, 1905.

                                        Matilda Bench
Witnesses To Mark:
{

Subscribed and sworn to before me this   28th   day of   April   , 1905

                                        Guy A Curry
                                        Notary Public.

Applications for Enrollment of Choctaw Newborn
Act of 1905   Volume XVII

AFFIDAVIT OF ATTENDING PHYSICIAN OR MID-WIFE.

UNITED STATES OF AMERICA, Indian Territory,　}
　Western　　　　　　　DISTRICT.

I, Elizabeth Quinton, a mid-wife, on oath state that I attended on Mrs. Matilda Bench, wife of Sam Bench on the 8th day of January, 1903; that there was born to her on said date a Male child; that said child was living March 4, 1905, and is said to have been named Charley Bench

　　　　　　　　　　　　　　　　Elizabeth Quinton

Witnesses To Mark:
{

Subscribed and sworn to before me this 28th day of April, 1905

　　　　　　　　　　　Guy A Curry
　　　　　　　　　　　　Notary Public.

7--3024.

Muskogee, Indian Territory, May 10, 1905.

Sam Bench,
　　Quinton, Indian Territory.

Dear Sir:

Receipt is hereby acknowledged of the affidavits of Matilda Bench and Elizabeth Quinton to the birth of Charley bench, son of Sam and Matilda Bench, January 8, 1903, and the same have been filed with our records as an application for the enrollment of said child.

　　　　　　　　　Respectfully,

　　　　　　　　　　　　　　Commissioner in Charge.

Applications for Enrollment of Choctaw Newborn
Act of 1905 Volume XVII

Choc. New Born 1322
    Miley Silvan[sic] Beams
    (Born Aug. 31, 1904)

NEW-BORN AFFIDAVIT.

Number..............

Choctaw Enrolling Commission.

IN THE MATTER OF THE APPLICATION FOR ENROLLMENT, as a citizen of the Choctaw Nation, of Mila[sic] Sloan[sic] Beames[sic]

born on the 31 day of August 190 4

Name of father Isom Beams   a citizen of Choctaw
Nation final enrollment No 9763
Name of mother Maggie Beams   a citizen of Choctaw
Nation final enrollment No 1002

Postoffice   Armstrong I.T.

AFFIDAVIT OF MOTHER.

UNITED STATES OF AMERICA, }
   INDIAN TERRITORY,   }
Central   DISTRICT   }

I   Maggie Beams   on oath state that I am 23 years of age and a citizen by marriage of the Choctaw Nation, and as such have been placed upon the final roll of the Choctaw Nation, by the Honorable Secretary of the Interior my final enrollment number being 1002 ; that I am the lawful wife of Isom Beams , who is a citizen of the Choctaw Nation, and as such has been placed upon the final roll of said Nation by the Honorable Secretary of the Interior, his final enrollment number being 9763 and that a female child was born to me on the 31 day of August 190 4 ; that said child has been named Mila Sloan Beams , and is now living.

                              Maggie Beames

WITNESSETH:
  Must be two   } Louis S. Hutchison
  Witnesses who }
  are Citizens.   Willie Roberson

Applications for Enrollment of Choctaw Newborn
Act of 1905   Volume XVII

Subscribed and sworn to before me this   16   day of   January   190 5

James Bower
Notary Public.

My commission expires   Sept 23, 1907

Affidavit of Attending Physician or Midwife.

UNITED STATES OF AMERICA
INDIAN TERRITORY
Central   DISTRICT

I,   Robt A Lively   a   Practicing Physician on oath state that I attended on Mrs.   Maggie Beams   wife of   Isom Beams on the   31   day of   August   , 190 3 , that there was born to her on said date a   female child, that said child is now living, and is said to have been named   Mila Sloan Beams

Robt. A. Lively   M.D.

Subscribed and sworn to before me this, the   16   day of   Jan.   190 5

James Bower
Notary Public.

WITNESSETH:

Must be two witnesses who are citizens and know the child.
{ Louis S Hutchison
  Willie Roberson

We hereby certify that we are well acquainted with   Robt A Lively a   Practicing Physician   and know   him   to be reputable and of good standing in the community.

{ Louis S Hutchison
  Willie Roberson

BIRTH AFFIDAVIT.

DEPARTMENT OF THE INTERIOR.
COMMISSION TO THE FIVE CIVILIZED TRIBES.

IN RE APPLICATION FOR ENROLLMENT, as a citizen of the   Choctaw   Nation, of   Miley Siloan Beames   , born on the   31st day of   August   , 1904

Name of Father: Isham[sic] Beames   a citizen of the   Choctaw   Nation.
Name of Mother: Maggie Beames   a citizen of the   Choctaw   Nation.

Postoffice   Armstrong, Indian Territory

Applications for Enrollment of Choctaw Newborn
Act of 1905   Volume XVII

AFFIDAVIT OF MOTHER.

UNITED STATES OF AMERICA, Indian Territory, }
   Central   DISTRICT. }

I, Maggie Beames, on oath state that I am 24 years of age and a citizen by marriage, of the Choctaw Nation; that I am the lawful wife of Isham Beames, who is a citizen, by blood of the Choctaw Nation; that a female child was born to me on 31st day of August, 1904; that said child has been named Miley Siloan Beames, and was living March 4, 1905.

                                              her
                                    Maggie x Beames

Witnesses To Mark: mark
  { W.T. Bennett Durant I.T.
    J.T. McIntosh   "   " "

Subscribed and sworn to before me this 26th day of April, 1905

                                    L.B. Wilkins
                                    Notary Public.

AFFIDAVIT OF ATTENDING PHYSICIAN OR MID-WIFE.

UNITED STATES OF AMERICA, Indian Territory, }
   Central   DISTRICT. }

I, R.A. Lively, M.D., a Physician & Surgeon, on oath state that I attended on Mrs. Maggie Beames, wife of Isham Beames on the 31st day of August, 1904; that there was born to her on said date a female child; that said child was living March 4, 1905, and is said to have been named Miley Siloan Beames

                                    Robt A Lively MD

Witnesses To Mark:
  {

Subscribed and sworn to before me this 26th day of April, 1905

                                    L.B. Wilkins
                                    Notary Public.

Applications for Enrollment of Choctaw Newborn
Act of 1905 Volume XVII

7-3422.

Muskogee, Indian Territory, May 10, 1905.

Isham Beames,
    Armstrong, Indian Territory.

Dear Sir:

    Receipt is hereby acknowledged of the affidavits of Maggie Beames and Robt. A Lively to the birth of Miley Siloan Beames, daughter of Isham and Maggie Beams, August 31, 1904, and the same have been filed with our records as an application for the enrollment of said child.

Respectfully,

Commissioner in Charge.

---

7 NB-1322

Muskogee, Indian Territory, July 7, 1905.

Isham D. Beams,
    Armstrong, Indian Territory.

Dear Sir:

    Receipt is hereby acknowledged of your letter of June 21, 1905, and replying to that portion of it in which you ask if you can file for your child Miley Solvan[sic] Beams you are advised that the name of your child Miley Silvan Beams has been placed upon a schedule of citizens by blood of the Choctaw Nation prepared for forwarding to the Secretary of the Interior, but pending the approval of the enrollment of said child no selection of allotment could be permitted in her behalf.

Respectfully,

Commissioner.

Applications for Enrollment of Choctaw Newborn
Act of 1905   Volume XVII

Choc. New Born 1323
    Guy McMurtry
    (Born May 27, 1904)

NEW BORN AFFIDAVIT

No ....

CHOCTAW ENROLLING COMMISSION

IN THE MATTER OF THE APPLICATION FOR ENROLLMENT as a citizen of the Choctaw Nation, of   Guy McMurtry   born on the 27" day of   May   190 4

Name of father   Lora McMurtry   a citizen of   United States   Nation, final enrollment No. ....
Name of mother   Irene McMurtry   a citizen of   Choctaw   Nation, final enrollment No.   13984

Atoka, I.T.   Postoffice.

AFFIDAVIT OF MOTHER

UNITED STATES OF AMERICA
    INDIAN TERRITORY
DISTRICT   Central

I   Irene McMurtry   , on oath state that I am 19 years of age and a citizen by   blood   of the   Choctaw   Nation, and as such have been placed upon the final roll of the   Choctaw   Nation, by the Honorable Secretary of the Interior my final enrollment number being   13984   ; that I am the lawful wife of   Lora McMurtry   , who is a citizen of the   United States   ~~Nation~~, and as such ~~has been placed upon the final roll of said Nation by the Honorable Secretary of the Interior, his final enrollment number being~~ and that a   male   child was born to me on the 27" day of   May   190 4; that said child has been named   Guy McMurtry   , and is now living.

Irene McMurtry

WITNESSETH:
  Must be two witnesses   Thomas D. Lee
  who are citizens   John Frinzel

Applications for Enrollment of Choctaw Newborn
Act of 1905   Volume XVII

Subscribed and sworn to before me this, the   6" day of   February   , 190 5

D.N. Linebaugh
Notary Public.

My Commission Expires:

Affidavit of Attending Physician or Midwife

UNITED STATES OF AMERICA, }
INDIAN TERRITORY,
Central   DISTRICT

I,   J. S. Fulton   a   Practicing Physician on oath state that I attended on Mrs. Irene McMurtry   wife of   Lora McMurtry on the   27"   day of   May   , 190 4, that there was born to her on said date a   male   child, that said child is now living, and is said to have been named   Guy McMurtry

J.S. Fulton   M. D.

Subscribed and sworn to before me this the   8"   day of   February   1905

D.N. Linebaugh
Notary Public.

WITNESSETH:
Must be two witnesses who are citizens and know the child.   { John Frinzel
Amelia McMurtry

We hereby certify that we are well acquainted with   J.S. Fulton a   Practicing Physician   and know   him   to be reputable and of good standing in the community.

Must be two citizen witnesses.   { John Frinzel
Amelia McMurtry

BIRTH AFFIDAVIT.
DEPARTMENT OF THE INTERIOR.
COMMISSION TO THE FIVE CIVILIZED TRIBES.

IN RE APPLICATION FOR ENROLLMENT, as a citizen of the   Choctaw   Nation, of Guy McMurtry   , born on the   27th day of   May   , 1904

Name of Father: Lora McMurtry   a citizen of the   Choctaw   Nation.
Name of Mother: Irene McMurtry   a citizen of the   Choctaw   Nation.

Applications for Enrollment of Choctaw Newborn
Act of 1905   Volume XVII

Postoffice   Atoka, Ind. Ter.

AFFIDAVIT OF MOTHER.

UNITED STATES OF AMERICA, Indian Territory, }
Central   DISTRICT.

I, Irene McMurtry, on oath state that I am 19 years of age and a citizen by blood, of the Choctaw Nation; that I am the lawful wife of Lora McMurtry, who is a citizen, ~~by~~ of the United States ~~Nation~~; that a male child was born to me on 27th day of May, 1904; that said child has been named Guy McMurtry, and was living March 4, 1905.

Irene McMurtry

Witnesses To Mark:
{

Subscribed and sworn to before me this 5 day of May, 1905

J.W. Jones
Notary Public.

AFFIDAVIT OF ATTENDING PHYSICIAN OR MID-WIFE.

UNITED STATES OF AMERICA, Indian Territory, }
Central   DISTRICT.

I, J. S. Fulton, a physician, on oath state that I attended on Mrs. Irene McMurtry, wife of Lora McMurtry on the 27th day of May, 1904; that there was born to her on said date a male child; that said child was living March 4, 1905, and is said to have been named Guy McMurtry

J.S. Fulton

Witnesses To Mark:
{

Subscribed and sworn to before me this 7 day of May, 1905

J.W. Jones
Notary Public.

Applications for Enrollment of Choctaw Newborn
Act of 1905 Volume XVII

7--NB--1323

Muskogee, Indian Territory, June 2, 1905.

Lora McMurtry,
    Atoka, Indian Territory.

Dear Sir:

    There is enclosed you herewith for execution application for the enrollment of your infant child, Guy McMurtry, born May 27, 1904.

    The affidavits heretofore filed with the Commission show the child was living on February 6, 1905. It is necessary, for the child to be enrolled, that he was living on March 4, 1905.

    In having these affidavits executed care should be exercised to see that all names are written in full, as they appear in the body of the affidavit, and in the event that either of the persons signing the affidavit are unable to write, signatures by mark must be attested by two witnesses. Each affidavit must be executed before a Notary Public and the notarial seal and signature of the officer must be attached to each separate affidavit.

    This matter should receive your immediate attention as no further action can be taken relative to the enrollment of said child until the Commission has been furnished these affidavits.

    Respectfully,

DFK-Enc-3   [sic]

7-NB-1323.

Muskogee, Indian Territory, June 10, 1905.

Lora McMurtry,
    Atoka, Indian Territory.

Dear Sir:

    Receipt is hereby acknowledged of the affidavits of Irene McMurtry and J. S. Fulton to the birth of Guy McMurtry, son of Irene and Lora McMurtry, May 27, 1904, and the same have been filed with our records in the matter of the enrollment of said child.

    Respectfully,

                                                      Commissioner in Charge.

Applications for Enrollment of Choctaw Newborn
Act of 1905   Volume XVII

Choc. New Born 1324
  Lucie Moore
  (Born Sep. 18, 1903)

NEW-BORN AFFIDAVIT.

Number............

...Choctaw Enrolling Commission...

IN THE MATTER OF THE APPLICATION FOR ENROLLMENT, as a citizen of the Choctaw Nation, of Lucy Moore

born on the 18th day of September 190 3

Name of father Lewis Carnes   a citizen of   Choctaw
Nation final enrollment No. 13972
Name of mother Lily Moore   a citizen of   Choctaw
Nation final enrollment No. 717

                                           Postoffice   Featherston, IT

AFFIDAVIT OF MOTHER.

UNITED STATES OF AMERICA
INDIAN TERRITORY
  Western   DISTRICT

        I   Lily Moore   , on oath state that I am
   33   years of age and a citizen by   blood   of the   Choctaw   Nation,
and as such have been placed upon the final roll of the   Choctaw   Nation, by the Honorable
Secretary of the Interior my final enrollment number being   717 ; that I am the ~~lawful wife~~
~~of~~ not married   Lewis Carnes   , who is a citizen of the   Choctaw   Nation, and as
such has been placed upon the final roll of said Nation by the Honorable Secretary of the
Interior, his final enrollment number being   13972   and that a   female   child was
born to me on the   18th   day of   September   190 3; that said child has been named
Lucy Moore   , and is now living.   her
                                          Lily x Moore
Witnesseth.   mark
   Must be two ⎫ Calvin Lewis
   Witnesses who ⎬
   are Citizens. ⎭ Wesley McCoy

313

Applications for Enrollment of Choctaw Newborn
Act of 1905 Volume XVII

Subscribed and sworn to before me this 7th day of Jan 1905

Guy A Curry
Notary Public.

My commission expires:
Apr 27-1907

AFFIDAVIT OF ATTENDING PHYSICIAN OR MIDWIFE

UNITED STATES OF AMERICA
INDIAN TERRITORY
Western DISTRICT

I, Silvia Carney a midwife on oath state that I attended on Mrs. Lily Moore ~~wife~~ of *not married* on the 18th day of September, 1903, that there was born to her on said date a female child, that said child is now living, and is said to have been named Lucy Moore

Silvia x Carney
her mark

Subscribed and sworn to before me this, the 7th day of January 1905

WITNESSETH:
Must be two witnesses who are citizens { Calvin Lewis
Wesley McCoy

Guy A Curry Notary Public.

We hereby certify that we are well acquainted with Silvia Carney a midwife and know her to be reputable and of good standing in the community.

Calvin Lewis

Wesley McCoy

BIRTH AFFIDAVIT.

DEPARTMENT OF THE INTERIOR.
COMMISSION TO THE FIVE CIVILIZED TRIBES.

IN RE APPLICATION FOR ENROLLMENT, as a citizen of the Choctaw Nation, of Lucie Carnes, born on the 18th day of September, 1903

Name of Father: Lewis Carnes a citizen of the Choctaw Nation.
Name of Mother: Lily Moore a citizen of the Choctaw Nation.

Applications for Enrollment of Choctaw Newborn
Act of 1905   Volume XVII

Postoffice   Quinton, Indian Territory

AFFIDAVIT OF MOTHER.

UNITED STATES OF AMERICA, Indian Territory,
Western   DISTRICT.

I, Lily Moore, on oath state that I am 33 years of age and a citizen by blood, of the Choctaw Nation; that I am the lawful wife of ———, who is a citizen, by _____ of the _____ Nation; that a FeMale[sic] child was born to me on 18th day of September, 1903; that said child has been named Lucie Carnes, and was living March 4, 1905.

                       her
                  Lily x Moore

Witnesses To Mark: mark
   { Ella Carney
   { Allen Carney

Subscribed and sworn to before me this 23rd day of May, 1905

                  Guy A Curry
                  Notary Public.

AFFIDAVIT OF ATTENDING PHYSICIAN OR MID-WIFE.

UNITED STATES OF AMERICA, Indian Territory,
Western   DISTRICT.

I, Silvia Carney, a midwife, on oath state that I attended on Mrs. Lily Moore, ~~wife of~~ _____ on the 18th day of September, 1903; that there was born to her on said date a Female child; that said child was living March 4, 1905, and is said to have been named Lucie Carnes

                       her
                  Silvia x Carney

Witnesses To Mark: mark
   { Ella Carney
   { Allen Carney

Subscribed and sworn to before me this 23rd day of May, 1905

                  Guy A Curry
                  Notary Public.

Applications for Enrollment of Choctaw Newborn
Act of 1905 Volume XVII

BIRTH AFFIDAVIT.

DEPARTMENT OF THE INTERIOR.
COMMISSION TO THE FIVE CIVILIZED TRIBES.

IN RE APPLICATION FOR ENROLLMENT, as a citizen of the Choctaw Nation, of Lucie Moore, born on the 18th day of September, 1903

Name of Father: Lewis Carnes   a citizen of the Choctaw Nation.
Name of Mother: Lily Moore   a citizen of the Choctaw Nation.
                  Postoffice   Quinton, Indian Territory

AFFIDAVIT OF MOTHER.

UNITED STATES OF AMERICA, Indian Territory, }
     Western   DISTRICT. }

I, Lily Moore, on oath state that I am 33 years of age and a citizen by blood, of the Choctaw Nation; ~~that I am the lawful wife of~~ ~~who is a citizen, by of the Nation~~; that a female child was born to me on 18th day of September, 1903; that said child has been named Lucie Moore, and was living March 4, 1905.

                                     her
                                Lily x Moore
Witnesses To Mark: mark
   { Chas Bascomb
   { Moten Carney

Subscribed and sworn to before me this 26th day of June, 1905

                               Guy A Curry
                               Notary Public.

AFFIDAVIT OF ATTENDING PHYSICIAN OR MID-WIFE.

UNITED STATES OF AMERICA, Indian Territory, }
     Western   DISTRICT. }

I, Silway[sic] Carney, a mid-wife, on oath state that I attended on Mrs. Lily Moore, ~~wife of~~ on the 18th day of September, 1903; that there was born to her on said date a female child; that said child was living March 4, 1905, and is said to have been named Lucie Moore

                                     her
                               Silway x Carney
                                   mark

Applications for Enrollment of Choctaw Newborn
Act of 1905   Volume XVII

Witnesses To Mark:
  { Chas Bascomb
  { Moten Carney

Subscribed and sworn to before me this 26th day of   June   , 1905

Guy A Curry
Notary Public.

7-NB-1324.

Muskogee, Indian Territory, May 29, 1905.

Lily Moore,
  Quinton, Indian Territory.

Dear Madam:

There is enclosed you herewith for execution application for the enrollment of your infant child.

In the affidavits of January 7, 1905, heretofore filed in this office, the name of the applicant is given as Lucy Moore, while in those of May 23, 1905, her name appears as Lucie Carnes. In the enclosed application the name of the child is left blank. Please insert the correct name of the [sic] and return the affidavits, when properly executed, to this office

In having these affidavits executed care should be exercised to see that all names are written in full, as they appear in the body of the affidavit, and in the event that either of the persons signing the affidavit are unable to write, signatures by mark must be attested by two witnesses. Each affidavit must be executed before a Notary Public and the notarial seal and signature of the officer must be attached to each separate affidavit.

Respectfully,

Chairman.

VR 29-11.

Applications for Enrollment of Choctaw Newborn
Act of 1905 Volume XVII

7 NB 1324

Muskogee, Indian Territory, June 30, 1905.

Lily Moore,
    Quinton, Indian Territory.

Dear Madam:

    Receipt is hereby acknowledged of your affidavit and the affidavit of Silway Carney to the birth of Lucie Moore, daughter of Lewis Carnes and Lily Moore, September 18, 1903, and the same have been filed with our records in the matter of the enrollment of said child.

                  Respectfully,

                            Chairman.

Choc. New Born 1325
    T. Beal
    (Born Jan. 8, 1903)

NEW-BORN AFFIDAVIT.

        Number..................

Choctaw Enrolling Commission.

    IN THE MATTER OF THE APPLICATION FOR ENROLLMENT, as a citizen of the Chocktaw   Nation, of   T. Beal

born on the   8   day of   February   190 3

Name of father   William Albert Beal   a citizen of   Chocktaw
Nation final enrollment No   15718
Name of mother   Sallie Beal   a citizen of   United States
Nation final enrollment No ....

                  Postoffice   Durant I.T.

Applications for Enrollment of Choctaw Newborn
Act of 1905   Volume XVII

AFFIDAVIT OF MOTHER.

UNITED STATES OF AMERICA,
INDIAN TERRITORY,
Central   DISTRICT

I   Sallie Beal   on oath state that I am   22   years of age and a citizen by blood of the Choctaw Nation   of the   United States Nation, and as such have been placed upon the final roll of the   Nation, by the Honorable Secretary of the Interior my final enrollment number being   ; that I am the lawful wife of   William Albert Beal   , who is a citizen of the   Chocktaw   Nation, and as such has been placed upon the final roll of said Nation by the Honorable Secretary of the Interior, his final enrollment number being   15718   and that a   Male   child was born to me on the   8   day of   January   190 3 ; that said child has been named   T. [sic]   , and is now living.

                                        Sallie Beal

WITNESSETH:
  Must be two } (Name Illegible)
  Witnesses who
  are Citizens.   (Name Illegible)

Subscribed and sworn to before me this   20   day of   Jan   190 5

                        FM Kizer
                                    Notary Public.

My commission expires   Mar 10 1907

Affidavit of Attending Physician or Midwife.

UNITED STATES OF AMERICA
INDIAN TERRITORY
  Central   DISTRICT

I,   Mary Cathrene Brantley   a   a midwife on oath state that I attended on Mrs.   Sallie Beal   wife of   William Albert Beal on the   8   day of   January   , 190 3 , that there was born to her on said date a   Male child, that said child is now living, and is said to have been named   T. Beal

                        Mary Cathrene Brantley   Midwife
Subscribed and sworn to before me this, the   20   day of   Jany   190 5

                        F M Kizer
                                    Notary Public.

WITNESSETH:
  Must be two witnesses   { A.B. Beal
  who are citizens and
  know the child.   Rosa Dills

Applications for Enrollment of Choctaw Newborn
Act of 1905 Volume XVII

We hereby certify that we are well acquainted with A.B. Beal a nd Rosa Dills and know them to be reputable and of good standing in the community.

{ George Beal
  Ada Bell Moore

BIRTH AFFIDAVIT.

DEPARTMENT OF THE INTERIOR.
COMMISSION TO THE FIVE CIVILIZED TRIBES.

IN RE APPLICATION FOR ENROLLMENT, as a citizen of the Chocktaw[sic] Nation, of T. Beal, born on the 8 day of January, 1903

Name of Father: William Albert Beal   a citizen of the Chocktaw Nation.
Name of Mother: Sallie Beal   a citizen of the United States Nation.

Postoffice   Silo Ind Territory

AFFIDAVIT OF MOTHER.

UNITED STATES OF AMERICA, Indian Territory,
Central DISTRICT.

I, Sallie Beal, on oath state that I am 22 years of age and a citizen by ...., of the United States Nation; that I am the lawful wife of William Albert Beal, who is a citizen, by Blood of the Chocktaw Nation; that a male child was born to me on the 8 day of January, 1903; that said child has been named T. Beal, and was living March 4, 1905.

                         her
                     Sallie x Beal
Witnesses To Mark: mark
{ B F Brantley
  William Albert Beal

Subscribed and sworn to before me this 1 day of May, 1905

                     F.M. Kizer
                         Notary Public.

Applications for Enrollment of Choctaw Newborn
Act of 1905   Volume XVII

AFFIDAVIT OF ATTENDING PHYSICIAN OR MID-WIFE.

UNITED STATES OF AMERICA, Indian Territory,
   Central   DISTRICT.

    I, Mary C Brantley, a "an attendant", on oath state that I attended on Mrs. Sallie Beal, wife of William Albert Beal on the 8 day of January, 1903; that there was born to her on said date a male child; that said child was living March 4, 1905, and is said to have been named T. Beal

                                    Mary C. Brantley

Witnesses To Mark:

    Subscribed and sworn to before me this 1 day of May, 1905

                                    F.M. Kizer
                                        Notary Public.

---

                                                        7 NB 1325

                  Muskogee, Indian Territory, May 18, 1905.

William Albert Beal,
    Silo, Indian Territory.

Dear Sir:

    Receipt is hereby acknowledged of the affidavits of Sallie Beal and Mary C. Brantley to the birth of T Beal, son of William Albert Beal and Sallie Beal, January 8, 1903, and the same have been filed with our records as an application for the enrollment of said child.

                                Respectfully,

                                              Chairman.

Applications for Enrollment of Choctaw Newborn
Act of 1905   Volume XVII

7--NB--1325

Muskogee, Indian Territory, June 1, 1905.

William Albert Beal,
    Silo, Indian Territory.

Dear Sir:

    Referring to the application for the enrollment of your infant child, T. Beal, born January 8, 1903, it is noted from the affidavits heretofore filed in this office that the applicant claims through you.

    In this event it will be necessary for you to file in this office, either the original, or a certified copy of the license and certificate of your marriage to the mother of the applicant, Sallie Beal.

                      Respectfully,

                        Chairman.

FVK

Choc. New Born 1326
    Bicy James
    (Born March 21, 1904)

NEW-BORN AFFIDAVIT.

                Number

...Choctaw Enrolling Commission...

    IN THE MATTER OF THE APPLICATION FOR ENROLLMENT, as a citizen of the Choctaw Nation, of Bicy James

born on the 21st day of March 1904

Name of father	Joseph James	a citizen of	Choctaw
Nation final enrollment No.	*not citizen*		
Name of mother	Betsy James	a citizen of	Choctaw
Nation final enrollment No. 5563			

Applications for Enrollment of Choctaw Newborn
Act of 1905   Volume XVII

Postoffice   Blanco I.T.

AFFIDAVIT OF MOTHER.

UNITED STATES OF AMERICA
INDIAN TERRITORY
Central   DISTRICT

I   Betsy James   , on oath state that I am 23 years of age and a citizen by blood of the Choctaw Nation, and as such have been placed upon the final roll of the Choctaw Nation, by the Honorable Secretary of the Interior my final enrollment number being 5563 ; that I am the lawful wife of Joseph James , who is a citizen of the Choctaw Nation, and as such has been placed upon the final roll of said Nation by the Honorable Secretary of the Interior, his final enrollment number being .... and that a Female child was born to me on the 21st day of March 190 4; that said child has been named Bisy[sic] James , and is now living.

Witnesseth.

Must be two Witnesses who are Citizens.   Stanton Kemp

Ben Moses

Subscribed and sworn to before me this   2^d day of   March   190 4[sic]

A.E. Folsom
Notary Public.

My commission expires:
Jan 9-1909

AFFIDAVIT OF ATTENDING PHYSICIAN OR MIDWIFE

UNITED STATES OF AMERICA
INDIAN TERRITORY
Central   DISTRICT

I,   Joseph James   *The Fæather of Bisy James*
on oath state that I attended on Mrs. Betsy James wife of Joseph James & Father & husband on the 21st day of March , 190 4, that there was born to her on said date a Female child, that said child is now living, and is said to have been named Betsy[sic] James

Joseph James *The Father*   M.D.

WITNESSETH:
Must be two witnesses who are citizens and know the child.   Stanton Kemp

Ben Moses

Applications for Enrollment of Choctaw Newborn
Act of 1905   Volume XVII

Subscribed and sworn to before me this, the   2^d day of March   190 5

A.E. Folsom   Notary Public.

We hereby certify that we are well acquainted with   Joseph James   a   The Father & Husband   and know   him   to be reputable and of good standing in the community.

{ Stanton Kemp
  Ben Moses

BIRTH AFFIDAVIT.

DEPARTMENT OF THE INTERIOR.
COMMISSION TO THE FIVE CIVILIZED TRIBES.

IN RE APPLICATION FOR ENROLLMENT, as a citizen of the   Choctaw   Nation, of   Bicey James   , born on the   21   day of   March   , 1904

Name of Father: Joseph James   a citizen of the   Choc   Nation.
Name of Mother: Betsy James   a citizen of the   Choc   Nation.

Postoffice   Blanco I.T.

AFFIDAVIT OF MOTHER.

UNITED STATES OF AMERICA, Indian Territory,
Central   DISTRICT.

I,   Betsy James   , on oath state that I am   26   years of age and a citizen by blood   , of the   Choctaw   Nation; that I am the lawful wife of   Joseph James   , who is a citizen, by blood   of the   Choctaw   Nation; that a   female   child was born to me on   21   day of   March   , 1904; that said child has been named Bicey James   , and was living March 4, 1905.

                her
Betsy x James
                mark

Witnesses To Mark:
{ *(Name Illegible)*
  OL Johnson

Subscribed and sworn to before me this   28   day of   April   , 1905

OL Johnson
Notary Public.

Applications for Enrollment of Choctaw Newborn
Act of 1905   Volume XVII

AFFIDAVIT OF ATTENDING PHYSICIAN OR MID-WIFE.

UNITED STATES OF AMERICA, Indian Territory,
    Central   DISTRICT.

    I, Elizabeth James, a midwife, on oath state that I attended on Mrs. Betsy James, wife of Joseph James on the 21 day of March, 1904; that there was born to her on said date a female child; that said child was living March 4, 1905, and is said to have been named Bicey James

                                                  her
                                          Elizabeth x James
Witnesses To Mark: mark
  { *(Name Illegible)*
    OL Johnson

    Subscribed and sworn to before me this 28 day of April, 1905

                                      OL Johnson
                                          Notary Public.

                        Muskogee, Indian Territory, May 2, 1905.

Joseph James,
    Blanco, Indian Territory.

Dear Sir:

    Receipt is hereby acknowledged of the affidavits of Betsy James and Elizabeth James to the birth of Bicey James, daughter of Joseph and Betsy James, March 21, 1904.

    It is stated in the affidavit of the mother that she is a citizen by blood of the Choctaw Nation. If this is correct you are requested to state the name under which she was enrolled, the names of her parents, and if she has selected an allotment of the lands of the Choctaw or Chickasaw Nation please give her roll number as it appears upon her allotment certificate.

                        Respectfully,

                                              Chairman.

Applications for Enrollment of Choctaw Newborn
Act of 1905   Volume XVII

7-NB-1326.

Muskogee, Indian Territory, June 14, 1905.

Joseph James,
    Blanco, Indian Territory.

Dear Sir:

    Referring to the application for the enrollment of your infant child, Bicy[sic] James, born March 21, 1904, it is noted from the affidavits heretofore filed in this office that you claim to be a Choctaw by blood.

    If this is correct you are requested to state when, where and under what name you were listed for enrollment, the names of your parents and other members of your family for whom application was made at the same time, and if you have selected your allotment give your roll number as the same appears upon your allotment certificate.

    This matter should receive your immediate attention as no further action can be taken until this information has been furnished the Commission.

                        Respectfully,

                                    Chairman.

Index

ABBOTT
  Dr W E 134
  W E 134
ADAMS
  G H 49
  J H 47
ADKINS
  Frank 150,151,153,154,155
  John A 150,151,152,153,154,155
  Mrs John 150
  Roscoe 150,152,154
  Tobitha 150,151,152,153,154,155
ALLEN
  L D 28,30
  Nicey 44,45
ALSABROOK
  Sims 300,301
AMOS
  Sidney 42
ANDERSON
  Kibbie 291,292
  Lizzie 10
  R F 260,261,262
  Robert 11,12,19,20,79,80,131,
  140,141,142,252
  Z D 128,129
ANGELL
  Geo 15
  Malina 15
  W H 14,15,40,187,188,189,228
ANGLIN
  J B 258,259
ARCHER
  Arthur O 187,228
ARNOTE
  A J 13,129,139
ATKINS
  Ethel 232,233,234,235
  Jewel Edward 232,233,234,235
  John E 232,233,234,235
AUSTIN
  Everdige 301
  Everidge 298,299,300
  Louie 298,299,300,301
  Louir 299
  Pauline 298,299,300,301
  Willis 299,300

BAKEN
  L E 112,113
BARNETT
  Louvicy 231
  William 92,93,97
BARNNETT
  William 98
BASCOM
  Chas 176
  Jincy 176
BASCOMB
  Chas 316,317
BATTICE
  Marcus 65
BATTIEST
  Stephen 80,81
BATTLE
  Frank 64
  H F 64
BEAGLES
  Myrtle 31
BEAL
  A B 319,320
  George 320
  Sallie 318,319,320,321,322
  T. 318,319,320,321,322
  William Albert 318,319,320,321,322
BEAMES
  Cora Bell 236,237,238,239
  Isham 306,307,308
  Lavina Victory 237,238,239
  Maggie 306,307,308
  Mila Sloan 305
  Miley Siloan 306,307,308
  William T 237,238,239
BEAMS
  Cora Bell 236,237
  Isham D 308
  Isom 305,306
  Lavina Victoria 236,237
  Maggie 305,306
  Mila Sloan 305,306
  Miley Silvan 305,308
  Miley Solvan 308
  William T 236,237
BELL
  G E 66

Index

Kinnie May 203,204,205
Mary Viola 203,204,205
Thomas Edward 203,204,205
Thomas W 203,204,205
BELT
  Malinda 99,100,102,104,105
BEN
  Bettie 44,45,46,47,49,51
  Betty 48,53
  Bittie 51,52
  James 44,45,46,47,49,50,51,52,53
  Saleyan 44,45,46,47,49,50,51,52,53
  Salyan 48
BENCH
  Bettie 145
  Charley 301,302,303,304
  J D 145,146
  Matilda 301,302,303,304
  Sam 146,301,302,303,304
BENNETT
  W T 307
BENSON
  Mary 213
BENTON
  Theodore 217,218
  Wesley 257,258,259,260
BILLEY
  Rebecca 38,39
BILLINGTON
  D A 124
BILLS
  Aimie Lee 211
  Annie Lee 214
  R C 241
BILLY
  Siney 80
BIXBY
  Tams 89,96,266,278
BOBO
  Lacey P 95
BOHANNON
  Joseph 28,29
  Mary 28,29
BOLLING
  John F 296
BOWER
  James 43,109,233,306

BOWLIN
  Gracie Marie 244,245,246,247,248, 250,251
  Gracie May 247,250,251
  R M 245,246,247,248,250,251
  Susie 245,246,247,248,250,251
BRANDY
  Cornelius 199,200,201,202
  Mettie 202
  Nettie 199,200,201,202
  Oscar 198,199,200,201,202
BRANTLEY
  B F 320
  Mary C 321
  Mary Cathrene 319
BREAKER
  J J 106,107,108
  J J, MD 106
BREEDLOVE
  E C 258,259
  R T 257,258,259
BRIANS
  R E 203,205
BRITTINHAM
  Lester 121
  Miss Lester 116
BROWN
  Dwight 223,224,225
BUSWELL
  W P 208
BYINGTON
  Annie 185,186,187,188
  Sallie 185,186,187,188
  Simeon 94
  Simpson 185,186,187,188
BYRD
  B F 169
  Mamie E 169
BYRN
  Alice M 1
CARLTON
  H B 148
  W T 148
CARNES
  B B 174
  Lewis 313,314,316,318
  Lucie 314,315,317

Index

CARNEY
  Allen 315
  Ella 315
  Joseph 175,176
  Lizzie 253,254
  Morton 175,176
  Moten 316,317
  Siliway 175,176
  Silvia 314,315
  Silway 316,318
CARTER
  Christanie Bele 262
  Christanie Bell 256,260,261
  Christanie Belle 263
  Crissannie Belle 257,258
  Ella 257,258,259,260,261,262,263
  J D 266,267
  Lillie E 272
  Minnie Elsie 256,258,259,261,262, 263,264
  T L 257,258,259
  Thomas L 260,261,262,263,264
CARUTHERS
  J H 291,292
CAUDILL
  W C 107,108
CHARLES
  R J 164
CHASTAIN
  J C 269
  J D 268
CHIKA
  Annie 299,300,301
CHOTAU
  George 211,214
CHRISTIE
  Carlison 54,55
  Jesse 54
  Jesse L 54,55
CLARK
  E O 30
  Mr E O 30
COCHNAUER
  D W 107
  David W 106
  Rhoda 106
COCKE
  John 21
COFFEY
  Dr O F 246
  O F 248,251
COLEMAN
  R B 133,134
  W A 3,4
COLEY
  Frank 28,29
COLLIN
  Bettie 44,45,46,49
  Buckner 43
COLLINS
  Bettie 47
  Jake 191,277
CONLEY
  W J, MD 39
  William J 40
  William J, MD 40
CORDLISH
  Beulah 266,267
COVINGTON
  W P 95
COWEN
  Dorsey Edmond 165,166,167
  Francis 166,167
  S B 165,166,167
  Susan 165,166,167
CRAIG
  John 211
CRAWFORD
  D M 296
CRIPS
  M E 103,104
CRISMAN
  Dr T L 83
  T L 83
CRISP
  M E 101
CRISSMAN
  T L 85
  T L, MD 83,84
CROUTHAMEL
  A H 132
  CRUTCHFIELD
  Evelynn 72,73,74,75,76,77,78
  Gertrude 72,73,74,75,76,77,78

Index

J W 77
John 78
John A 78
John W 72,73,74,75,76,77,78
CULBERTSON
   W T 66,68,69,70
CUNNINGHAM
   William H 187,189
CURRY
   Guy A 123,176,303,304,314,315,
   316,317
DAUGHERTY
   Beulah 195,197,198
   Buena 195,196,198
   John F 196,197,198
   Lillian 196,197,198
DAVENPORT
   George A 242
   Narcissa 242
   S P 12,13,139
   Wyle E 242
DEVENPORT
   George A 239,240,241,242
   Narcissa 241,242
   Narcissa S 239,240
   Wyle E 239,241,242
   Wyley Edmond 239,240
DICK
   Malina 14
DIFENDAFER
   Chas T 35,36,164,191,229,230,231
DILARD
   Marie 25
DILLARD
   Leflore 25
   Marie 23,25
DILLIARD
   Cora 24
   Le Flore 24
   Marie 24
DILLS
   Rosa 319,320
DRAKE
   Beulah 280,281,282,283
   Bula 279,280,281
   Edith M 279,280,281,282,283
   George 279,280,281,282

George W 283
DRIVER
   Lillie 170,173
DUER
   Isaac 255,256
   Martha 255,256
   Valley May 255,256
DURANT
   Z W 83
DURR
   Frances 233,234
DYER
   E E 233,234
   Elliston E 82,83,84,85
   Louis 3,4
   Nancy J 82,83,84,85
   Sallie 95
   T D 122
   Winnona 82,83,84,85
DYKES
   N T 172
EARLY
   C W 160
EDWARD
   Cely 80,81
   Emeline 79,80,81
   Wesley 80,81
EDWARDS
   Emeline 79,80
   Sealy 79,80
   Wesley 79,80
ELLIOTT
   J E 180
   J H 181
ELLIS
   C L 276
   Charles V 87,88,91
   Chas V 85,86,89,90
   Delphin 87
   Delphine 85,86,87,88
   Puahmataha 87
   Push-ma-ta-ha 88,91
   Push-ma-taha 87
   Push-Ma-Ta-Ha F 85
   Pushmataha F 85,86
ERVIN
   H E 204,205

M E 204
EVERIDGE
   Thomas W 210,211
FANNIN
   E G 89
   E J 90,266,267
FARLEY
   J C 100
FARR
   Arthur T 22,23
   Lena Eliza 22,23
   Texanna 22,23
FIELDS
   Brady Effelet 295,296
   Brady Efflet 294,295,297,298
   Cora 295,296
   Cora Bell 294,295
   Cora Belle 297,298
   W E 295,296
   William Efflet 294,295,297,298
FILLMORE
   Gipson 263
   Isabelle 263
FINLEY
   Su 80,82
FOBB
   Eastman 92,93,94,95,96,97,98
   Louie 91,92,93,94,95,96,97,98
   Sallie 92,93,94,95,97,98
FOLSOM
   Alie H 67
   Caroline 216,218
   Catherine 219,220,221
   Cletus A 64,65,66,67,71,72
   A E 74,75,87,88,168,183,190, 216,217,323,324
   Lillie P 70
   Mrs O P 69,71
   O P 65,66,67,70,71
   Peter 199,200
   Rosa 66,70,72
   Rose 67,69,70
   Rosie E 69
   Rosie L 65,66,68,71
   W S 66,67,70
   William E 64,68,69,70,71,72
   William W 64,65,66,68,69,70,71,72

   Wm W 66,67,69,70
FOOSHEE
   Geo A 40
FOWLER
   H L 300,301
FRANCIS
   R D 49
FRANKLIN
   Wirt 1,11,12,18,19,20,23,24,25,26, 41,80,127,130,131,140,141,142,143, 144,253
FRAZIER
   Josephine 184,191,277,278
   Lucy 183
   Wilson 182,183
FREENEY
   R C 170
FREENY
   Josephine 170
   Mary 170
   Robert C 170,173
FRENCH
   D 157
FRINZEL
   John 309,310
FULKER
   J W 246
   Jno W 248,249
FULLER
   F M 5,6,46,47,48,49
FULTON
   Eliza 67,68,69
   J S 30,310,312
   J S, MD 310
FUNK
   E C 276
FUNKHOUSER
   A M 49,53
GARDNER
   Annie 99,101,105
   Daniel H 105,106,107,108
   Eliner 98
   Elmer 102,103,104,105
   J B 99,100,101,102,103,104,105
   J J 83
   J T 212
   Jack Griffin 105,106

Index

Jeck Griffin 107
Joch Griffin 107,108
Malinda... 99,100,101,102,103,104,105
Minnie 106,107,108
Robert 268
Stella 98,99,100,101,105
GIBSON
   Cillian 109,110
   Earnest J 108,110,111
   Emma 11,12,13
   Ernest J 108,109
   Harrison 11,12,13
   John 38,39
   Malissa 20
   Melessa 21,22
   Morris 21
   Sallie 108,109,110,111
   Sallie Ann 10,11,12,13
   Sam 109,110,111
   Sillen 111
   Thenton 108,109,110,111
GILL
   Charles F 100
GLENN
   W T 117,118,119,210
GOLD
   S M 237
GOLDSTON
   C L 243,244
   Estelle 243,244
   James William 243,244
   Viola Bell 243,244
GRAHAM
   Lawrence 63
   Mary J F 63
GRAMAN
   Jackson 19,20,21,22
   Sallie 19,20,21,22
   Sophia 19,20,21
   Sophie 22
GRAY
   Archie M 14,15,16,17
   Geo 16
   George W 14,17
   Malina 14,16
GREENWOOD
   Allen 21

GRIGGS
   Mary 137
   Willy 136,137,241
GRIGSLEY
   J E 168
GUESS
   Bettie 86,87
GULTON
   J S 311
GUYRE
   Sarah J 106
HAMMOCK
   T J, Jr 157
HAMPSON
   Aaron 48
HAMPTON
   Aaron 46,47
   Frances 143
   Johnson 143
   Nancy C 272,274,275
   Ollie 143,144
HANCOCK
   Willis 177,178
HARRIS
   John E 2
   Sadie Aline 1,2,3
   Sarah E 1,2,3
   Walter C 1,2,3
HARRISSON
   Wood 263
HENSAL
   T W 224
   Thos W 225
   Thos W, MD 224
HENSEL
   T W 223
   Thos W, MD 223
HICKS
   V 228
HINSLEY
   F M 132
   T M 166
HODGES
   D W 16
HOLBROOK
   W H 199,201,202
HOLM

Aaron 190
HOLMES
   Sissey 208
   Sissie 207
HOMER
   Jacob 93,94
   Sol J 171
HOMES
   Sissie 207
HOOVER
   J T 212,213
HOPKINS
   D M 200,201
HORTON
   L D 233
HOWARD
   Dr W E 235
   W E 235
HOWELL
   J L 168
HOYT
   Lizzie 144,145,146,147,148,149
   Milo A 144,145,146,147,148,149
   Olin 145
   Olin V 144,145
   Olin Vernon 144,146,147,148,149
HUBERT
   J C 110,111
HUDSON
   Charles H 61
   Chas H 56,57,58,59,60,61
   J F 199,200
   Lydia Mai 58
HULSEY
   Wm J 34,268,269
HULSEY & PATTERSON 271
HUME
   W M 14,16,273
   W M, MD 16,273
   Waverly M 273,274
   Waverly M, MD 274
HUNTER
   E F 285
HURT
   Annie 33
HUTCHISON
   Louis S 305,306

IMPSON
   Isaac 167,168,170,171,173,174,175
   Isaac C 169,170,172
   Lillie 167,168,169,170,171,172, 174,175
   T J 107
   Teddie 167,168,174
   Theodore Roosevelt 167,169,170, 171,172,173,174,175
ISH
   W W 177,178
JACKSON
   S W 102,103,105
   S W, MD 102,103
JACOB
   H B 299,300
JAMES
   Annie 113,114,116
   Betsy 322,323,324,325
   Bicey 324,325
   Bicy 322,326
   Bisy 323
   Charley 112,113,114,115,116
   Ed D, MD 280
   Edward D 280
   Elizabeth 54,55,325
   Elsie 188
   Ester 221,222,223,224,225,226,227
   Joseph 322,323,324,325,326
   Levi 54,55
   Louisa 27,29
   N C 223
   Rhoda 223,224,225,227
   Rhoda N 222
   W C 222,223
   William 112,113,114,116
   Willie 113
   Willie C 223,224,225,226,227
   Winnie 55
JEFFERSON
   Salina 135
JETER
   R C 286,287
JIM
   Sadie 229,230,231
JOEL
   Hampton 252,253,254

Index

Jim 252,253,254
Sallie 252,253,254
JOHN
   W N 26
JOHNSON
   Alexander 28
   Jess 83
   O L 32,33,35,36,164,184,192,
   229,230,231,277,284,324,325
   P S 297
JOHNSTON
   P S 295,296,298
   P S, MD 295,296
JOLLY
   Edward R 280
JONES
   Celissie 43
   Celizzie 41,42
   Cellissie 43
   Dr A G 67
   Ellen 290,292
   Ellis 241
   A G 66,71
   A G, MD 66
   J W 311
   Lotin 151,152
   Lottie 41,42,43
   Luella 289,291,292,293
   Lula 289,290,292,293
   Osborn 290,291,292
   Osborn N 293
   Osgorn 293
   Virginia 290,291,292
   Willie 109,110
   Zenobia V 65,66,68,69
KEMP
   Girdie 189,190
   Guertie 189,191,192,193,194,195
   Jennie 190,191,192,193,194,195
   Jinnie 189
   Richard E 243,244
   Standley 190
   Stanton 189,190,191,192,193,
   194,195,323,324
   Stenton 190
KENDRICK
   Lester 117,118,119,120

Mrs William W 119
Sylma 116,117,118,119,120
W W 116,121,210,211
William A 120
William W 117,118,119,120
KENNEDY
   D S 186
KERR
   J R W 240,241,242
   James R W 242
   James R W, MD 240,242
KING
   Jack Evelyn .. 121,122,123,124,125,126
   L L 123,124,125,126
   Luther 121,122,125
   Mamie 122,123,124,125,126
   Mamy 121,122
KIRBY
   W R 2
KIZER
   F M 319,320,321
LAFLORE
   Chas 16
LANDI
   Lucy 144
LANDIS
   Lucy 143
LARECY
   W E 136,240,241,242
LARGEN
   R T 216,218
LAUGHLIN
   Dora Maud 244,245,246,247,248,
   249,250,251
   J A 245,246,247,248,249,250,251
   Susie 245,246,247,248,249,250,251
LEE
   E 42
   Minnie 87,88
   Robert E 42,43
   Thomas D 309
LEFLORE
   Alice 207
LENTZ
   John M 124,125,145,146,
   147,148,302
LEWIS

Anderson 266,267,268,269,270,271
Bulah 268,269,270
Calvin 313,314
Cyntha 270
Cynthia 269
Dorothy..............................265,271
Emeline.. 271
Emoline 265,268,269,270,271
Minie 178
Nancy 11,13
O G.. 48
Silas.........................46,47,48,49,51
Winsie..................................93,98
LILLARD
   Minnie 170
LINEBAUGH
   D N... 310
LIVELY
   R A, MD....................................... 307
   Robt A..................................306,308
   Robt A, MD..........................306,307
LONG
   John M... 122
LOWTHER
   R D 151,152,154,155
   R D, MD....................150,151,152,154
LUKWELL
   J A.............................287,288
   Jane A... 288
LUNSFORD
   T B.. 7,8
LUTTREL
   Eddie..227,228
   Elzy..227,228
   Ida..227,228
MCCLARD
   C C 290,291,292
MCCLURE
   Alfred W.................................31,33
MCCOY
   Wesley..................................313,314
MCCULLOUGH
   P 111
MCCURTAIN
   Osborne 177,178
MCDANIEL
   Alma Mae..........................131,132

   Kate 131,132
   Thomas.. 131
   Thomas E...............................131,132
   Tom 132
MCDONALD
   Joseph R 287,288
   Joseph Richard....................286,287
   Lucy E 286,287,288,289
   Verna Austin............286,287,288,289
MCINTOSH
   J T... 307
   Juston...................................185,186
MCKENZIE
   Mack.. 81
MCKINZIE
   Goodman 80,81
MCMURRAY
   Beckey...................................133,134
   Ervin......................................133,134
   O M.......................................133,134
MCMURRY
   Beckey... 134
   Ervin.. 133
MCMURTREY
   Joseph B 269
MCMURTRY
   Amelia 310
   Guy..........................309,310,311,312
   Irene.......................309,310,311,312
   Lora 309,310,311,312
MANNING
   A F...74,75
   F..74,75
MANSFIELD, MCMURRAY &
   CORNISH.................................... 96
MARSHALL
   Annie Palmer....................38,39,40
   Pearl.....................................38,39,40
   W H... 222
   William Henry..................38,39,40
MATHEWS
   O H......................................260,261,262
MAYS
   Malinda Spring......................211,214
   Malinda Springs........................... 211
   Malinda... 212
   Melinda.........................209,210,213

Index

Molinda 212,213
Molinda Spring 214
Rosa Anna 209,211,212,213,214
Rosana 209,210
Rose Anna 211,213,214
Will 209,210,211,212,213,214
MEEKS
   Margaret 156,157
MELTON
   W J 73,74,76,77,78
   W J, MD 74
MERRYMAN
   Benjamin C 63
   G V 64
   Gibson B 62
   Gibson V 56,58,59,60,61
   Gipson B 61
   Gipson V 57,58,61,62
   Grace Ella 55,60,61,62,63
   Marion Francis 63
   Pairlee 57,58,59,61
   Paralee 56,60,61
   Sherman 55,56,57,58,59,61,62,63,64
MIDDLETON
   Agnes 156,157
   Charles 156,157
   Mary 157
   May 156,157
   Mrs 156
MOORE
   Ada Bell 320
   Christopher D 188
   Clorentine 59
   E W 285
   Joe 276,277,278
   Lily 313,314,315,316,317,318
   Lucie 313,316,318
   Lucy 313,314,317
   S J 211
MOREMAN
   B F 158,159,160,162
MORRIS
   H 136,137,138
   S E 1
MOSES
   Ben 222,323,324
MUGLER

Delphine 85,86,89,90,91
Theodolia 87,88,168
NAIL
   Alice Eva 157,158,159,160,161,
   162,163
   Beulah 160
   Beulah M 158,159,161,162,163
   Edward J 158,159,160,161,162,163
   Jennie 195
   Jimmie 193
NAKISHI
   David 112,113
NEAD
   James A 56,60
   Saphronia 61
   Sophronia 56
NEED
   James A 61
   Saphronia 60
NELSON
   Bertha Elizabeth 141,142
   Eastman W 65
   Eden 141,142
   Gabriel 13
   Laura 141,142
   Lula 142
   Melvina 34,37
   Molsey 141
   Mulsie 139,140
NEVINS
   Floyd 200,201
NICHOLS
   Emma 17,18
   Escar 17,18
   Levi 17,18
NOAH
   Georgeana 182,183
   Georgeanna 182
   Rena 182,183
NOEL
   Agnes 276,277,278,279
   Ella 278
   Georgianna 182
   Georgie Ann 183,184
   Jennie 192
   Lynes 278
   Nancy 182,183,276,277,278

Natsy...................................278,279
Rena..............................182,183,184
NOELS
   Rhoda.. 285
NOLAN
   Rhoda.. 285
OTT
   Alfred...............................34,35,36,37
   Johnson....................................... 273
   Lizzie................................34,35,36,37
   Martha Jane....................34,35,36,37
   Samuel A.................................... 273
OWEN
   Amanda............................128,129,130
   C C...................................128,129,130
   Martha..............................128,129,130
   Martha P...................................... 130
PARK
   J F.. 132
   J F, MD...................................... 132
PARTAIN
   W S...................................260,261,262
PATE
   Jane......................................255,256
PATTERSON
   W R.. 270
PEARSON
   Robert T..........................236,237,296
PEBWORTH
   Dora E..................................272,273
   Dora Ella...............................274,275
   Henry.......................272,273,274,275
   Henry Lee...........272,273,274,275,276
PERKINS
   Cora Belle.............................297,298
   Hattie Adaline............................. 297
   L H..................................236,237,238
   Lyman Humes............................ 297
PERRY
   Charles T..................................... 43
   Guy A... 122
PHILLIPS
   Charles A..............................255,256
PICKEN
   Isom.. 193
PICKENS
   Isom.. 195

PIERCE
   Bell... 136
   Belle...............................136,137,138
   Doglas J..................................... 136
   Douglas J..................135,136,137,138
   Ed..............................135,136,137,138
POTTS
   Amanda..................................116,117
   J E.................................116,117,121
   L E... 116
PRICE
   ? T... 248
   J D......................................247,248
   O B.. 248
PRINCE
   J N.......................................146,147
QUINCY
   Daisy Bell........................179,180,181
   James Dewitt...................179,180,181
   Jerome Ervin...................179,180,181
QUINTON
   Elizabeth..........................302,303,304
   Katie....................................302,303
   Sallie.. 302
RABON
   O A... 176
RAIL
   Hester May............................284,285
   Mary......................................284,285
   William..................................284,285
RANDELL
   Eddie.....................................126,127
   Gus..126,127
   Janey... 127
   Mattie....................................126,127
RAPPOLEE
   J L..76,86
REASOR
   J M..156,157
REED
   E L.. 238
REID
   Inez.........................215,216,217,218
RICE
   T J..238,294,295
RIDDLE
   Ed.. 59

Index

Richard 59
ROBERSON
  Willie 305,306
ROBERTS
  Sam T, Jr 9
ROBERTSON
  L L 219,221
ROGERS
  John 30
  Miss John 30
ROSE
  C C 223
  Vester W 11,12,19,20,79,80,131,
  140,141,142,252
ROWE
  S D 247,249
ROWELLS
  R E 47
ROWLEY
  H B 99,101,102,103,104
  J B 100
ROWLIN
  R M 250
ARCHER
  Arthur O 189
RUTNER
  J M 125
  J M, MD 125
RYAN
  T J 71
SANFORD
  Thomas J 52
SATON
  Pheby C 238
SAVAGE
  Martin 193,194
SCHLICHT
  J C 205
  J C, MD 205
SEXTON
  Dixon 101,103,104
SHEPPERD
  Ada 228
SHERRED
  Wesley 81
SHILLINGS
  Mary 25,26

Virgie Lou 25,26
William C 25,26
SHOATE
  Robinson 49
  Rollinson 51
SHONEY
  W A 3,45,55,83,92,93,97,98,113,
  222,299,300
SHORT
  Robinson 49
SIMMONS
  T W 118
  Thomas W 119,120
  Thomas W, MD 118
  Thos W, MD 119
SIMPSON
  Isaac 13
SISIMOORE
  Clorentine 58
  Florentine 56,61
SITTER
  Edward D 204,205
SIZEMORE
  Ester 57
SMALLWOOD
  Robert 240
SMITH
  Chas P 234,235
  Dan 216,218
  J H P 216,218,219,220,221
  Laura 2,3,4
SOCKEY
  Ben 177,178
  Eliysabeth 177
  Elysabeth 177,178
  Rosey 177,178
SPAGLE
  John F 2
SPRING
  B J 28
  Isaac 117,118,210,211,213
  Malinda 212
  Melinda 209,210,213
  Molinda 212,213
  Willie 117,118
STANLEY
  W M 300,301

Index

STATON
  Pheby C 238,239
  Phoeby C 237
STEPHENS
  Eva... 207
  J J 159,160,161
  J J, MD 159,160
  John J 163
STEWART
  Levi... 44,45
STONE
  Mattie 196,198
  W B 89,90
STORIE
  N A 181
STORRIE
  Mrs N A 181
STORY
  Mrs M A 180
  N A 180
STRACHAN
  Dr H 136,137
  H, MD 136
STRACHEN
  H 138
  H, MD 138
SULLIVAN
  B F 170,171,172,174
  B F, MD 170
SUTHERLAND
  B F 168,169
  B F, MD 168
SWINK
  William 206
SYMOTH
  Wm 151,152
TAYLOR
  Agnes 41,42,43
  Mamie 123,124,126
  Mamy 121
  Wilburn 41,42
  Wilkin 190
TELLIO
  William 54,55
TERREL
  Houston 29
  Jessie James 29

Louisa 29
TERRELL
  Houston 27,28
  Jesse James 27,28,30
  Jessie James 29
  Louisa 27,28,30
  Louisa James 28
THATCHER
  Rosa L 64,65,72
THOMAS
  Emma 232
THOMPSON
  Cyrus R 273
  Green 158,159
  Jesse 4
THREADGILL
  C M 38,39
THREDGILL
  F F 90
THURSTEN
  Lovina 164,165
TIGERT
  Bertha M 215,220,221
  Bertha May 217,218
  Julia A .. 215,216,217,218,219,220,221
  Samuel .. 215,216,217,218,219,220,221
  Samuel C 215,216,218,219,221
TODD
  Edna 233
TURNER
  J J 128,129
  J M 123,126
  J M, MD 122,123
  James M 122
  T B 145,146,147,148,149
  T B, MD 145,148
VAUGHAN
  J H 124
  John H 196,197,198
VAUGHT
  F T 61
VINSON
  M A 223
  Rhoda 223
  Rhoda N 222
VON KELLER
  Theo 273,274,275

Index

WADE
  Eli 228,229,231
  Emma 229,230,231
  Lily 228,230,231
  Willis 229,230,231,232
WALKER
  I D 129
  I D, MD 129
WALLACE
  Ione 31,32,33
  Myrtle 31,32,33
  Robert 31,32,33
WALLS
  Jess 302,303
  T J 122,302
WALSHE
  Geo W 166
WARD
  J P 211
  W S 92,93,97,98
WESLEY
  Edmond 138,139,140,141
  Elias 179,180
  Houston 138,139,140,141
  Rhoda 138,139,140,141
WHEAT
  J W 6
  Mary 6
WHEELER
  Louisa 163,164,165
  Lovina 163,164,165
  William P 163,164,165
WHITLOCK
  Isabelle 261,262
  Isibel 258,259,260
  W P 263
WILCOX
  Maud 58
WILHELM
  P E 16
WILKINS
  L B 307
WILKINS
  T B 84,85
WILKINSON
  J T 30
WILLIAMS
  Ann J 280
  Henry 136,137,240
  J E 245,246,288
  Joe B 185,186
  John 5
  Minnie 6
WILLIS
  Betsy 253
  Cillin 254
  Janey 139,140
  Mary 35
  Minnie 257,258,259,260
  Mose 34,36
  Rayson 253
  Silen 253
  William 139,140
WILSON
  Carlo 206,207
  Carlo A 207,208,209
  E M 83
  Fannie 215,216
  McVay 206,207,208,209
  McVey 206,207
  Margaret 206,207,208
  Margette 207
  Margrette 206
WIMBISH
  Robt 169,171
WISE
  M J 18,23,24
WITT
  Jesse Thomas 5
  Jessie Thomas 6
  Marion 5,6
  Peggy 5,6
WIZMORE
  Clemintine 61
WOODS
  Beulah Grace 7,8,9,10
  Bulah Grace 7,8
  Ella 257,258
  Gilbert W 7,8,9,10
  Kizzie F 8,9
  Lizzie 7,8,10
  Lizzie (Anderson) 7,8
  Lizzie Anderson 9
  Lizzie E 8,9,10

Index

R A 137
WOODWARD
   C A 83
WOOLERY
   Annie 112,113,114,115,116
   Charley James 115
   James 206
   Nancy 113,114,116
WOOLEY
   S L 181
   Samuel L 179,180
   W L 181
WORCESTER
   Alfred 182,183,184
WYERS
   John W 199,200
YOUNG
   J M 285

www.ingramcontent.com/pod-product-compliance
Lightning Source LLC
Chambersburg PA
CBHW020241030426
42336CB00010B/576